Person in Progress

Person in Progress

A Road Map to the Psychology of Your 20s

Jemma Sbeg

RODALE

NEW YORK

Rodale Books
An imprint of Random House
A division of Penguin Random House LLC
1745 Broadway, New York, NY 10019
rodalebooks.com | randomhousebooks.com
penguinrandomhouse.com

A Rodale Trade Paperback Original

LIBRARY OF CONGRESS CATALOGING-IN-PUBLICATION DATA
Names: Sbeg, Jemma, author.
Title: Person in progress / Jemma Sbeg.
Description: First paperback edition. | New York, NY: Rodale, [2025] |
Includes bibliographical references and index.
Identifiers: LCCN 2024051278 (print) | LCCN 2024051279 (ebook) |
ISBN 9780593735732 (trade paperback) | ISBN 9780593735749 (ebook)
Subjects: LCSH: Young adults--Life skills guides. | Young adults--Psychology.
Classification: LCC HQ799.5.S325 2025 (print) | LCC HQ799.5 (ebook) |
DDC 646.70084/2--dc23/eng/20241207
LC record available at https://lccn.loc.gov/2024051278
LC ebook record available at https://lccn.loc.gov/2024051279

Printed in the United States of America on acid-free paper

1st Printing

BOOK TEAM: Production editor: Cara DuBois • Managing editor: Allison
Fox • Production manager: Chanler Harris • Copy editor: Nicholas Lo Vecchio •
Proofreaders: David Goehring, Alicia Hyman, Zora O'Neill, Tess Rossi •
Indexer: Gina Guilinger

Book design by Diane Hobbing

Interior art from stock.adobe.com: krissikunterbunt (abstract head), Pixel
Craft (map navigation route)

First Paperback Edition

The authorized representative in the EU for product safety and compliance is
Penguin Random House Ireland, Morrison Chambers, 32 Nassau Street,
Dublin D02 YH68, Ireland. https://eu-contact.penguin.ie.

To Ellie and Hannah,
Hopefully you make the same mistakes I did,
but make them your own.

Contents

SECTION III
Work in Progress

SECTION IV
Everybody Is Healing from Something

Introduction

I spend a lot of my time thinking about my twenties: This infamous decade known for being as chaotic and frustrating as it is exciting and divine. This fleeting chapter in our lives that promises nothing but uncertainty. The strange vacuum between adolescence and adulthood where we feel like we still have a foot in each world, torn between diving into the responsibility of adulthood and clinging to those last remaining moments of complete, unadulterated freedom.

Our twenties are my bread and butter, my biggest source of anguish, but also my greatest source of curiosity. I have examined this decade every which way; I have heard thousands of stories of how lost we all feel, how challenging it is to navigate love in such an unstable period, the mistakes and failures that haunt us, the endless decisions that feel exceedingly important and permanent. I have spent hours in the academic literature looking for some scientific explanation for why this is all so hard. At the time I am writing this, I am still very much in this period myself, trying my best to give advice to fellow travelers while still not having all the answers.

When I began my podcast, *The Psychology of Your 20s,* it acted as a permanent way to preserve my experiences and what I was going through at the time, almost like a digital diary. Since I was very young, I have been haunted by this idea that our memories are not permanent and can be reshaped and forgotten. I always used to think, "How can I know any of my experiences were real if I can't remember them?" So I would frantically keep logs and notebooks and journals of all my most noteworthy, but also boring, day-to-day experiences.

The podcast was born from that desire to hold on to the past by keeping track of the present. There was something already so special about my twenties that I knew I would want to look back on someday. It turned out that a lot of people could relate to what I was going through, and as more and more people joined our community, the podcast only grew, until it transformed from a passion project to my full-time job. You listened on as I graduated university, had my heart broken for the first time, and then the second (and then the third), lost friends I considered soulmates, moved cities, fell in love again, struggled with my mental health, experienced great loss, death, and unemployment, and tried to work through all I was feeling using the thing I trusted most: the science. This book is a culmination of all my experiences, along with those of so many of my friends and your own, to create a guidebook for this confusing decade so we can, hopefully, feel less alone.

This book is also not just for twenty-somethings. The more I've explored the milestones and experiences of this decade, the more I've realized how universal and lifelong they are. You could be in your thirties, your forties, maybe even your seventies, and still be struggling with love, trying to discover your purpose, healing childhood wounds, or wondering who you really are. It's also for the people who are trying to better understand the tales and turmoil of this generation and why we see things differently than those who have come before us. Parents, teachers, colleagues, bosses, mentors, friends, loved ones: there is a lot you may not know or that has changed since your time.

As with any book, there may be parts you don't relate to.

Maybe you've already found the love of your life, so you don't need to learn about the woes and psychology of breakups, or you don't work a nine-to-five, so the existential dread that accompanies that work doesn't apply. That's okay. You can read this book from cover to cover, or selectively. The message remains the same: **This decade is hard, but there is an explanation as to why.** More importantly, **there is also a way through.** So many of the things we experience in isolation—the fear, the uncertainty, the heartbreak, the loneliness—become much more manageable when we understand what's really occurring below the surface and, also, when we have company. For all the hard moments, this period is one of extreme and wonderful growth, even if it doesn't always feel like it. All those times you feel like you're falling behind or wish you had all the answers are the times you look back on and say, "The person I am now was created in those moments." There is great joy to be felt, serious elation and companionship to be found, that makes all the uncertainty worth it. If you knew how this decade would turn out or if you had all the answers, there would be no room left for surprises. That's where we have the most fun, even if your twenties don't end up being the "best years of your life."

So, to all my fellow twenty-somethings: welcome. To all those a bit older: welcome back. Let's uncover what this decade is really all about and unravel the elusive psychology of our twenties.

Person in Progress

The Quarter-Life Opportunity

It happens like clockwork—we hit our mid-twenties and suddenly everything we thought we knew flips. The quarter-life crisis is a rite of passage for each of us where we are forced to seriously consider if the life we have created so far is the one we want to continue with. In my mind, it is a season of shedding—shedding old friends, old values, old dreams, old places, and most of all the version of us we were before. As with any kind of transformation, it's going to be painful because we are saying goodbye to a lot of what we were comfortable with and had grown accustomed to. On top of that, there is naturally a period between when we shed the old version of ourselves and when we discover the new version of ourselves. Moving from one to the other requires risk, mistakes, and doing some real deep soul-searching about who we are and what we want. Understandably, we feel very lost during those moments. A therapist of mine once described it as having a faulty compass in a desert and just having to place your bets on going in one direction, without having any clue where you might end up.

But what if we reframe the quarter-life crisis to be a quarter-life opportunity?

There is something so romantic about new beginnings and fresh starts. It would be a tragedy to stay the same for your whole life, to be the same version of you at eighty that you were at eighteen, and that is the opportunity provided by your quarter-life crisis: the capacity to evolve. This is not a crisis. This is an opportunity. Let's discuss why focusing on four defining elements of our twenties—**mistakes, risk, decision paralysis, identity**—can help us embrace the opportunity provided by the quarter-life crisis.

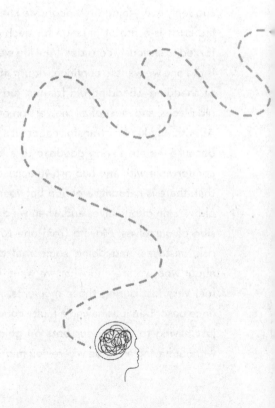

CHAPTER I

Welcome to Your Quarter-Life Crisis

WHEN I WAS six, I wanted to be a lawyer. At fifteen I wanted to be prime minister, when I was nineteen my dream job was consultant even though I wasn't quite sure what that was, at twenty-two I just wanted to pay my bills and avoid overdrawing my account each month. By twenty-three I had somehow found myself running a podcast full-time, and at twenty-five I have absolutely no clue what I want to be, whether I should drop everything and move to Costa Rica, go back to school for another three years of grueling study, find some job security, maybe get married and raise a family, or sell everything and become a nomad. All I know is that I'm writing this book and that, if it's not obvious already, I'm having a quarter-life crisis.

Red Sports Car?

We all know what it means when someone is having a mid-life crisis. The term has become part of our collective psychobabble, associated with fast red cars, affairs, excessive spending, a new hair color, a nose piercing at fifty. It's also associated with people who are quite a few years past their twenties, people facing the existential reality that life is a lot shorter than they once thought.

What the mid-life and quarter-life crisis have in common is the uncertainty and insecurity around the core pillars of our lives: career, relationships, finances, health, and the future. They also both occur at the cusp of a significant new chapter, a new developmental phase in our lives when we are forced to answer a number of really unsettling questions. What do I actually want from life? Am I happy where I am now? What am I missing? Will those things I'm missing actually make me happy? How do I get the most out of my years on this earth, or what I have left of them? What results is a period of panic, uncertainty, and the overwhelming urge to do something drastic in our lives so that we can reinstate a sense of control over our destiny.

Maybe you think it's a bit dramatic to suggest twenty-somethings are entitled to these fears. For many of us, our twenties are the period when we should feel the most free and fearless. The world is beckoning to us with opportunities, and our youthfulness and enthusiasm give us an advantage. We are young enough to still have some of our childhood dreams intact; we are optimistic about the future while still having a bit of knowledge and life experience in our back pocket to feel like adults. And yet we are also thoroughly unprepared for what this decade is about to throw our way.

Maybe you've already gotten a taste or lived through it. The confusion, the heartbreak, the sense that everyone else has it all figured it out while you don't know what tomorrow will bring. The changing friendships, loneliness, watching parents get older, worries about money or about finding purpose while the world is changing every moment. The future feels daunting, but the present feels equally chaotic and unstable. While everyone is telling us to enjoy this decade—the period when we are not quite adults, but not quite children either—we are struck by the deeply disquieting feeling that we are completely lost and no one can tell us where to go next, or at the very least what comes next.

The Moment of Crisis

Welcome to your quarter-life crisis. Millions have completed this pilgrimage before you, and you will not be the last. While it might be comforting to know you're not alone, I think it's equally disconcerting to realize you have to forge your own path, and regardless of all those who have come before, no one is going to give you the answers. Unfortunately, you are on your own. I say unfortunately, but there is also something so uniquely exciting about the prospect that you get to make your life your own. **This discomfort you're feeling is actually a sign that you are growing into a new version of yourself, undergoing a metamorphosis, and your old skin, your old self, just doesn't fit any longer.** Because there is no rule book to play by, no one can tell you what is right or wrong if it makes you happy.

However, what complicates this crisis are the opposing types of decisions or life paths to consider. On one hand, we face these societal expectations to settle down, have some five-year plan for the future, and progress toward that outcome. Society expects stability and a story they can understand, normally one that follows the traditional blueprint of graduating or completing some kind of study, finding a nice partner and getting married, holding a steady full-time job, having children, getting promoted, retiring, and then dying. That's a nice story, but I'm sure I'm not the only one who also finds it incredibly suffocating. Not only is that not everybody's dream (even if that kind of future is what will make you happy), but our generation has the added complication of facing one of the biggest recessions in decades, rising inflation, a climate crisis, a global pandemic, and increasing inequality. Yet we still wonder why we feel less like the adults society expects us to be at this age. When we are unable to find our path the way our parents or those around us have, we feel an increased sense of urgency to have all the answers. **That urgency is exactly what creates the quarter-life crisis.** Our brains are not particularly great at managing uncertainty, because uncertainty signals the unknown—which, evolutionarily, could mean danger. Think about our ancestors for who a dense forest was a lot more uncertain, and contained a lot more potential danger, than a flat and empty plain. We prefer outcomes we can predict or can see, and so the chaos of this decade and the decisions we need to make can, naturally, trigger a great deal of psychological stress and discomfort.

And then maybe we do it—we have everything we've ever wanted, what everyone told us we needed to be happy. We are on the right path but feel remarkably unsatisfied. This is also a trigger for the quarter-life crisis. One of our foundational psychological needs is a sense of fulfillment or purpose. The American psychologist Abraham Maslow, best known for his eponymous Hierarchy of Needs—a pyramid that reflects our most universal needs as humans—believed that purpose and achieving our potential was so important that he put it at the very top of his pyramid. The science confirms it as well. Purpose is good not just for our emotional and psychological well-being, but for our physical health as well. In 2020, a group of researchers dove into the health data of 13,770 recent retirees who had been assessed five times over the eight years after they retired. It was hypothesized that a lot of them, having finished their working lives, would be suffering from a lack of purpose. But what the researchers found was that the retirees who continued to have goals and a sense of direction, or who found greater meaning to their lives, were not only happier but more physically active and less likely to smoke, drink excessively, or report sleep problems. In other words, a sense of purpose is as psychologically nourishing as it is good for our physical health.

A sense of purpose, in the plainest terms, means we have something personally meaningful to strive toward. This in turn gives us direction, long-term goals, a sense of accomplishment, and a way of organizing our life. It may seem obvious, but we find purpose when we align our behaviors and actions with our mission, values, or desires. Someone who cares deeply for others finds purpose as a nurse because it aligns with their deeper desire to be helpful. Someone who values material success above all else finds purpose in seeking to increase their investment portfolio or reputation. It's entirely subjective, but each of us has something that feels "bigger" than us and bestows a sense of meaning to life.

When we don't know how to align our behaviors with our mission, values, or desires, we experience the mental discomfort that comes with the territory of a quarter-life crisis and needs to be resolved by changing either our values or our actions. If you value adventure and helping others but are working in a sedentary job that feels very self-serving, you are going to experience a conflict between the value and the behavior. The alternative of being a park ranger or a conservationist or an adventure tour guide would align better and reduce your internal sense of crisis, even if it means shifting directions. If you are in a relationship with someone and it is no longer fulfilling, but you always imagined the kind of love that could burn down the world, you are going to experience conflict. Leaving that relationship for one that matches your deeper desires would, again, reduce the sense of crisis. That unconscious conflict is what is making you so uncomfortable. It is a feeling of claustrophobia, a sense that you cannot escape the life you have created, perhaps the life you were forced to start working toward when you were only a teenager, or just so happened to fall into. You're trapped. You're stuck in your full-time job, you're stuck in your relationship, you're stuck in an unfulfilling environment. And this sense of entrapment is often accompanied by depression and panic.

This is the beginning of the crisis. **While it's terrifying to feel like everything you wanted isn't fulfilling anymore, it also means you are at an important crossroads where you can change everything.** You can start over again. In fact, we know that our twenties are perhaps the best time to change. Congratulations! Instead of suppressing these feelings for another twenty-odd years, you have the gift of being able to explore new beginnings when they are easiest. At our age, many of us don't have children, mortgages, businesses, or the types of familial relationships that keep us tied to one place. We aren't yet facing the stigma and discrimination that people may face when trying to start a new career at fifty or a new relationship at sixty-five. You are poised for transformation. In fact, I believe this decade requires it.

The Silver Lining

When you reach this crisis point, you're forced into a place of reflection and value realignment to resolve the panic. You gain humility. You see that life is not black-and-white, and you let go of the things you can't control for the things you can. That renewed sense of agency causes you to make changes—whether dramatic or "micro"—that are necessary for breaking out of the rut you find yourself in. The biggest antidote to a crisis is movement in any direction that feels meaningful. If you are in this place right now, focus on changing just one thing about your life that feels stale. You don't need to tear the whole house down right away, but choose one area where you could do something differently or align your behavior with a greater desire, dream, or value you have. There are four broad categories most people choose from:

- **Work and career**—Look for new opportunities, leadership roles, or promotions in your current workplace; start applying for new jobs elsewhere; reach out to someone you admire to network with; start volunteering for a cause that you've always felt a pull toward.

- **Routine**—Try a new workout routine; set a new fitness goal; start prioritizing sleep or finding more time for friends on the weekend; stop drinking for a month; journal before bed rather than going after the quick dopamine hit you get from bingeing a TV show or social media.

- **Environment**—Swap the indoor workout for one outdoors; redecorate your space and bring more vitality into it; move to a new neighborhood, or even to a new city; book weekend trips to the national park the next city over; declutter.

- **Relationships**—Break into a new group of friends by going to social events; stop waiting for someone else to plan the outings or invite you; join a new sport; start dating again, or stop for a while; begin a new passion project with your partner.

Remember: Nothing changes unless you do. That is such basic advice, but sometimes the simplest statements hold the most truth. When you start going about things differently and challenging what you've grown comfortable with, doors will begin to open for you. It's a slippery slope—one day you're making the conscious daily choice to apply for new jobs in your evenings, pretty soon you'll be ready to leave the job you hate, forge new friendships, dye your hair one way and then another the week after, say goodbye to old relationships, explore your childhood dreams, or book the one-way flight because you have embraced the possibility and the opportunity of the quarter-life crisis.

Without this discomfort, there's no telling how many of us would end up in lives that still don't fit twenty years later. So, once again, I am here to formally welcome you to your quarter-life crisis and, hopefully, introduce you to the person you are becoming—that person in progress who is born the moment you accept the chaos of your twenties.

Things are a lot different for us than for the generation(s) before us who set the standards for what our twenties supposedly should look like.

It's okay to feel lost. Everyone else is feeling the same way.

The fear and discomfort you are feeling is a sign that you care about your future. That is a good thing! Without chaos, we have no incentive to grow.

Millions have come before you and survived. You will figure it out.

CHAPTER II

The Art of Fucking Up

As FRUSTRATING AS it is, we learn the most from our mistakes. The times we slept through an alarm, the words we said to a friend that we didn't mean, a failed exam, not proofing an email before it was sent out to all the new staff in the company, only to realize it said "Welcome to our orgasm" instead of "Welcome to our organization" (this is a true story).

We are all works in progress. No one comes out of the womb completely flawless and excellent at everything—at least I haven't had the privilege of meeting this kind of superhuman! Half the learning process is incorporating the times you didn't get everything right and adapting from those mistakes. It's harder than it sounds, as anyone who has ever made a mistake would know, myself included. Mistakes often feel like dark, ominous clouds that never go away and, what's even worse, that everyone can see.

Mistakes reveal that we are not as perfect as we'd like others to think. They make us insecure about our abilities, our competence, our intelligence, even our kindness or thoughtfulness. The worst thing we can do is let those mistakes define us, especially during our twenties. When our identity is already unstable, slight missteps and failures can become magnified in our minds until we think our mistakes are all anyone will ever see. The truth is, no one is ruminating on your missteps for months afterward; no one else is spending hours thinking about them. There are people out there, still alive right now, who have made bigger mistakes than you have—and they recovered. The Olympic snowboarder Lindsey Jacobellis, who fell two seconds before victory at the 2006 Olympic Games, only to return sixteen years later and win the gold. People who have made terrible investments and lost it all, only to rebuild successful businesses. Ex-cons who did decades in jail who are now inspirational speakers or CEOs of charities. The list goes on. Reminding yourself of these stories brings perspective to what probably feels so major for you.

Again, no one is thinking about your actions as much as you are, and we have proof of this.

Back in 1997, researchers Robin Dunbar and Anna Marriott wanted to know what most people were thinking about throughout the day. By observing what people talked about, they found that 78 percent of conversations were about ourselves, our thoughts, our fears, our desires, our perceptions. Only a relatively small proportion dealt with topics like work, money, or negative opinions about others, despite our false beliefs to the contrary.

When we make a mistake, we think there is a gigantic spotlight shining directly on us and that everyone must be thinking about it the way we are: with regret or secondhand embarrassment, cringing at our behavior. When we start to realize this is not the case, we can master the art of fucking up and accept all the realities of being human—of being fallible, flawed, clumsy, and sometimes confused. **A lot of beauty lies in those imperfections,** a lot of humor lies in our mistakes, and a lot of learning exists in our errors.

Accepting Our Mistakes

Not many of us learn how to fail correctly, because society is so obsessed with success and accomplishment. Bragging about your achievements is totally normal, but discussing your failures and what you learned is definitely not. So we only know how to respond with shame, because we are taught that mistakes are "taboo" or need to be hidden. However, by not accepting the grace in failure, we are missing out on many valuable life lessons that could prevent us from making the same mistakes again and again. **Mastering the art of fucking up, especially in our twenties, releases us from the additional mental and emotional punishment we inflict on ourselves.** It frees us from perfectionism and expands our capacity to grow and improve. Building this skill requires an entire mindset and attitude shift from viewing mistakes as failures to seeing them as opportunities, which you will learn so much more from than if you were perfect all along. The art of fucking up is a three-step process:

1. Identify what kind of mistake you've made.

2. Decide whether to absorb or release this mistake.

3. Focus on the teachable content of this mistake.

Let's walk through this together.

Different Types of Mistakes

First, mistakes are not just one big basket of all the silly things people can do. Mistakes have different origins, and those origins help us decide how much blame or shame we really need to take on and what negative thoughts we can ignore instead.

In the 2015 study "What Is Stupid? People's Conception of Unintelligent Behavior," three researchers set out to understand how people conceptualize mistakes. They wanted to know what it is about certain behaviors that make us feel idiotic or silly and the mental roots of this interpretation. They showed participants a number of news stories from sources like *The New York Times,* TMZ, the BBC, and *The Guardian* in which people had done things we might label "stupid"—including a story about a thief who broke into a house to steal a TV, only to forget the remote. Or a man who robbed a bank by putting lemon juice on his face because he thought that would obscure the CCTV footage (he obviously was mistaken). The researchers asked the participants to then rate these stories and identify what led to this idiotic behavior.

What they found was that there are broadly three categories of mistakes. First, **arrogant mistakes** occur when our confidence outstrips our ability, a phenomenon also known as the "Dunning-Kruger effect." In short, we often think we are much more skilled than we are. A few years ago, there was a TikTok trend in which people asked their boyfriends, fathers, and male colleagues whether they thought they could land a plane, never having done any pilot training. A large majority of these men said yes. That is an arrogant mistake.

Second, there are **impulsive mistakes,** when we act in the heat of the moment only to calm down later and realize we've really messed up and could have made a better decision. We let our desires guide our behavior in a way that is inappropriate, like gossiping about a colleague to someone you know isn't trustworthy because you just can't contain yourself.

Finally, **inattentive mistakes** occur when you're just not concentrating or thinking straight, such as turning off your alarms on exam day or sending out an email without seeing your massive typo ("Welcome to our orgasm"–type mistakes).

We can use these three categories—arrogant, impulsive, and inattentive—to define our mistakes and learn how to prevent ourselves from repeating them. For example, arrogant mistakes require us to rethink our abilities and judge them realistically before we act. Impulsive mistakes can be rectified by emotional regulation, while inattentive mistakes can be fixed by prioritizing what is most important and having a mental checklist of what needs to be done. The *source* of our mistakes thus seems to contain the solution. This is our first way of categorizing the many mistakes we make in our twenties.

We can also arrange mistakes by severity. Tripping over your words on a date is not the same as accidentally missing your final exam, which is not the same as crashing a plane. There is a difference in scale that we need to acknowledge in order to forgive ourselves and move forward. I like to think of mistakes as being "littles," "mediums," or "massives." We can determine this based on the significance our actions and their outcomes have for our future, and their significance for others.

Littles are the small things you can easily forget by the end of the week. These are the most common type of mistake. From personal experience, I can say that about 90 percent of the mistakes we spend time worrying about are littles. They typically do not impact your future or damage relationships beyond repair and, therefore, are negligible in the long term, if not valuable lessons. For example, forgetting you've double-booked plans and canceling on a friend is a mistake, but it's easy to see you were just being inattentive or disorganized. You can apologize and move on. Another example is missing a deadline. It feels embarrassing in the moment, but within a week you can recover, apologize to your boss, give your reasons, and move on. Littles become significant only when they are continuously repeated or become a habit. But we can move past most littles.

Mediums are mistakes that may have an impact on your future or on the people around you; they could take a few months to recover from, but no longer than a few years. If 90 percent of our mistakes are littles, I'd say 9 percent of our mistakes are mediums. They are mistakes we have a right to feel worried about because they can be incredibly stressful in the moment, but we will recover from them in time. Mediums might include a poor investment or financial choice, choosing the wrong university, dating the wrong person for longer than is healthy, selecting the wrong friends, or wasting time in dead-end jobs. These are all choices we would rather avoid, but we don't always know better. The only way we can learn is through experience. In the grand scheme of life, mediums may change our current life trajectory, but not destroy it.

Finally, **massives** are mistakes that impact both those around us and our future and will become part of our life story. Massives occur less than 1 percent of the time, and some of us may never even experience a massive. These are the kinds of mistakes you would get prison time for, like fraud, murder, theft, or assault. Those kinds of mistakes are life-altering or irreparably harm others—emotionally, physically, or mentally. Massives result from an accumulation of bad decisions and impulsive actions we can't take back.

I have never had a massive—and fingers crossed I don't—but the problem is that we often confuse littles or mediums with massives and treat them with the same level of life-ending alarm. Those small hiccups everyone experiences can create a significant amount of stress if you don't put them in perspective, especially if you are a catastrophizer, a perfectionist, or a people-pleaser. The very act of doing something wrong, accidentally, makes us feel like our entire personhood is damaged beyond repair, when all it takes is time and another distraction to come along for us to realize it really wasn't that big a deal. If I asked you what you were worrying about six months ago, you probably couldn't tell me. But you most likely learned something from that experience that is still visible in your behavior today. We have more to learn from that situation than to lose. Very few mistakes are going to be so memorable that you're thinking about them in five or ten years' time, and very few of us have the capacity to even create this kind of upending chaos if we simply pay attention.

The first step to mastering the art of fucking up in your twenties is to be able to distinguish between your arrogant, impulsive, and inattentive mistakes, as well as your littles, mediums, and massives. Then taper your reaction to be in proportion.

Once you have determined what kind and severity of mistake you're facing, next you need to decide whether you benefit more from **absorbing or releasing that mistake.** Here's a spoiler: Very rarely should we absorb a mistake in its entirety, because often our interpretation of a mistake is clouded by a need to find blame: by excessively blaming ourselves or others, neither of which is particularly helpful. When we absorb the mistake, we think it says something about who we are, which it doesn't, or otherwise we don't learn anything at all, because we look to others to make our mistakes sting less.

Getting Comfortable with Your Mistakes

Instead of absorbing the mistake, you want to approach mistakes in your twenties with neutrality: break down what happened, why it happened, and what you have to learn from it. When examining the why, focus on what you know to be objectively true, rather than subjective.

You can tell yourself, "I spent too much money on that piece of clothing because I didn't properly budget and think about my future expenses," rather than "I spent too much on that item of clothing because I lack any self-discipline and I'm stupid and have no impulse control." One of these statements is actionable because you can rethink how you manage money for a better outcome, while the other lowers your self-esteem and belittles your qualities as a person, rather than addressing the mistake itself. You have no incentive to improve if you already believe that deep down you are this flawed person who can never change. As I always say, you can't hate yourself into changing your behavior. But if you release the mistake and take what you need from it, you can focus on what this moment can teach you instead.

Here's what common mistakes in your twenties can teach you:

The mistake: **Spending too much money.**
What it could teach you: The importance of budgeting and calculating your expenses for short-term and long-term financial freedom.

The mistake: **Ignoring your physical and mental health until the point of burnout.**
What it could teach you: The signs that it's time to rest to prevent future exhaustion.

The mistake: **Messing up at work.**
What it could teach you: What your boss expects of you and how to impress them.

The mistake: **Dating the wrong person for too long.**
What it could teach you: What you do need in a future partner.

The mistake: **Hurting a friend.**
What it could teach you: How to take accountability and apologize.

The mistake: **Getting too drunk on a night out.**
What it could teach you: Rethinking your relationship with alcohol and knowing where your limits are.

When I look at those lessons, they all sound like some of the most important skills to gain during this decade. They sound like the crucial stuff—the key takeaways from our twenties. I wouldn't want to miss out on any of them just because it might make me more comfortable now. Being comfortable now often means greater discomfort in the future when we either a) haven't realized something crucial that would have helped us a lot sooner or b) are learning the same lesson only when we are considerably older. In fact, not having these experiences may be more harmful than having a healthy dose of mistakes in your twenties.

Professors at Stanford and Harvard coined the term **"failure deprived"** to describe students they were encountering who had never been exposed to a healthy amount of error in their childhood, teen years, and even early twenties. When failure-deprived young people eventually make a mistake that a parent or teacher isn't there to help them with, they have no idea how to cope, because they have never become accustomed to trying and failing. They only know what it means to try and succeed, or to be told, "Good job!" They may be more likely to drop out of university, suffer poor mental health, or see a huge decline in their self-esteem. I never thought I'd say this, but maybe we should thank our lucky stars for the opportunity to fail—to fuck up and have to fix it, to make the wrong decisions and get comfortable with the discomfort. I know that sounds simple, but discomfort is sometimes like cold water: we get more used to it when we just let ourselves be submerged, and the next time we're less afraid of it.

When we get comfortable with making mistakes, we also get comfortable with failure, because "failure" is not a bad word. In fact, saying someone "failed" implies that they at least tried. It may not be as good as "They succeeded," but it's definitely better than "They did nothing." Getting comfortable with failure means that you can push yourself to new levels, because large goals are no longer frightening. Expanding beyond your comfort zone doesn't have to be all-or-nothing—failure is an acceptable outcome because at least you're further ahead than before. Sometimes you can find better outcomes than you ever expected by learning from your failures and mistakes.

What Comes Next?

When I was twenty, all I wanted was a consulting internship for some big-shot firm. To be honest, I didn't know what the job title "consultant" even entailed, but everyone who had studied what I did seemed to be applying for these jobs. So I put everything into my interviews, and got rejected from every single one. In one of them, I read the wrong case study, so I answered all my questions wrong. For another, I couldn't answer the question "Why do you want this job?" beyond the basic responses (because I didn't really), and for the other two I fumbled through my interviews, completely held up by my nerves. As everyone around me seemed to be advancing, I spent the summer with my grandma and had never felt more like a failure. But because of those failures, I started thinking about a podcast. I didn't get into a graduate program the next year, so I applied for a different job that made me move to Sydney and gave me three months off after university to focus on this tiny show called *The Psychology of Your 20s* I was nurturing. Those mistakes were the gateway to an entirely different life I would have missed out on if everything had gone according to plan. What are your mistakes preparing you for? What if that failure is just a redirection?

Sometimes it's hard to have that kind of positive attitude when nothing good seems to have come from your errors. That's okay—there are plenty of times when that's happened to me too. It's at this point that we need to embrace radical self-compassion and practice forgiving ourselves for the times we didn't know any better.

Self-forgiveness has two components: compassion and accountability. You need to master both. The first step is to show yourself the compassion you would have for others if they were in the same situation. Imagine it was your best friend, your sibling, your partner—anyone you love dearly—who made this mistake. Wouldn't you want them to forgive themselves? What advice would you give them? Can you take your own advice in this situation? What kind of love would you show them at that moment? You should be showing yourself that same love. Just like you accept their doubts and mistakes, you can accept that you are equally as deserving of self-forgiveness. Second, take accountability. We all know that the best kind of friend is the one who is willing to tell you when you've messed up. They're not going to sugarcoat your actions or immediately tell you everything's fine, because, honestly, sometimes it isn't. You need to be that friend. Take responsibility for the ways you perhaps objectively acted against your instincts, the errors you overlooked, and learn from them. Most people find it easier to bury their head in the sand or find excuses—it's a lot more comfortable to think this way. But it also does little to help you in the long term, meaning the mistake loses its transformative power. It then becomes nothing more than a source of shame and embarrassment you'd rather ignore—when it could have the potential to make you into a better person.

Becoming more comfortable with your mistakes will make you a better person if you practice the art of fucking up: identifying the type of mistake you have made, releasing rather than absorbing it, and using this situation as a teachable moment.

If it won't matter in five years, don't spend more than five minutes thinking about it.

No one is paying that much attention to you. There is no spotlight on all the things you've done wrong.

Most mistakes are littles and mediums, not massives. Treat them as such.

When we choose to learn from our mistakes, they become valuable. When we choose to internalize our mistakes, they are worthless.

- - - -- -- -- --

CHAPTER III

Risky Business

YOUR TWENTIES ARE your decade for taking risks. Moving to a new city or a new country, starting over fresh in a new career, approaching that new person, leaving that stagnant relationship, quitting the toxic job and doing freelance, putting everything you've got into a passion. Each of us has something in mind that we think is a bit too risky to be realistic. But risks are our way of aligning our lives with our values and our dreams and saying to ourselves: "I care enough about my future to do the scary thing now, rather than face missing out later."

There has never been a better time for you to do something that pushes you out of your comfort zone, to do something fueled by passion rather than reason, or to do something unexpected. Playing it safe may keep you comfortable, but it also keeps you in a predictable timeline. What often emerges from predictability is boredom. If you have never gotten accustomed to being a little bit scared by your decisions and the possibility of what comes next, it gets harder to embrace risk the older you get. The risks you choose to take in your twenties don't necessarily have to be dangerous (they don't even need to be spontaneous), but if you are going to take a huge leap of faith, there is no better decade than this one. Let me explain why.

Why Twenty-Somethings Should Take Risks

Why is a healthy level of risk-taking especially important in your twenties? First, risks can be the biggest catalysts for changing your life and the entire direction it goes in. Risks are sometimes the decisions with the biggest payoffs, if you can get past your initial fears. When you move beyond that fear and do the hard thing anyway, you become part of the elite 1 percent who get to say, "I did that, I tried, I went where others wouldn't."

Second, risks are essential for your growth and self-development—for figuring out who you are. The best memories and growth occur when you put yourself in a position where you are unsure about what comes next. As a result, you have more room for exploration, can test yourself, and build greater confidence in your abilities and resilience. I found this to be true when I quit my full-time job to speak about my twenties for a living. I was completely terrified but ready to try anything, and with more room to say yes, I could see where that took me. Now, with the gift of hindsight, I can see why that was one of the best decisions I ever made. I think I'm back in that phase right now: uncomfortable with what my future has in store but holding space to be open to possibility. The previous experience of quitting my job taught me that fear, uncertainty, and spontaneity are part of the process. Being a little bit afraid might even be the most necessary part. As the saying goes: Diamonds are made under pressure!

Risks are also an essential part of an exploratory mindset for your future. They allow you to see what is out there and what is possible, especially at an age when society is a lot more tolerant of a spontaneous and free-spirited attitude. And taking risks will give you something to be proud of the older you get. They give you the gift of a good story and a life well lived. Even if you're in your twenties now, fifty years from now you'll have something to tell your grandchildren or friends in the retirement home that makes them think, "They really got everything out of life." But even more important, risks give you a sense of agency over your life. You are the driver, you are the decision-maker, you are in control of your destiny.

As the years go by, it becomes so much easier to do what is convenient and obvious, because there is less friction. We become a lot less active in our own decision-making, and to be honest, we get used to just being comfortable and not much else. But true growth and true happiness occur when we push beyond what is comfortable, beyond what feels safe, and into a place of expansion. I've also found that what is easy isn't always what is best. It's easy to spend your days watching TV, but that won't make you feel great at the end of the night. It's easy to do what is expected of you, but then you're not really living your life for you. It's easy to never move and stay in the same city or company your entire life, but that won't necessarily leave you feeling fulfilled. It's easy to put away your big hopes and creative dreams because it's scary to think about failing, but how will you know unless you try?

Naturally, the risks you choose to take will look different based on your own values and life vision. It might mean going back to school at twenty-nine, taking a year off to travel solo, starting a business, moving to a new city where you know nobody, quitting your terrible job without a solid plan for what comes next, choosing to invest that time in a hobby or passion you love, or building something. On an even smaller level, risk can also show up in your daily interactions with those around you by being more honest about your feelings, introducing yourself, doing something that scares you, putting your hand up even if you're unsure, going to events alone, or having difficult conversations. It all comes down to being able to say yes to an opportunity, even if you don't feel prepared.

On paper, these things don't seem too hard. And if taking those risks offered everything we're promised—great payoffs, amazing memories, self-growth, fulfillment, excitement, a better future—it's difficult to imagine why anyone would ever play it safe. But anyone who has ever contemplated a risky bet will know the fear that comes along with it.

Fear is the killer of dreams. Fear is what keeps us stagnant. We're scared of failing, we're scared of things not working out, of giving our dreams our everything and having nothing to show for it. We're scared of feeling lonely, out of place, or insecure, of not being capable enough. We're scared of what people might think: the judgment, potential embarrassment, or letting others down. Underneath it all is the fear of the unknown. If you've lived your life one way for the first two decades of your existence, what would it mean to turn it all upside down for an outcome you can't predict? There is nothing safe or familiar about this level of uncertainty.

Why We Fear Risks

In order to take risks, we need to reframe our relationship with fear. Fear is actually a valuable emotion, and it serves a function like any other emotion we may experience. Fear is what keeps us safe by alerting us to the dangers around us—whether those are physical, social, or psychological. When we encounter something that could potentially harm us, an automatic process in our body is set off that will increase our chances for survival. It starts in the fear center of the brain, the amygdala, sending a distress signal to our command center, the hypothalamus, which then alerts the rest of the body to be prepared. It's known in psychology as the fight-or-flight response, which has recently been adapted to also include freeze.

Essentially, if a giant predator is coming toward us, we can do one of three things: fight it off, run away, or freeze and hope it doesn't see us. While we are making this decision, our sympathetic nervous system—the part of us that responds to dangerous and stressful situations—is doing everything it can to make sure we get through the situation. It's flooding our body with adrenaline, increasing our heart rate to get more oxygen to all those crucial areas of our body, and shutting down all those other functions that aren't immediately important, which all leads to that state of arousal and panic.

That fear response has evolved alongside our changing modern environment and the stressors and dangers that come with it. It's no longer activated just by external threats, but by internal threats—fear of judgment, worries about the future, existential anxieties, social comparison—that we predict will harm our sense of stability and security. That includes real or imagined scenarios like: *I'm going to fail and lose everything. I'll make the wrong decision and end up alone or broke or lost.* Our fears keep us stuck because we instinctively don't want those mental predictions to come true, and it is easier to imagine failing than succeeding because our brain wants to keep us more alert to the outcome that poses the bigger threat.

The easiest way for our fears to never be realized is to never do anything risky. Great—we've found the solution! Fear, begone. Unfortunately, doing nothing is also the easiest way to be incredibly bored. Sure, you can stay in your safe bubble your entire life and never have to encounter any of those worries. But at the end of your life, you'll have to face an even more terrifying reality: a life you never truly lived. There's no taking that back. What you need to recognize and embrace is that nearly every decision you make in life can be reversed—except for the decisions you didn't make.

Struggling with taking risks is not all about fear; it's also about our perception of the different options and outcomes. Some people are more aware of what could go wrong than others. They pay closer attention to the level of uncertainty in their decisions and how terrible the imagined worst outcome would be, and this holds them back from risks. There are three kinds of people when it comes to risk-taking: the **risk-averse,** the **risk-neutral,** and the **risk-loving.**

The **risk-loving** are willing to bet more on a risk even if they're not promised any real outcome or the promise of a potentially huge payoff. These individuals drop everything to take a job overseas without any certainty it will even exist when they arrive, or quit jobs whenever they feel the need, even if they're not entirely sure a new opportunity will fall into their lap. Most of us don't think this way. Instead, we are either risk-neutral or risk-averse.

Risk-neutral individuals could either take the risk or leave it. They are not influenced by how uncertain an outcome is, whether it is more or less likely to happen; they just choose what has the highest payoffs in their mind. If they have to choose between staying at their secure job or betting it all on their big new business idea, they won't be thinking about how likely they are to succeed or the risk involved. They'll simply choose whatever is going to give them the most of what they desire, whether that's freedom, money, community, or fame.

Risk-averse individuals are very reluctant to jeopardize what they currently have for something that might be better or worse. Certainty is an important factor in their decision-making and may be worth more than any unpredictable payout. A paper by researchers at the University of Pennsylvania argued that this kind of risk aversion may be more common in anxious people. Reading that was like reading something I already knew was fact—like someone telling me, "The sky is blue" or "We need oxygen to survive." Of course we anxious individuals are going to be more scared of taking risks, because we have already imagined every possible worst-case scenario and we have overthought every possible outcome. That is the nature of anxiety: we want to be prepared for absolutely everything that could ever possibly occur in the hopes of being more prepared if it actually occurs. Very rarely do our imagined hypotheticals come true, but they don't need to come true for us to still be scared of the possibility. So we choose the outcome we can be sure of, which is the one we already have.

Fear and risk aversion are two factors that stop us from taking risks, but there is also an innate competition between **passion and practicality**. The average twenty-something is not necessarily off chasing the sunrise; they are also caretakers, parents, indebted to banks or loved ones, providers. You may want something more than anything else in the world, but there are money, security, health, family, and responsibilities to consider. It's very easy to look at someone who has "abandoned" a dream and jump to the conclusion that they were just too scared. But not everyone is born with the same privilege to be able to take a year off to travel or move across the world or quit their nine-to-five for a side hustle.

Risks often require giving up something. Perhaps it's a previous dream you have outgrown, or parts of your life that make you comfortable. For other people, it may mean giving up a whole way of survival and living. For most of us, practicality wins out over passion. But when we conceptualize risk differently, we begin to see that maybe our assumptions about the cost or compromise that comes with risk are misguided, and risk can be a club that welcomes everyone, even in small ways.

How to Take More Risks

There is no denying that risks are life-changing, but they also don't have to be necessarily significant or spontaneous. We can put conscious thought into our risks and select them carefully. I think it's a major misconception that taking risks means throwing all caution to the wind or having no plan whatsoever. There are **two types of risks** we can take, and one type is definitely preferable to the other, at least in my mind. Let's talk about the distinction between **bounded and unbounded risk.**

Bounded risks are amazing and are the ones you should be taking. They have limited downside yet unbounded upsides or gains. Basically, this means there is a limit or cap to how much you can lose. Normally, bounded risks require some initial investment to get started, but that is all they will cost. That is a one-off temporary loss, but once you begin, there is no ceiling on what you can gain from this decision. Starting a podcast, building a new skill, committing to running a marathon, booking a nonrefundable flight—these are all examples of bounded risks. If it doesn't work out, you won't lose more than what you've already invested. Think about the plane ticket. If you don't go on the trip, the most you lose is the cost of the fare, but you could gain a whole wealth of experiences from just pulling the trigger on your dream. Or take the decision to learn a new programming skill or language. You can walk away at any time. But if it does work, it could mean a new career, a new facet of your identity, a whole new lifestyle.

In contrast, there are also **unbounded risks.** There is nothing stopping this risk from getting out of control and no limit to how much you can lose. The example I always give is choosing to jump out of a plane. There is no limit to how much you could potentially lose in this situation, considering that you could die. Another example is putting all your money and savings into a poorly planned business idea. Or posting controversial things online. It could end up costing you your reputation, your friends, your career—a big risk with an unpredictable payoff. Hopefully you get the picture.

The equation to remember is this:

Bounded risks: small and contained cost, big wins.

Unbounded risks: unlimited cost, unpredictable wins.

It's important to still maintain some level of rationality in our twenties. Taking a risk requires judgment. Yes, there are risk-loving people who will tell you how it was the best decision they've ever made, all about their riches and dreams coming true, but that fantasy is not one you should buy into without thinking it through. When we plan and think them through, our unbounded risks can become bounded.

Planned Risks

Risks don't have to be inherently spur of the moment to still be risks; they can be planned. You can take your time, prepare, and talk it through with family and friends. Just make sure that your preparation is not actually an unconscious form of avoidance whereby you are constantly in the planning stage and always have a reason to not take action.

You're never going to feel fully ready for anything, ever. There will always be some doubt, there will also always be things we can't account for, but these hidden surprises aren't always terrible. They're exciting, as things often turn out better than expected. To get comfortable with the unknown while also testing the feasibility of your risk, take small risks in preparation. If you want to change careers, start by networking and applying for new jobs with bigger salaries and more responsibilities before you quit your current job. If you want to start your own business, take a solid look at your finances and see if you can launch just one successful product or service. If you want to solo travel but are afraid of feeling lonely or unsafe, go on a solo camping trip in preparation. If you want to move cities, visit first and spend a week there to actually see how you feel about it. You don't have to jump in the deep end to take a chance on yourself. You can paddle out instead and still be in the same position, but taking the same risk at your own pace.

One of the other huge misconceptions I hear about taking risks in your twenties is that they have to be something you never saw yourself doing or something completely shocking in order for them to "count." You went from working a desk job to hiking Mount Everest; that makes you a risk-taker. You shaved your hair off and did ayahuasca.

Instead of thinking about risks as these big decisions that will forever alter your life, think about them as a value realignment. **Risks are a way for you to shift your life back in the direction that aligns with how you see yourself, what you value from life, and what you want from the future!** Maybe you see yourself as a creative, someone who has a true eye for beauty and producing work that moves people. Maybe you are missing the kind of risk that takes you out of your comfort zone, so you pursue this more deeply in a way that the stakes are high enough to motivate you. The risk is to just create, no matter the threat of judgment or even failure. At least you can say you did it and have something to be personally proud of.

Maybe you value being really adventurous—you're a bit of a nomad. You've perhaps felt stuck post-pandemic and felt the need to work full-time to make money for your dreams. Here the risk you need to take is to get back out on the road, to say: Fuck it, this is what I actually want from life even if it's difficult at times, even if people don't understand it. The risk is to book weekend trips, to find a way to make this a priority.

Risks are a catalyst not just for change but for realigning yourself with your purpose, taking yourself off the path that was expected of you—and that may seem like the one of least friction—and finding your way back onto your unique path. The one that might change everything and unlock your dream future. The worst that can happen is you fail, in which case you're back at square one anyway, the same place you never would have left if you hadn't tried.

You have a responsibility to yourself to make decisions that might leave you temporarily feeling a bit out of place but will significantly change your life and set you on a new course. You have the responsibility to make friends with fear, because you know something better is on the other side. No one is going to come and suddenly make your life amazing for you. You are the only one who can do it. Maybe not everyone will understand your motivations, but it doesn't matter because, luckily for you, it's not their life. It's yours—treat it as such.

> The biggest risk you can take is playing it safe and hoping life happens to work out the way you want it to... without doing anything to make that your reality.

> When you choose to play it safe, you let fear become your master. When you embrace risk, you acknowledge the fear but do it anyway.

> Risk doesn't have to be scary and spontaneous; it can be slow and planned.

> Give yourself this decade to dream big and see what happens, and the rest of your life to reap the rewards.

- - - - - - - - - -

CHAPTER IV

The Paradox of Choice

IN OUR TWENTIES, we enter the stage where we are expected to make significant decisions about our future career path and begin formulating the "plan" we have for our life. If this decade is our period for exploration, the pressure to reach a conclusion about what we want next intensifies throughout and leading up to our thirties. But that one unanswerable question remains: "What do I actually want to do with my life?"

It might not surprise you, but there truly isn't one right answer to this question. Not only does everyone have a different interpretation, it's possible to feel like you hold multiple answers at the same time. While that might feel liberating, it's also terrifying because the lack of a straightforward answer presents more options than you are prepared to deal with. With options comes the need to make a choice. And it can feel like with each choice you make, you close a lot more doors than you open, leading to fears that maybe the path you are taking might not, ultimately, be the right one.

Choice Overload

When it comes to the amount of choice we have for our careers, this generation of twenty-somethings is perhaps the luckiest in history, even if it doesn't always feel like it. The possibilities for future jobs, travel, passions, and projects are endless, primarily due to a rapid expansion in technology that has created an entire new category of potential professions and simultaneously opened our eyes to what is out there.

Previous generations at our age were limited to a handful of career options, even fewer when we consider the family tradition of passing on a trade or business. People worked the jobs that their community needed, and the somewhat strict and antiquated class divisions also further limited what they could actually do: farmer, soldier, maybe a trade. For women, the options were even fewer: mother, wife, spinster, widow. Maybe the occasional secretary, housemaid, or poet (of course writing in her husband's name).

These days, the path we get to take through life is not so strict or confined. Never in history have there been so many kinds of jobs, but also types of life paths to take that are becoming accepted as a valid way to live. This might seem like it would contribute to greater satisfaction and more freedom to choose, but in many ways it has made that choice harder, because we are more aware of the different lives we have to decline in order to pick the one we think is best. In our twenties, the gravity of this decision is particularly profound.

Do I want to travel the world? Do I want to go back to university? Do I want to settle down? Do I want to save money while working my nine-to-five? Do I want to quit my dead-end job? Do I want to learn a new trade? Do I want to pursue my creative passion?

These are only a few possible choices, but what do we do when two of our dream lives contradict, meaning that we might not be able to do both? Which do we choose? You are not the first person to encounter this dilemma, nor will you be the last. In her book *The Bell Jar,* the poet Sylvia Plath talked about this feeling of being claustrophobic in one's own life, ironically limited by one's freedom and imagination.

Life is like one giant fruit tree, and from each branch hang thousands of delicious fruits, or potential futures that could be, each one beckoning us. One fruit is a partner and a happy home, another is a famous author, a parent, an eccentric single aunt, an athlete, a mysterious artist with a dozen lovers in Italy, a world traveler, an executive, a retail worker. The question is, which fruit to pick? Which future do we want most? The longer we wait, the more of these fruits rot away and leave us with fewer options, lamenting over all the fruits we could have eaten. We are very aware at this moment in our lives that commitment to one comes at the price of freedom and flexibility for another. So we remain suspended, paralyzed in time and unable to decide.

You might find yourself endlessly researching different industries, job roles, and companies, trying to identify the one that will bring you the most fulfillment and success. In another case, you may find yourself unable to settle down or commit for extended periods of time, jumping from place to place, quitting jobs as soon as you feel bored.

A close friend of mine—let's call her Chloe—fits this very profile. When I first met her, I had mutual friends say, "To love Chloe is to see her leave and never really know what's going on in her life." I didn't quite realize what they meant. I thought it was a weird thing to say about someone you loved. As the year went on, she changed jobs so rapidly I could never keep up. By the end of the year she was living in Canada as a ski instructor; by mid-April she was doing her master's in Germany. That didn't stick and she moved home, only to buy a van and travel Australia. She didn't want to miss out on all the different lives she had contained in her. In other cases, though, we are faced with extreme dread and anxiety, sleepless nights worrying about what we give up with each decision we make.

What we are experiencing at this moment is known in psychology as the **paradox of choice.** This theory suggests that **the more options we have, the harder it is to make a decision.** Furthermore, having more options tends to predict how dissatisfied we are with our choice later on, because we have more opportunities to compare to and ruminate on the what-ifs. It turns out the best way to explain this is using jam.

In 2000, psychologists Sheena Iyengar and Mark Lepper conducted an experiment in an upscale grocery store. On day one, they presented shoppers with twenty-four types of jam. On the second day, they had only six. What they wanted to determine was whether people were more likely to buy jam when they had more options or fewer. Contrary to what they expected, more people purchased jam when they had only six flavors available compared to when they had twenty-four. With fewer options, they were also less likely to express dissatisfaction with their choice a few days later. How exactly does this apply to the life decisions we need to make in our twenties? This study shows us what we already know: **more choice doesn't necessarily mean greater freedom,** and therefore happiness. In fact, when we are presented with as many potential futures as we are now, it can produce choice paralysis.

You might hesitate to commit to a career path out of fear that there could be a better option out there. Or a new opportunity pops up, but it means giving up on the plan you have already decided, so you hold off. At that moment, you have so many more factors to weigh and consider that the level of mental energy required slows down your decision-making process. With only six options, the correct option becomes a lot clearer, because there is often a solid winner, compared to twenty-four equally good choices whose differences are harder to discern. With less choice, we feel less overwhelmed, but also more satisfied. This "analysis paralysis" is a big contributor to our sense of instability and anxiety toward the future in our twenties.

Moving Beyond the Fear of Regret

The second factor to consider is regret. Regret is one of the scary realities of aging because it makes you contemplate every potential version of you that could have been made with different choices. We don't want to feel like we have missed out, or to be haunted by the what-ifs of what could have been had we made a better choice. In a finite life, every opportunity for happiness, joy, wealth, love, and satisfaction seems precious, and we don't want to live with the acknowledgment that things could have been better for us if we had chosen differently. Furthermore, we understand that regret is so powerful because we know we aren't able to go back and correct our "mistakes." So our only protection is to be preventative, and that is where our chronic indecisiveness comes from. We face the cognitive fallacy that if we just think longer and harder about what the best option is, we will reach a conclusion and the correct answer will suddenly appear, when we know overthinking actually further contributes to a spiral of doubt and uncertainty.

That pressure to create a good life contributes further to our fear of regret, because we feel solely responsible for the outcome of our decisions, when really it's not as serious or final as our brains make it out to be. The worst thing we can do in the face of this fear is nothing. While it might feel safer in a place of inaction, studies have revealed that we are more likely to regret the decisions we didn't make, compared to the ones we did.

In one of my favorite studies of all time, researchers concluded that across our six biggest sources of regret—education, career, romance, parenting, the self, and leisure—the majority of individuals regretted inaction rather than action. In the cases where we do pick and devote our energy to a particular path, at least we are able to say we did **something.** Something will come from that choice, whereas no decision equals no outcome. What can we take from this research?

Not every option is going to be perfect, and it will require trade-offs. So we just have to choose what we feel is best at the time and see where it takes us, ignoring the tiny voice inside that wants us to wait out our uncertainty. It won't get any easier to make a choice. The further along we get with our decision, the happier we also tend to become, because we adjust to the life we have chosen and find happiness in things we didn't expect.

Let's address this idea that, once you choose a path, you are locked in for life. Destiny sealed. No going back. This fallacy maintains your fear of the future and the potential of committing to one dream, one career, one goal. The thing is, it's entirely false. **The average person tends to go through three to seven career changes before they retire, with that number only increasing within this upcoming generation of twenty-somethings.** Furthermore, you have the capacity for change at any moment if you develop a healthy relationship with fear and uncertainty.

Say you decided at eighteen you wanted to become a lawyer, but now at twenty-five you realize that life isn't for you: you want more flexibility and maybe want to try hospitality work or start your own café. That is going to be scary because you are challenging a way of thinking and a goal you had for over half a decade. All your thoughts have been centered on this goal and they no longer have a destination. But it's not as scary as waiting another five years and realizing, for all your excuses, you've just wasted your time. **There is no shame in deciding that something you once wanted is no longer for you.** In fact, I believe it takes incredible bravery to start again, not just in your twenties but at any age. You are unburdening your future self of the regret that may result from your inaction.

Overcoming the Paradox of Choice

When you are overwhelmed by the paradox of choice, it's important to reframe how you visualize the next forty to fifty years of your life. I'm not talking about what your future house will look like or all the milestones you want to reach. More specifically, how do you conceptually see those years?

Each of us has a way of imagining the structure, size, color, and movement of our days, months, and years. For example, some people see a year as a loop, months as different colors, or days as a hill. This is due to a phenomenon known as "calendar synesthesia." We are going to borrow this type of visualization and mental processing to help us overcome our analysis paralysis and fear of making the wrong choice. What I want to prove is that we can live all the lives and timelines we want, just not at the same time.

Most of us tend to think of our lives as one big chunk of time or years that stretch out before us. There is where we are now, and then there is the end. When we think about our lives this way, it feels especially daunting, because there is very little acknowledgment and room to appreciate the many different twists, turns, and chapters contained in that giant lump of years in our future.

Instead, I want you to think about your life as a series of seasons, starting in your twenties, whereby each new season is going to contain a new plot, new characters, new locations, new jobs, new opportunities, and new challenges, almost like a long-running TV show—a sitcom, say, to add an element of humor.

Season one occurs when we're between twenty and twenty-two. These are our founding years, when we come of age and make the majority of our mistakes.

Season two is from twenty-two to twenty-four, our settlement years. We think we're getting our feet under us; maybe we land our first "big" adult job. Perhaps we move to a new city or a new home. Although we start to feel distinctively "adult," we've probably never felt more lost.

Season three is from twenty-five to twenty-six, or our leap of faith. This is our time to take a big risk or a collection of small risks as we emerge from our quarter-life crisis.

Season four is twenty-seven and twenty-eight, our renaissance years, when we gain more confidence and branch out of our preexisting social circles.

Season five, at twenty-nine, is the finale. The grand party at the end of this decade where we get to look back and fully appreciate that ten years is a very long time. We have done so much, and we have five or six more times to try again as we enter our thirties, forties, and beyond.

In our twenties alone, we get to experience five different seasons of our very own TV show—and then, as we enter our thirties, we get to do it again, hopefully with more money and stability as well. Life is not just one long line of years strung together by the same experiences, the same locations, the same people over and over again.

Life is exciting and nuanced and there are thousands of opportunities to change paths and directions. In fact, in each new season, I think it's important to change at least one thing about your life, whether that's leaving a job you hate, creating a new goal for yourself, making new friends—anything to remind yourself that you are not a passive, stagnant entity. That way, you can look back at each year and say, "This was the year I moved cities," "This was the year I got my first tattoo," "This was the year I traveled alone for three weeks." Then your years will be bookmarked rather than floating past.

It's also valuable to remember that you are alive and you have agency. If something about your life and your choices frustrates you or isn't satisfying, you have time to adjust and shift to an entirely new plotline. The paradox of choice occurs because we fear making the wrong choice. The antidote is to acknowledge your own power to live out every version and timeline life has to offer, recognizing that you are not restricted because of one decision or choice.

There is no one perfect path. You will find happiness in whatever you choose to do.

You are more likely to regret the decisions you DID NOT make, compared to the ones you DID make.

You are not locked into the choices you made at eighteen, let alone twenty-five, or any age.

You can do it all, just not all at once. Luckily, you have multiple seasons of life to try it all.

CHAPTER V

The Battle for Authenticity

OUR TWENTIES ARE one massive journey to discover our true selves against a backdrop of all the people we think we should be, or who others want us to be. We are in search of our authentic selves, and the certainty that we know who we are and what we want. Who are you when you remove all the extraneous variables and factors you think define you: your job, your partner, your friends, where you live, your appearance? When you strip that back, what's left at your very core?

More than that, the battle for authenticity is about pushing back against conformity, the version of yourself that makes others happy, the version of yourself you're convinced is your "true self" but actually makes you really uncomfortable, the version of yourself you've concocted in order to be accepted. During this decade I would like to think we begin to get better at accepting all the versions of us from the past who we thought were cringe or who we denied or we told to keep quiet and now get back to who we actually are, without the frills and the pretending. It's a significant shift from our teenage years, when we spent most of our time trying our hardest to blend into the group.

As we enter our twenties, everyone is trying to be different from the next person, no one wants to feel like they are "basic," and so we go about trying on a million different identities, seeking the one that fits best. Throughout all the noise of this decade, the most important thing you can do is take the time to reflect on who you are at your core. Ignore the opinions and the trends that are trying to pull you in a million directions, and focus on who you are without the distractions.

What Does It Mean to Be Authentic?

We often think of authenticity and identity in terms of archetypes and stereotypes, as if we were a one-dimensional character in a book or TV show: Am I the studious one, the eclectic one, the career-driven one, the nomad, the caregiver, the artist? Your true self is so much more than that. It is multifaceted; it is the part of you that only you can truly observe and, therefore, can never be contained by a label. But you know it when you feel it, and you know what it feels like to be in perfect alignment with who you truly are. You also know it when you see it in other people—those folks who know they'll be fine even if people dislike them, who seem so unlike anyone else we have ever met, who carry themselves with the grace of total self-assurance. There is an essence of complete release and expression. That's your authentic self, a mixture of self-awareness, confidence, and honesty, and it's the part of you that would exist regardless of others' expectations, regardless of where you are in the world or who you are with.

I know this all sounds rather intangible and not quite the scientific explanation or definition you may be looking for. That's because psychology has, for a long time, really struggled to observe and measure authenticity, due to its highly subjective nature. How would it be possible to design an experiment to

measure what it means to be "authentic," when the very definition of that term is different for everyone? It doesn't mean psychologists haven't given it a go.

Researchers normally list a few core ingredients of the authentic self: our values, beliefs, judgments, desires, our tempera-
ment, our mission, our creativity, and at the end of the day our
free will to express all these things. Free will is perhaps the most
important component, because being authentic means choosing
to be in control of who you are and the actions you take to make
that known. Authenticity is not just a checklist of things you are
and aren't, or a big black box of some obscure beliefs and un-
nameable values. **Authenticity is a verb and requires action to
realize.**

Authenticity is also not just something that you happen across.
It can take years, sometimes even decades, for some people to
fully discover and embrace who they are. It's also going to be
uncomfortable: when you are used to playing a character for
others, being yourself can sometimes feel like a lie. It might bring
up feelings of guilt about "tricking" those around you or about
abandoning yourself for too long. But once you commit to your
true self, it is one of those things that never go out of style, it
never loses its merit. In that way, it is one of your greatest assets.

The Danger of Being Inauthentic

What occurs when you deny your authentic self? When you hide
your authentic self or are disconnected from this version of you,
it elicits feelings of shame and immorality. Essentially, you feel
like you are constantly lying to yourself and those around you.
We have been told since childhood to be honest, so lying makes

us feel icky. But at the same time we were taught not to lie, we were also told to behave and be polite and were delivered a litany of things that weren't socially acceptable. Whether implicitly or explicitly, society has a way of impressing on us norms about how it wants us to behave. It may have been a comment from a friend's parent about someone's outfit, derogatory language, news articles villainizing certain people, or even the trends that are pushed on us constantly across social media. We are trained from birth to behave in a specific way based on what people expect. Act this way, be good, this is what people find attractive, this will make you likable, don't stir up trouble. So we experience this cognitive dissonance: Do we lie and adopt a false persona, or be authentic and risk being shamed for who we are?

In those moments, we adopt a defensive facade or disguise to protect us from judgment, to conform and be who others want us to be. This is known as the **"false self,"** a term coined by psychotherapist Donald Winnicott to describe the superficial versions of us that exist in daily life, which emerge from a place of duty rather than freedom.

In contrast, the **true self** is unchanged by expectations and the pressure to conform—it's spontaneous, free, and creative. When people behave as their false self, there are emotional consequences that come along with that. You might experience negative feelings, ranging from feeling a bit uncomfortable in a situation to chronic guilt about everything and anything. Everyone can remember a time when they've acted in a way they knew contradicted who they truly were at their core. We all know this feeling, this tug in our chest, the panic, the distress, the discomfort. That feeling is shame, and in that moment it serves a purpose. It indicates that you are acting in a way that goes against who you really are. Aside from this momentary guilt and discomfort, it takes a lot of everyday mental energy to pretend to be someone you're not. That exhaustion has some pretty real consequences. Imagine if every single moment of your life you were acting out some character, someone else who you didn't really understand, who you didn't really believe in. Constant method acting. It's exhausting. It's like having a full-time job that the clock never stops on.

Refusing your authentic self also impacts your relationships. When you are living out this false character or persona, the people you are attracting aren't seeing what exists behind that facade. They're only attracted to what you choose to show them. You end up developing friendships and romantic relationships based on something you can't sustain, which will inevitably create distance. You also, sadly, don't give yourself the opportunity to really find your tribe and open up. Recent studies have shown that when people perceive we aren't being authentic, it affects their judgment of us. Although we might be suppressing our true selves out of fear or because we crave acceptance, those around us might interpret this as insincerity or manipulation. These people are "fake" or "try-hards." I think we deserve more empathy than that. We all want to belong and be part of the illusory group, whatever that might look like in our context. It can be hard to face that vacuum between when we leave our old friends and false self behind and find our true self, and true friends. It has been shown that when we do choose to act in a way that serves the true self—when we show up authentically—our relationship satisfaction improves, we do better at work, and our social anxiety may even decline.

Why We Deny Our Authentic Selves

We don't always have a choice when it comes to being in touch with our true selves. There are so many factors imposed on us that stop us from being authentic. I've already mentioned a few, but others that come to mind are situational, such as changing who you are based on the context you're in. Part of conforming with society's behavioral norms is acknowledging that you need a variety of masks for different situations to match what is expected of you in a particular context.

Who you are at work is not who you are when you're drunk with your friends or having dinner with your parents. The example I always think of is how weird it is when you overhear a friend's "work voice" and how quickly they can shape-shift into this professional person you've never met. This is quite typical and necessary to exist in a society that cares a lot about perception, but the problem occurs when we let one version of ourselves subsume the others beyond the specific context. Especially when that version is false. It is common, but problematic, to let the version of you that your family expects dictate your decisions, your career, or your love life. The older we get, the more dissatisfied we become with the life we created to keep others happy.

Social comparison contributes to suppressing your authenticity in favor of a self you think others will like. In the social media age, we have thousands of opportunities to compare ourselves to someone's curated version of the self they present online. We think, "Would my life be better if I was more like them? What am I lacking that they have?" We tend to evaluate our worth, form our identity, and identify where we stand in the social hierarchy through these acts of comparison. This comes in two forms: downward social comparison and upward social comparison.

Downward social comparison involves comparing yourself to someone you perceive as "less" than you for a self-esteem boost or self-enhancement. **Upward social comparison** involves comparing yourself to people you believe are "better" than you. This can make you feel lacking and motivate you to change to be more like the object of comparison. You end up trying to "improve" parts of yourself to be more in line with this "better" version of you. In that process, you give up what makes you authentic in exchange for conformity or similarity. The problem with that—if it's not already obvious—is that you try to force and mold yourself into a person and a life that don't fit. It's like forcing yourself into an outfit that's too small. This can actually hurt your self-esteem even more and leave you feeling empty, because in pursuit of an unrealistic version of yourself, you become detached from the parts of you that are real and easy to access. It also creates a "spotlight effect," where the more you engage in acts of comparison, the more you believe people are doing the same with you. All eyes are seemingly on you. You begin to feel more noticed, like your imperfections and insecurities are on full display, so you burrow further into your false self for safety.

How can you avoid this? Frankly, being told to "just be yourself" is often entirely unhelpful. How do you even know who that self is when you've spent years trying to hide it? When people tell you to be yourself, what does that really mean? Does that mean you need to do whatever you want without thinking of others, that you should be honest or direct, talk more about your beliefs, wear quirky clothes? Well, not exactly. We can learn a lot about how to be truly authentic by looking at people who are already acting in alignment with the highest versions of themselves.

There are a number of attributes that connect these individuals. First, they know their core values. They act in accordance with these values. They don't base their self-worth on the opinions of others. They are open about their interests and passions. They have boundaries. They don't compare themselves to others, and they have a strong internal validation system. They are unique and passionate about something.

What would that look like for you? How do you become that person?

Embracing Your Authentic Self

First, you must get clear on what matters to you by examining your values. It can be really difficult when someone asks you to just outright identify what you stand for, because you have a million things to choose from in the moment.

Instead, spend ten minutes identifying just five of your core values. Start with a big list you can find anywhere online, and then choose twenty of those values that resonate most with you. These might include gratitude, kindness, creativity, success, loyalty, intelligence, passion, power, or playfulness. Once you have that list, take it down to ten, and finally five. At your core, what are five things about yourself you are absolutely sure of?

When I did this exercise myself, I landed on: independence, creativity, generosity, community, and joy. These are the values that I need to keep at the front of my mind because they are core to who I am, and therefore they're core to my authentic self.

Each day, do one thing that channels the values you selected. If you value kindness, show an act of kindness to a stranger: a compliment to someone on the bus, an "I'm thinking of you" message to a friend, a kind comment on a video. If you value curiosity, make listening to a daily podcast part of your routine, or read an opinion piece on your commute. If you value ambition, work on a side hustle or new project. **Remember, authenticity should be a verb, not just a noun.**

Second, reflect on what activities, people, and situations make you feel the most alive—that is when your true self is unlocked. The best way to identify this is by noticing the times you have entered your **flow state.** Your flow state is when you feel so completely engrossed in an activity that what's going on around you and everything else in your life fades away. In this state of mind, you are equally energized and focused; all the energy in your body seems perfectly aligned and channeled into what's in front of you. The flow state is one of the highest states of consciousness you can be in, the closest you may get to inner peace, and it indicates that you are doing something that aligns with your authentic self.

The coiner of this term, the Hungarian American psychologist Mihaly Csikszentmihalyi, discovered the flow state by interviewing and observing a number of highly self-actualized people, such as mountain climbers, ballet dancers, chess players, and surgeons. These individuals weren't just highly disciplined, successful, and hardworking, but were also deeply in touch with what made them unique and who they were. We may not all end up as elite athletes or millionaires by finding our flow, but, on a smaller scale, flow can bring us closer to our true selves—what we are all about.

Think about the friends you can talk to for hours about everything and anything without looking at your phone or worrying about the outside world. Those are the people to hold close, because in their presence you can be authentic. Think about the hobbies you can be consumed by and effortlessly find yourself wrapped up in, whether it's painting, hiking, knitting, reading self-help books like this, or cooking. For me, flow has always meant doing something with my hands. I feel most in tune with my true self when I'm crafting something—removed from myself in dedication of making something beautiful or at least unique. Ceramics, bad painting on $5 canvases, wind chimes from shells—that is when my flow state activates.

These are the things that you should be doing more of, so find time to do them in your daily life, or at least weekly. Set aside time to actively engage in the activities and hobbies that make you feel alive. It does amazing things for your brain. It does amazing things for your well-being. It refreshes you, and it connects you with your authentic self.

Third, your authentic self is not just who you are right now, but who you are preparing to be. **There is a future version of you who is relying on you doing the hard work now to bring them into existence.** How can you get in touch with the future you? Through visualization. Without guidelines or structure, it is very hard to simply picture what your ideal or actual self will look like in five years. The secret is in the details.

Picture your most authentic self on a random day in five years' time using as much color and as many details as you can. What are you wearing, what colors, what textures, what styles? Where are you living, what pictures do you have on the wall? Who is the first person you message in the morning and what does your day look like? How do you get to work, what have you got planned, what emails are you replying to, who are you getting dinner with? At the end of the night when you come home, what does your room look like, what are you thinking about, what are you dreaming about, what are you looking forward to?

It might sound imaginary, but this version of you exists! You just need to show up as that person—as *you*—in your present life, every day. How would your authentic future self handle what you're going through? How would they respond to that comment, or to a nasty voice in your head? How would they want you to be spending your energy to best serve the future you? It's going to take effort, time, and commitment to get there, but you already have an excess of these things—it's just that you're currently using them to try to be someone else. Imagine how much emotional space you'd have if you gave up trying so hard to be a character who is, frankly, not you.

A great deal of peace comes when you shift from pleasing others to investing in your truest, highest self. Part of that process is also identifying when you are relying on **external validation versus internal validation.** Internal validation occurs when you are able to encourage yourself by focusing on your strengths and achievements, and acting in a way that feels truthful and good. External validation occurs when you look to others to provide that encouragement through approval and praise, even things like social media likes. **External validation is fickle.** When you rely too heavily on others to legitimize who you are, you are basing your self-worth on something that can quickly be taken away. In contrast, internal validation is consistent: it is controlled entirely by you, so you can trust it will be a constant source of confidence.

It's not that your authentic self will eliminate all insecurity. Your false self will sometimes reappear. You'll naturally still care what others think about you from time to time. But this shift will keep you centered on the opinion that matters the most to your life: your own.

The journey to realizing your authentic self is a long, sometimes arduous one. It might feel selfish to let others down, especially when they feel particularly connected to who you used to be. Some people will be disappointed because they have become accustomed to someone who wants to please them and make them happy. But to gain anything, sometimes you need to lose something in return, whether that is false relationships, a people-pleasing crutch, or the comfort and safety of keeping yourself hidden.

Life is too short to not be exactly who you are. Too many people spend their whole lives masquerading as their false selves. You don't want to wake up in twenty years and contemplate how your whole life could have been different if you'd had the courage to embrace authenticity. You want more for yourself than that, and you should be looking for it right now.

Some final questions for discovering your authentic self:

What are the experiences or moments that have shaped who I am, for better or worse?

What are the things I like about myself when no one is watching?

If everyone's memory of me would disappear in ten years, what would I choose to do in this time—what kind of life would I create?

What does my ideal self look like and what needs to change to transform me into that person?

Love on the Brain

Love is arguably the most talked-about subject on the planet. From sonnets to movies to speeches to entire text-books and careers: all based on trying to figure out what it is about love that drives us so mad but also keeps us so sane. What is it about love that we need so much, but can equally be so hurtful and brutal? It all comes down to the ways our brain creates bonds, processes emotion, and craves a sense of belonging. A lot of love is actually neuroscience and, of course, psychology.

When we dive into this psychology, behind the biggest love dilemmas of our twenties we find a lot of the answers we're looking for. Why am I attracted to the wrong people? Attachment theory can tell us a lot. Why is it so hard to make new friends in adulthood? The principles of attraction make it a lot easier to understand. Why is unrequited love so pain-ful? Does everyone else feel the pressure to settle down? Is it just me who is losing friends? The answers become clearer when we discover how our minds work, and also zoom out to examine these problems in the broader context of this tran-sitional decade. Let's talk about why love in our twenties al-ways seems to be in every corner we look.

CHAPTER I

The Psychology of Attraction

WE THINK ABOUT love and relationships more than anything else in our twenties. We obsess over the people we're dating, we fear being single forever, we question whether the person we chose at twenty or twenty-one can last us a lifetime, we worry about sex, whether we're having enough of it or too much, whether they like us back, whether we even like them.

It's more than just our romantic relationships that take up this much mental real estate. Another huge insecurity for us is our friendships and the constant friendship roller coaster we seem to be on during this decade. I recognized this phenomenon a few years ago: my fellow twenty-something friends and I never seem to be completely secure in the quantity or quality of our friendships for an extended period of time. One day you are at the peak of the roller coaster, feeling fulfilled and loved, overjoyed by how deep and meaningful your friendships are, and the very next day you can be at the bottom of the roller coaster, despairing how you have "no one," wanting the kind of friendship groups you see plastered everywhere online, and feeling utterly alone.

Often, in these moments, the only thing that changes is our internal state. Everything outside is unchanged, our external relationships have remained the same, but we are just overwhelmed with an innate social insecurity that seems to define our twenties.

It's a constant longing for more—more connection, more security, more friends, more love, better love—because without these things we feel like a lone ship in a terrible storm. **Our relationships are truly what make or break our twenties.** We want to know: What connects us as people? What makes us attractive to others? What is the difference between someone we want to be around and someone we don't? How do I find my people? To answer these questions, the science of attraction is incredibly important to understand. When we understand what brings people together, either romantically or platonically, we can dispel a lot of the mystery around what we feel we're missing in our twenties—and learn how to obtain it.

Understanding Attraction

We normally think of attraction as purely romantic, sexual even. We think of the fireworks, the instant connection, or an invisible string that draws us to someone across a room. It's euphoric and electric. Attraction is absolutely a powerful substance, but it can also be a lot simpler and subtler than that.

To me, attraction is that force that pulls people into the same orbit, whether a friend or a love interest. We need that attraction to alert us to the things that aren't immediately obvious about someone else: their little quirks, the values we share, their unique sense of humor, their kindness and personality. Attraction is the catalyst, but it's those little traits that truly get us to bond on a deeper, more substantial level.

There's been plenty of research on what attracts us to others. Of course, when we're talking about intimate relationships, physical attractiveness is perhaps the most studied. Things like scent, facial symmetry, and even voice draw us to someone based on our personal preferences. Those personal preferences come from a mix of genetics and biology (for instance, men with a deeper voice are more attractive to some heterosexual women because a lower voice indicates greater testosterone levels, which might make them better for mating), but are also informed by our preexisting relationships and past partners.

Some have even suggested that attraction has to do with our parents. We've all heard the myth that we are more attracted to people who look like our parents, and even more notorious is Freud's idea of the "Oedipus complex," which basically assumes that young boys find their mother attractive and therefore later in life will pursue women who have her same physical and psychological traits. For women and girls, this phenomenon in reverse is known as the "Electra complex." Not only is this all somewhat gross, for lack of a better word, but so many of these theories fail to explain how sexual preferences emerge in people who are queer—so they don't have much legitimacy to me. A lot of the modern studies that examine outdated Freudian-based theory find the truth is a lot more nuanced: we are really attracted to what seems familiar and similar. It's not attraction but a sense of recognition and therefore safety that seems to explain these strange models for attraction.

At its core, the formula for attraction comes down to four things: proximity, similarity, familiarity, and reciprocity. When we have these things, it seems like a relationship is destined to happen.

Proximity means how close we are to someone, not just geographically but functionally: how often we see them and talk, the frequency of our interactions, and how convenient the relationship is in the beginning. Physical nearness gets us in someone's orbit from the start and explains why so many of our primary friendships are with people we meet in high school or at university, in our dorms or apartment buildings, or at work, where we have the greatest opportunity and likelihood of seeing someone more days than we don't.

One of my favorite studies of all time, published in 2022, tested this hypothesis in the classroom. It looked at how seating arrangements—something largely arbitrary and probably given no second thought by teachers or students themselves—impacted friendships. The students sitting next to each other were more likely to call their deskmate a friend compared to students sitting on the other side of the room. Other research conducted on this phenomenon has shown that students were more likely to communicate, email, and text people living in neighboring dorm rooms on campus compared to students who lived down the hall or in another building. They were also more likely to call these people friends. Two of my oldest friends lived in the same corridor of my dorm building when I was at university. Sometimes I wonder whether it could have been anyone living in those rooms and we would have the same bond. I would like to say that's not the case, but maybe the evidence is stacked against me.

The problem with proximity as the singular factor for a relationship with someone is that, as we age and get further into our twenties, we realize that some of our friendships are based on convenience. Someone just happened to be nearby and so we believed that we were meant to be lifelong friends. But as people move and the frequency of our interactions declines, so does the importance of the friendship. When I moved away from my university town to a bigger city three hours away, it became really apparent who was in my life because they wanted to be and who was there because it had just always been easy, for them as for me. When it comes to romantic connections, disentangling real connection from a mere exposure effect becomes more complicated. Do you actually like the person, or are they just the closest person nearby? Of course, it's hard to fall in love with someone you never have the chance to meet, but not everyone has the potential you see in them just because you happen to bump into them a few times a week.

Similarity is another major factor of attraction and, perhaps, quite self-explanatory. While many people assume that "opposites attract," we actually tend to like people who are similar to us. This is known as the "similarity-attraction hypothesis," and the psychology behind it is quite simple. Of course we are going to feel more connected to people who have similar values, life experiences, hobbies, attitudes, and daily realities as us, because a) we have more to talk about, and b) we don't feel we need to explain ourselves. So the relationship feels easier and less draining.

When it comes to romantic love, it's hard to feel connected, much less that you have a future, when your partner prefers partying and you prefer relaxing at home, or you value family and they don't, or you are optimistic and they are pessimistic. Other explanations are a bit more nuanced. When we share similar attitudes with someone, this validates our own judgments. Being similar to someone also means being more likely to predict what they'll do, which makes us feel secure and safe. Having similar personalities means less friction.

In a number of studies, researchers have observed that people are more likely to marry someone who shares similarities with them in age, race, education, values, and level of objective physical attractiveness. The same goes for friends. It's a lot easier to feel connected with someone who shares the same hobbies, because you always have something to talk about that bonds you.

However, relying too heavily on similarity as the basis for a relationship can actually prevent us from meeting some incredible people just because we initially believe we have nothing in common. There are so many fascinating, caring, and warm people who could become one of the loves of our lives if we stop basing relationships on our preliminary assumptions of affinity. If you only ever connect with people who are similar to you, you end up in a bubble and will keep going back to those preexisting relationships, unable to meet new people.

Psychologists Paul Ingram and Michael Morris observed this phenomenon in their study on people's tendency to seek out connections beyond what they found familiar. They invited a number of business executives to a cocktail mixer promoted as a "networking event." They found that the majority of them did not meet new people, but instead tended to spend most of their time interacting with the people they already knew. Similarity may be important, but it's not the be-all and end-all. When we rely too heavily on what we have in common, we miss out on what we could discover that is different.

Related to both similarity and proximity is the notion of **familiarity**. When we have had a chance to build a connection and a bond, our attraction increases, because the person sitting in front of us feels familiar and comfortable. Sometimes that just comes down to time. If you want a concrete estimate, some research suggests it takes about 30 hours to call someone a casual friend, 140 hours to call someone a good friend, and over 300 hours before we fall into the best-friend category. No wonder so many of us struggle to establish new friends or connections in our twenties—because where are we getting that kind of time?

So many of us judge the quality of our friendships based on the length of time we've known someone. The person we call our best friend is most likely the same friend we've known since high school or the early days of university, because we have had more time to really *know* them, including the good and the bad. We have seen them through multiple seasons and chapters and so, as our time together increases, so does our comfort in their presence, our willingness to be vulnerable, and our trust. It's why I am never surprised when I hear about people who have been friends for years suddenly ending up together. One estimate by a researcher at the University of Victoria suggests two-thirds of married couples start off as friends. Why wouldn't we want someone we are already familiar with, who we already have some preliminary love for?

Finally, there is **reciprocity**. To me, this is the most important foundation for attraction, because without it we are left with unrequited love—either platonic or romantic. **We are more likely to like someone who likes us, plain and simple.** We are more attracted to someone who puts the same amount of energy and attention into us as we do for them. If one person is distant or a taker, it takes a lot of mental gymnastics to continue to want them in our life, because the relationship no longer has a sense of equity. Another example of this is when a new friend, or someone you're dating or interested in, shows how much they care by making plans, messaging regularly, and celebrating you. We feel compelled to return that same level of effort and the relationship flourishes from there.

An important caveat: sometimes we have the opposite reaction, especially when it comes to romantic interests. Someone not returning our interest can occasionally feel like a challenge because of the magnetism of the "chase." I find this particularly common in the case of people who are high achievers or quite stubborn. We convince ourselves that the best things, the things worth having, take effort and time, and so we continue to pour more and more into a leaky cup. We don't want what comes easy, and so this relationship feels like something we need to earn. That's not attraction, though; that's suspense or unease. Sometimes, a small part of it is entertainment. The breadcrumbing—never fully giving our energy back, leaving us with just a taste—creates a sense of invariable reward, whereby sometimes they reciprocate, sometimes they don't, and so we never know when to expect a payout for our efforts, which keeps us invested.

It also comes down to this principle known as the "scarcity effect." We have a natural cognitive bias to value something that seems "rare," or scarce, because this makes it seem more valuable. Things that are in abundance seem more commonplace and, therefore, less shiny and worthwhile. When someone pulls away or offers us only short bursts of their time or energy, they immediately become more attractive to us. But that attraction and interest, that intrigue and excitement, the chase—these do not make a relationship. Eventually this will burn us out, and we will move on because there is nothing of substance to pursue. However, whether that takes weeks, months, or years is entirely dependent on our assessment of not just the other person's value, but our own.

Using Attraction to Our Advantage

We can use these principles of attraction to our advantage to foster better relationships and attract people to us. I've often found that the people who make friends the easiest or have those romantic interests chasing after them embody these rules for attraction.

They put themselves in proximity to others by doing multiple activities, being social, and being endlessly open to conversations and meeting new people. That might sound fairly obvious to say, but if you want more connection in your twenties, you're not going to achieve that by being comfortable and staying inside all day. These people also go searching for friendship in the places it is already readily available, such as in the workplace or with friends of friends.

Second, they search for things they have in common with people. They are quick to find commonalities, shared interests, and conversation topics, to build a sense of mutual likeness and liking. The easiest way to achieve this is by letting the spotlight fall onto someone else and being genuinely curious about who they are. You'll find something to bond over and then, as time progresses, even more similarities will become apparent. Building familiarity, even if it's a lot of added effort in the beginning, is another successful strategy of the highly sociable and connected. We all know what it's like to meet someone we immediately feel like we've known for years, and how magnetic this is. This reaction is no accident. Whether unconsciously or deliberately, people who are quick to open up foster closeness and familiarity a lot more quickly by being the first to be vulnerable, ensuring that we feel comfortable to do the same.

Of course, sometimes this backfires. Inadvertent trauma-dumping is one such example. This occurs when someone might not be prepared to hear our darkest secrets only days after we've met, even if we feel like we're at that level. It can also be a sign of an intensity addiction, whereby we speed up the process of becoming friends or dating too early, too soon, without laying the necessary groundwork first.

However, making an effort to become familiar with someone's

life—such as by asking them questions about something they mentioned a few weeks back, remembering those small details—usually makes them feel more attracted to us. We are likely someone they want to have in their life.

Finally, the golden rule of reciprocity ties this all together. It's not the glue, but the cherry. It doesn't have to be mathematical or mechanical—they call, we must call back in return; they invite us to something, we now have to initiate next time; they give us a birthday present, we should too. That can sometimes feel slightly manipulative, or as if we have a scoring sheet we're paying close attention to. Friendships and relationships don't need to have these kinds of rules, but by ensuring that we match someone's energy and showing them we are invested, we provide that necessary positive reinforcement for the relationship to continue and grow beyond the initial attraction period.

Beyond Attraction

We all have preferences for the type of partner, love interest, or friends we want in our lives. We know what it feels like to have those butterflies in our stomach, to feel alive with passion. But pursuing a person based on chemistry sometimes ignores the need for compatibility and something more than just a "spark."

One theory always drives this home for me. It's known as the "triangular theory of love." Developed by psychologist Robert Sternberg, this theory proposes that love—whether platonic or romantic—needs three things to be sustained: intimacy, passion, and commitment. Attraction might fulfill only one of these criteria. We equally need to feel a sense of closeness to someone, a vulnerability, a gentleness and depth. That would be intimacy.

We also want commitment, the knowledge that someone is dedicated to keeping us in their life and promises to be there for us, to be a stable force for the future. Even in open or polyamorous relationships, this is a necessity, though it may look a bit different from the outside.

At the core there is an understanding that your partner is loyal to you emotionally, has you in their plans, and wants the best for you. If you just have passion, you are really only experiencing infatuation. If you have passion and commitment, you don't have the openness. Passion and intimacy give you a situationship— maybe a friends-with-benefits situation—but without commitment, can you really call it a relationship? Look beyond physical appearance, lust, and excitement, because these things are flimsy and exhausted by time, but intimacy and commitment don't wane and can be rebuilt again and again.

> Attraction, including for friends, is based on the principles of proximity, similarity, familiarity, and reciprocity. Fostering these factors helps create opportunities for connection.

> Relationships need more than fleeting excitement or lust to flourish. All good relationships thrive on emotional intimacy.

> It gets harder to make friends the older we get because people have less time to invest in new connections. Seeking opportunities to foster closeness, find similarities, and build familiarity helps speed up this process.

> Match the energy even if it feels extra! Trust me!

CHAPTER II

Myth-Busting Your Attachment Style

ATTACHMENT STYLES HAVE received a surge of attention in recent years thanks to the circulation of the idea across social media platforms like TikTok and Instagram. Viral videos and content geared toward diagnosing your attachment style have made this concept part of our collective psychobabble. However, as terms and concepts gain popularity, their true meaning often becomes misconstrued and misunderstood. The truth about attachment styles is a lot more nuanced than what we gain from a thirty-second video.

Many people incorrectly diagnose themselves as being anxiously attached or avoidant in relationships, when the majority of us—some 65 percent—are securely attached. This misdiagnosis can create a self-fulfilling prophecy whereby we act out how we expect ourselves to be in a relationship (i.e., anxious, avoidant) when we actually have all the underlying necessities to be securely attached. Furthermore, we tend to believe the myth that our attachment style is unchangeable after we reach twenty and that this will, ultimately, determine the success of all our romantic relationships in the future. We think we are doomed. This is neither true nor useful in helping us better understand how we approach relationships.

Having a proper understanding of what it means to be securely or insecurely attached in a relationship—whether romantic, platonic, or familial—is important to identifying patterns of behavior that either sabotage or elevate the quality of these connections. This is especially the case during our twenties, because we have a unique opportunity to address and release some of the trauma we encountered in childhood while we are in the midst of forming some of our most life-changing relationships. I think it's about time we set the record straight and got attachment theory correct.

The Attachment Style Basics

Let's begin with a history lesson on what is possibly one of the most well-known theories in psychology. The idea of attachment styles emerged from the work of the pioneering psychiatrists and psychoanalysts John Bowlby and Mary Ainsworth. The essential premise is that children need to have a stable, affectionate relationship with their caregivers, who in turn provide them with safety, security, and protection along with their other basic human needs. As children, we are vulnerable and highly dependent on an adult caregiver to provide for us in every capacity. Our attachment to the adults in our lives emerges from a place of survival.

When this attachment is disrupted due to neglect, abandonment, or abuse, a child learns that they cannot trust those who are meant to love and protect them. This results in a number of distinct behaviors in a child that carry on into adulthood. Such behaviors are indicative of an anxious, avoidant, or disorganized attachment style.

Ainsworth demonstrated this in her "strange situation" experiments, in which researchers observed how the children reacted when their parents left them in a room to interact with strangers and play with toys. The researchers then observed the children's subsequent reactions to their parents returning. They sought to measure children's willingness to explore, their levels of separation and stranger anxiety, and their reunion behavior. What the researchers began to notice in the initial experiments was that the children reacted in one of three ways across these four measures.

The strange situation experiments were thus the basis for articulating the three primary attachment styles: secure, anxious-ambivalent, and anxious-avoidant. While the initial studies were conducted on children, further research began to produce evidence that the attachment styles displayed in childhood subsequently informed our adult behaviors in terms of relationship seeking, intimacy, vulnerability, connection, and rejection. Our early patterns of relating and attaching to others become wired into our brains as children, then repeated in adulthood as our attachment style.

Secure Attachment

Securely attached children are willing to explore their environment. Although they are moderately distressed by seeing their caregiver leave the room and by the entrance of the stranger, they are easily soothed by the reentrance of their parent and happy to be comforted and held by them. A child is most likely to be securely attached when their parents give them consistent care and are available to meet their needs. They see their parents as a safe space but, because they are not overly dependent, they are able to partake in play and exploration during their absence.

In adulthood, the secure attachment is most common. These individuals feel they are able to trust others but will be okay in their absence. They are confident and self-assured and seek out healthy love and social support from friends, family, and partners. When someone leaves them or a relationship ends, it may still be difficult, but they feel secure in their situation and the future. Their emotional stability is not dependent on someone else's availability or presence in their life.

Anxious-Ambivalent Attachment

Anxious-ambivalent children become extremely upset when their caregiver leaves and the stranger enters. During the parent's absence they are unwilling to explore and cannot self-soothe. Upon the reentrance of the caregiver, they seem ambivalent, or even become angry or unresponsive. This child sees their caregiver as emotionally unavailable or unresponsive to their needs. The care they give is unpredictable, perhaps because they work long hours, do not respond to a child's cries for attention, or are preoccupied with other children. The child may perceive them as pulling them in and then pulling away. They may be hot and cold and create an environment where it feels like their love needs to be earned, causing a child to both resent their inconsistency and crave their love, eventually becoming very clingy.

As adults, people with an ambivalent attachment style are distrustful of others and question whether their partner truly loves them, provoking feelings of panic, anger, or fear that the partner is going to leave. They feel anxious about the possibility of their partner leaving and tend to sacrifice boundaries in order to ensure they maintain closeness with their partner. When their partner asks for space, they need a lot of reassurance.

Anxious-Avoidant Attachment

Also sometimes called the "avoidant-dismissive" attachment style, anxious-avoidant children are entirely unfazed by their caregivers' absence and show little or no interest in their parents returning. They treat the stranger in an equally aloof manner and are very independent, not needing their caregiver to feel safe exploring their environment or to self-soothe. These children have likely learned to rely on themselves for their comfort and security needs, recognizing that their parents are unavailable and insensitive to their emotional distress.

As adults, these individuals push away opportunities for genuine, vulnerable connection. They tend to withdraw as the emotional connection deepens, and they appear perfectly happy to have a series of casual relationships that allow them to maintain emotional distance, in contrast to long, intimate ones. They are often hyperindependent and might claim they don't particularly need relationships and meaningful intimacy, because their early childhood experiences conditioned them to believe that, in these instances, they will just be left disappointed.

It's important to note that no single experience creates our attachment style. Instead, it is an accumulation of small experiences or a pattern of actions by our caregivers that teach us how to relate to others, particularly in those moments when we are seeking comfort, intimacy, and support. When we talk about what contributes to an insecure attachment style, this list extends beyond just abuse and neglect. It is anything that may have created irregularity or instability, such as divorce, substance abuse in the family, narcissistic or emotionally unavailable parents, constant moving, or having parents with mental health struggles. Most parents do not set out to cause this kind of damage to their children, but their emotional ceiling and what they are capable of providing may not align with what their child requires. This is another example of how attachment styles have been misconstrued within the current discourse—only malicious parenting can supposedly create insecurely attached individuals. Not true—a great number of factors are at play here.

Let's address some of the other myths that seem to follow this theory around.

Myth One: Your Attachment Style Is Unchangeable Once You Reach Your Twenties

There is no doubt that our early childhood experiences are powerfully impactful. Those early years are so formative because our neurological development is occurring very rapidly. A child's brain is like one big sponge, soaking up the environment, other people's emotions, tiny moments and big ones as well. But the first ten to fifteen years of our lives are not the determining factor of our relationship success as adults. While attachment styles tend to form in early life and can persist into adulthood, they are not fixed in stone. This means there is a lot of hope for people who may not have had the easiest childhoods or relationships with their parents.

Research in psychology and neuroscience consistently demonstrates that individuals possess a remarkable capacity for personal growth and change throughout their lives, including the capacity to "heal" their attachment style through psychotherapy and reparenting. Our attachment style will continue to be challenged as we mature, but it will also be changed by adult experiences.

In fact, recent studies into adult romantic relationships demonstrate that early dating experiences can also mold our attachment style. This can happen in both directions. That terrible boyfriend you had in high school or that girlfriend you spent a year chasing in university may have done more harm than you thought. Someone who was once secure can become anxious upon the entrance of a partner who is inconsistent, emotionally manipulative, or abusive, because their expectations for how they will be treated and what they can expect from the loving bonds they form are left irrevocably changed. Because our brains are not finished developing in our adolescence and early twenties, our attachment style is influenced equally, if not more, by these early experiences as by the bond we share with our parents.

Luckily for us, this change in attachment style can, of course, occur in the reverse. Someone who was once avoidant or ambivalent can shift to a secure attachment by deconstructing what they unconsciously learned in childhood from their relationship with their caregivers. This shift can be accomplished through conscious remembering, identifying the events that contributed to this pattern, and correcting the false beliefs they have created about their worth and capacity to be loved. Conscious remembering is especially powerful. It involves recalling core memories that contributed to your attachment style in childhood and re-explaining them to yourself as a self-aware adult. The time you watched a parent leave, or were yelled at, or faced cruelty—your childhood self could only blame you, but the healed version of you can understand that situation better. By dipping into your memories and consciously adding in some additional information, you stop relying on incomplete recollections to define yourself and your capacity to receive love.

You may also find that your attachment style slowly transforms when you finally encounter healthy love. A great deal of healing occurs when you have someone who is willing to understand how your injured inner child might approach love. You might still act from a place of fear, but a new loving partner may encourage you to communicate why that may be and stop you from pulling or pushing them away. That can be one of the greatest and most healing gifts, but also one of the most challenging examples of love we encounter.

A few years ago, I had dinner with a friend in Boston I hadn't seen in a few years. In our time apart, she had started dating someone new who she described as the love of her life. She said it was the deepest love she had encountered because it required her to dig deeper than ever before. It was the first time she saw any truth in that age-old wisdom that "love is hard work," a sentiment that had previously terrified her. That work involved her slowly learning that sometimes healthy love can be as triggering as unhealthy love because it gives you a reason to stare down your biggest fears in a relationship and work through them. She had to unpack the ways in which she was avoidant, baiting her partner to start fights that would give her a reason to leave for a few hours or for good, shutting down when things got too vulnerable, and avoiding big acts of commitment. She said she also now saw how those same behaviors had caused all her previous relationships to fail. She wondered whether maybe she wanted them to? But with this new person, that avoidance was no longer going to work. She wanted a future, and he made himself her teammate in this conscious reprogramming of her attachment style. They got married last year.

Her story gives me a lot of hope for those of us wondering whether we will always relate to people in the way we do now. Her example shows that if we have enough self-awareness to recognize how our avoidant or ambivalent patterns might cause us to self-sabotage, we can interrupt those habits before that occurs. Holding ourselves accountable when we find ourselves reverting to these childhood defense mechanisms and unlearning the false belief that these are what keep us safe will unlock a whole new level and depth of intimacy.

I'm also never someone to discourage therapy. That safe space, free from the shame we may be carrying from childhood or past relationships, free from the fear, is life-changing when it comes to healing an insecure attachment style.

Myth Two: Only Insecurely Attached People Struggle in Relationships

Being securely attached does not in any way predict relationship success. People whose parents showed them consistent care and were emotionally available can still be highly anxious in their adult relationships, push people away, experience rapid relationship breakdown, cheat, get divorced, go through endless situationships, or struggle to find genuine connection and love. How we approach relationships is a lot more nuanced than simply drawing a line between our childhood experiences and adult behaviors. It is shaped by our values, our self-esteem, and what we want from our connections.

I grew up with two loving parents who were consistent, drove me to my basketball games, and told me they were proud of me. But in my early twenties I still sought out plenty of emotionally unavailable people. I dated people who treated me pretty badly. I still had times when I would start fights when I really just wanted reassurance. I still had plenty of relationships come to messy ends. **I wasn't insecure or anxiously attached; I was just experiencing a moment of insecurity and anxiety.**

Relationship success does not hinge entirely on attachment style. Successful relationships still require mutual effort, effective communication, and compatibility—but also just emotional maturity. If you don't have those skills in your tool kit—regardless of your attachment style—you will be limited in your ability to show up in your relationships and be present, patient, successful, and self-aware. The truth is that people with insecure attachment styles may struggle more when it comes to finding a way through these obstacles and learning how to be a good partner. Yet that doesn't mean they are doomed to fail, nor does it mean those of us with a secure attachment style don't have weaknesses.

Myth Three: Only Romantic Relationships Are Impacted by Attachment Style

One of the most fascinating aspects of attachment styles for me personally is how they are reflected in our friendships, not just our romantic relationships. Attachment theory suggests that our attachment style is merely a reflection of our ability to bond with others based on childhood experiences and how we replicate our parental relationship with others in our lives. It makes a lot of sense that this would apply to all connections, including our platonic ones. Our friendships can be equally as complex, intimate, and vulnerable as romantic relationships, if not sometimes more so, because the rule book for relationships is so different than the one for friendships. Therefore, the same motivations we have for being clingy with a partner when we feel like they're pulling away or for seeking out shallow relationships because we're scared to be hurt or rejected are also reflected in our friendships. Friendships equally have the capacity for hurt but, additionally, require so many of the same emotional tools to be successful.

A friend of mine grew up with a father who was an alcoholic. He would go on long binges and disappear for days, only to re-emerge full of apologies, bearing gifts, swearing to never do it again. That would last for a couple of weeks and the same cycle would happen all over again. Due to that inconsistency from her primary caregiver, my friend developed an anxious-ambivalent attachment style. She would form these very close friendships with people, become overclingy—perhaps even codependent at times—and at the slightest sign someone was pulling away, she would spiral and become worn down by her constant anxiety and fear of abandonment. Eventually, she would have no choice but to push them away. The thing is, she didn't date until she was twenty-five, but her attachment style was still visible within her friendships. It was also creating a self-fulfilling prophecy. The more she tried to draw people in and hang on as tightly as possible, the more they would feel restricted and ask for space. To her, this sounded like "I hate you and I never want to see you again." The cycle continued; friendship after friendship ending, reaffirming exactly what she had always believed and exacerbating future anxiety that the same thing would happen again. **Love is not just reserved for romance. Sometimes your friendships are** your greatest relationships, and they challenge you in a manner that triggers those childhood memories and patterns.

Our attachment styles are extremely nuanced. Not everyone will fall neatly into one of the three categories. In fact, in recent years researchers have begun introducing entirely new attachment styles and variations to account for individual differences. Furthermore, they are a lot more complex than what we might assume. It's very easy to say you are anxiously attached or avoidant, but at the end of the day most of us are securely attached and just have additional habits and tendencies that are causing strife in our relationships. An anxiously attached person can have a fulfilling relationship or marriage, while someone who is securely attached continues to go through heartbreak after heartbreak because they haven't developed the necessary interpersonal skills that fall way beyond their attachment style.

Stop allowing the internet to diagnose your relationship problems, because it will give you the simplest (and often incorrect) answer. You have the agency to change how you relate to others, how you unconsciously sabotage opportunities for deep, meaningful connection, and how you choose to love—from a place of fear and scarcity or excitement and abundance.

> You can be securely attached and still act from a place of anxiety and avoidance.

> Your attachment style does not have the final say when it comes to your relationship success and fulfillment. Healthy and deep love is for all of us.

> Attachment styles may be influential, but they are also malleable. You are not cursed by your upbringing.

CHAPTER III

Repeating History in Relationships

"EVERY ONE OF my exes is exactly the same!" "I have such a type!" "Why do I always attract these kinds of people in my life?" I've said all of these at some stage in my dating life. For the longest time I couldn't figure out why every person I dated was a carbon copy of the person who came before and why I was dealing with the same issues: people who didn't want to commit, who seemed emotionally unavailable and confident to the point of arrogance. Most of them had even studied the same course, had the same interests and hobbies; two of them had even lived in the same house six months apart. It was beyond coincidental at that point.

I was constantly blaming them and putting it down to my terrible luck in dating. Eventually you have to wake up and smell the coffee. They weren't the problem; I was. They may have had faults that made them difficult to deal with, and they may have done the wrong thing, but so had I, and I was the common denominator in all these situations.*

I realized that all along I was doing the same things and choosing the same kinds of people. I was the one who found that same

---

* This does not apply to relationships that are abusive. That is never your fault. Full stop.

combination of aloofness, unavailability, and excitement attractive. I was the one who didn't trust my instincts. I was the one who was so scared of being alone I would let anyone in who knocked on my door. Yet I was expecting a different outcome every time. At some point, finding healthy love means recognizing when you are repeating history in your romantic relationships and getting the same outcome that you don't want. Coming to this realization changed how I approached dating in my twenties and reversed these age-old habits. It also meant I found someone who was exactly what I wanted all along. I had just been looking in the wrong places.

The Past That Haunts You

There are myriad ways you can repeat dysfunctional relationship patterns over and over again, including jumping from one relationship to another, or what we would call "serial dating." Always going for the person who won't commit because you think you can change them, unlike that person from your past. Finding that your relationships always end because you get too comfortable and neglect the emotional vulnerability that sustains your love. Continuing to date people with different religious beliefs from yours, even though you know you eventually want to marry someone of the same faith. Constantly finding your relationships breaking down due to poor communication because you initially find yourself attracted to people you need to "crack." Seeking out dependent connections where you never have the space to tend to your own identity. Being a parent or caregiver for your partner. Pushing people away when they get too close because they trigger your unmanaged avoidant traits. Perhaps you are always fighting with your partners about retroactive jealousy over people in their past because you haven't quite yet managed your own insecurity. It's a long list and these are just a few examples I've observed in myself and the people around me. There are thousands of other situations that match this pattern whereby we never stop to examine the root cause of our dysfunctional relationships or relationship breakdowns.

Repeating Patterns

It's crucial to understand how you may be sabotaging your own relationship success by choosing the same kinds of people who are just plain wrong for you. This is especially the case in your twenties, when you are establishing the foundations for your dating style, preferences, and wants. These early romantic experiences teach you what to expect from future partners and can become an ingrained pattern of thinking and behaving. Some might say it's a version of so-called "repetition compulsion."

Repetition compulsion occurs when we continue to repeat painful or stressful situations looking for a different ending. It's also known as "trauma reenactment." It has been proposed that the reason we unconsciously relive these experiences with new people is to prove to ourselves that, all along, there was a solution. Psychotherapists have tried to explain this for decades.

Perhaps it's because we repeat what we absorbed as children, or we are attempting to gain mastery over experiences in which we previously felt powerless? Maybe we just don't think we deserve love, and this is a form of self-punishment or self-sabotage? We become so convinced we are unworthy of love that we seek that truth in every situation we encounter. With that, there is never an opportunity to question those deeply rooted beliefs: *I deserve to suffer; this is what love is like; I don't deserve anything more.* This links very closely to the next explanation. Repeating history in relationships may also occur because we repeat what we have become accustomed to. We repeat what we find normal because it's familiar. We know what to expect with someone who is, for example, noncommittal because we've been through it before. The ups and downs, the stress, the anticipation, the expectation. If we were to experience something different, this would be too unpredictable because it doesn't match the narrative we have come to expect in love and relationships. As the saying goes, we choose the devil we know.

It may also be a reflection of the dysfunction we witnessed in childhood. We don't know anything else and, therefore, can't compute *having* anything else. On a more biological and neurological level, I often think of the saying **"Neurons that fire together, wire together,"** which describes a deeper process known as "long-term potentiation." The more frequently we repeat a pattern of behavior or a series of relational actions, or we think in a certain way, the stronger those connections between thought, behavior, and outcome become. Breaking these past relationship habits becomes trickier because we have a whole series of connections in our brain that keep taking us back to what we know and make it hard for us to seek out something to the contrary. It's not that you want to be unhappy and heartbroken and back on the dating apps for the third time in a year; it's that you have learned one way to love and need to relearn a new approach.

Fatal Fantasy Bonding

The final reason we may repeat dysfunctional or unhelpful relationship patterns has to do with the concept of fantasy bonding. Fantasy bonding occurs when we invest in the illusion of a connection between ourselves and someone else despite nothing of the sort existing. We do this to protect ourselves from truly recognizing what we are missing. It is a psychological defense mechanism that protects us from seeing the things we don't want to see about our partner. It is often seen in children growing up in dysfunctional or neglectful environments who have no choice but to idealize their parents as the people they are *not* in order to sustain their connection, which they rely upon for security and survival. What really exists underneath is something completely different, but the fantasy is so much nicer.

We fall in love with our initial idea of someone, only to realize, further into the relationship, that we had it all wrong. Sometimes someone looks so much better in our imagination and we become attached to their potential, rather than who they are. They just fit so well in the storyline we have already created for ourselves, and so we idealize all the wonderful, golden parts while ignoring the red flags and projecting our desire for a future and the perfect relationship onto someone who is either unable or unwilling.

As time goes on, we find it harder to ignore all the signs that things may not be what they seem, and the illusion begins to fragment and eventually shatter. The traits that initially attracted us to someone now seemingly disappear because they were never really there. According to fatal attraction theory, it may be that the things we love about someone at the start actually end up being the very things that cause a relationship to end.

In the pioneering study behind fatal attraction theory, conducted by sociologist Diane Felmlee in 1995, participants were asked to describe the characteristics that initially attracted them to someone they were dating. Some were pretty standard, like physical attractiveness, kindness, and dependability. However, when it came to traits like "fun," "exciting," and "different," these appeared to be fatal attractors, meaning they inevitably contributed to relationship breakdown. That makes a lot of sense, because people who are spontaneous and entertaining are often quite charismatic. But when it comes to establishing a long-term relationship, what was once fun and interesting might soon become difficult if this person can never take anything seriously or plan ahead and is always the life of the party when you just want them beside you. It's not that the "fun" guy is always going to be bad for you, but this shouldn't necessarily be the most important factor to base a relationship on.

Similarly, someone who seems very different from you is initially interesting and intriguing, but as the relationship progresses you realize you don't have anything in common that can sustain a future together. So that initial attractor becomes fatal.

About 29 percent of the relationships observed in this study ended because of these "fatal attractions." It seems that a lot of us can't actually trust our initial preferences when it comes to dating, because we are driven by the need for a "spark" rather than the qualities that will endure and keep us feeling safe and satisfied in the long term. We continue to be driven toward people who excite us rather than leave us feeling calm, and we wonder why our relationships keep failing. This disenchantment occurs because we are investing in someone's potential, rather than their truth.

Breaking the Habit

Repeating dysfunctional habits or behaviors in relationships gets pretty exhausting. We get tired of telling the same story, with the same outcome, unable to identify the root psychological and emotional cause. We don't like seeing our story as a string of failed relationships, platonic or romantic. But we are bound to repeat what we don't repair, whether that is the trauma of past relationships or our childhood, learned relational behaviors, fantasy bonding, self-sabotaging, or misunderstood personal preferences. Very rarely do we engage in these things voluntarily, but they operate in our subconscious, snaking their way into how and who we date.

This is our history, but it doesn't have to be our future. We all come into relationships with baggage and it's our responsibility to figure out how to unpack it. Otherwise, it ends up strewn all over the floor, leaving both people tripping over it and frustrated.

Breaking the cycle starts with acknowledgment. Recognizing the times you've made mistakes or dipped back into unhealthy habits doesn't make you the villain, and it doesn't mean you will never deserve or find good, stable love. I think we tend to suppress these darker parts of ourselves that we're ashamed of in order to protect our self-esteem, not realizing that two things can be true at once: "This is who I was" but also "This is who I am becoming." Recognizing those times you aren't proud of how you acted or were driven by fear will help you stop it from happening again.

All of us are people in progress, from the day we're born to the day we die. Take some time to really sit with your past. Why did those last few relationships end? What things did you ignore at the beginning that reappeared at the end? What past story or relationship acts were you reproducing? Is this person really your type, or do they just provide the emotional environment you've become accustomed to? Do your preferences match what you actually want out of a relationship in the long term? This self-guided, autobiographical history lesson is where you need to begin, because you can't begin treatment without a diagnosis—a self-diagnosis, in these circumstances.

Then it's time to get clear on what you want. Be honest with yourself. If you know you crave stability and want someone who will always be in your corner to grow alongside you, why are you giving second and third chances to people who don't want to commit? If you know you want a soft and gentle life alongside someone who helps you regulate your big emotions, why are you dating people who haven't done the work themselves or who are emotionally volatile? If you know you want a life of adventure and need a few more years before settling down, why are all your exes so eager to get married straightaway?

I think it's because we like to imagine we can be someone we are not in a relationship. We want to make this other person happy, so we force ourselves into a life we don't fit, and eventually that just gets too uncomfortable to sustain. We settle or lower our expectations and neglect our needs just because we want love in any form we can get our hands on, even if it drains us. We let love break us, thinking we can change someone or change ourselves. I don't think I need to tell you that this never works.

Instead, address the problem at its source. **Get super clear on your relationship wants and needs by making a list of nonnegotiables.** For example: I want someone calm. I want someone looking for commitment. I need someone who is emotionally mature. I need someone who has family values, who doesn't mind moving around, who is entrepreneurial, who is spiritual or religious . . .

This is going to look different for everyone. But each of us should have at least five requirements we wouldn't be willing to compromise, and if you don't, it might be worth examining why you are so unfussy about something so important. Make your list of five requirements and apply them liberally. When you meet someone, be deliberate about noticing whether they match up with what you need in a partner.

Ask yourself three questions: Is there anything about this person I feel the need to change to be satisfied? What if they never change? In five years, would this still be a problem for me? These questions help you decide whether there is a future with this individual. If you don't think there is but you still feel attached and want to "see where it goes," reflect on the past and remember how that turned out before. Do you need to learn that lesson again, or are you ready for a new story?

Be articulate with yourself and the people you are dating about your nonnegotiables, and give yourself a big enough window of time to see for yourself before you commit. The start of a relationship is always exciting, and sometimes we get wrapped up in that intensity, causing us to artificially speed up our closeness before we've had a chance to reflect on whether this person is good for us in the long term. Pause. Stop. Check your list and check it twice. You are the Santa Claus of dating. I think it's better to remain single for a bit longer or spend more time getting to know someone than to wake up at thirty or forty and realize you've spent the past years trying to force something that is so against your instincts, wants, and desires—only to end up back at square one.

Take a dating detox. Before I met my partner, I spent six months practicing being single. I decided that being alone was a skill I wanted to get used to, and instead of using temporary relationships and flings to distract me, I needed to go back to dating and relationship boot camp. It seems ironic that while I'm talking about establishing healthy patterns in your relationship, I'm also telling you to avoid dating. But I do think that a dating detox breaks the cycle of past partners and automatic behaviors we rely on in our relationships. If humans are creatures of habit, the only way to break the habit is to do the complete opposite of what you're used to. So give yourself time to explore the past, who you are and who you want, without becoming distracted by the excitement and task of building a new connection or the dizzying thrill of the honeymoon period, which makes us irrational and unable to make the best decisions.

Finally, be gentle with yourself. This is hard. Love is hard. Relationships are hard. You will not find the solution in self-hatred and self-blame, because you cannot hate yourself into a better version of you. There are so many unconscious reasons we repeat dysfunctional patterns or history in relationships, and we don't voluntarily choose them. Regardless of what happened or went wrong in the past, you are still at your core a vulnerable, sensitive human looking for the kind of love that can hold your dreams and hopes for the future and grow with you. You will find it, if you take the time to unpack, settle in, and set yourself up for success.

> Are they really your type, or are you just repeating a dynamic you already feel comfortable with, even if it's not best for you?

The fantasy of someone and their potential may be nice, but the stories we assign to others crumble over time.

You, and you alone, are responsible for unlearning the dysfunctional patterns you apply in relationships. That doesn't mean you're to blame, but you do owe a more successful future to yourself.

It's okay to take a break and rethink what you really want from love and, with that, a relationship. There is no rush, and the outcome will be more fruitful.

- - - - - - - - - -

CHAPTER IV

The Stigma of Being Single

IN THE STAGE between emerging adulthood and established adulthood, there are three major milestones that society expects us to reach: moving out of our childhood home, establishing a career, and meeting "the one." We've spoken a lot about society's blueprint for twenty-somethings and how restrictive it can be, and finding love in particular feels largely out of our control, since it's based on factors like fate, timing, destiny, emotions, and luck. Fairy tales are not written about promotions at work or securing a home loan; they are written about romance and the fantasy of finding your dream partner and never leaving them.

However, there is a deeper love we need to tune in to before we have any hope of finding "the one": the love we have for ourselves. We focus so much on wanting others to want us, without ever pausing to consider whether we actually like ourselves, or what we might need or want from others. You are your first love, and the longest relationship you will ever have is with yourself. So *you* deserve the same kind of time, energy, investment, and care that you put into your romantic relationships.

Unsurprisingly, the more we take care of ourselves, cultivate a strong sense of self, and build our confidence and self-assurance, the more **good** people we tend to attract. Focusing on yourself takes the pressure off trying to win over someone else, because then love is no longer a necessity, it's an addition. When you are focused on making your own life incredible, joyful, and fulfilling, you will only accept the things—and the people—who make it better. So if you want to find love, the first step is realizing that you already have all the love you crave from others—in yourself.

The Stigma of Being Single

The fairy tales aren't totally wrong. The person we choose to be our partner is one of the biggest predictors of future emotional health, happiness, and success. A stable marriage or partnership can even improve our life expectancy—not only are we going to live longer, but we are going to spend even more time with our partner. One 2019 study suggested that people who are happy with their spouse reduce their risk of an early death by 13 percent, even when controlling for other significant factors like socioeconomic situation and baseline health. The importance of making the right choice cannot be overstated by researchers, scientists, dating coaches, and matchmakers alike.

However, anyone who has dated in their twenties knows the chaos and upheaval of searching the dating pool for someone they are, at a bare minimum, compatible with, and just hoping someone likes them back. It can take years, dozens of failed first dates, medium-term relationships, second-guessing, breakups, and heartache before we feel ready to settle down. Maybe we never do. That possibility carries a lot of shame and fear. Society places relationships on a pedestal. The ultimate success story is a love story ending in marriage, children, and happily ever after. This narrative can create a panic as we get further into our twenties with no "success." It feels like a race to the finish line, perhaps even a competition to make it to thirty with someone by your side. Our society covets the idea of monogamy and partnership. Being single is not the norm. Therefore, by these standards, it becomes more acceptable to be in a relationship—even a dysfunctional one—than to be happy and content by yourself. This is the stigma of being single.

The stigmas and stereotypes about being single firmly paint people who choose to be single, or who might not feel they have a choice, as being inherently unhappy, unsatisfied, or deserving of pity. This stigma manifests in a lot of implicit judgments and phrases we've all heard: "The right person is out there for you," "It's just a numbers game," "Once you get to thirty it becomes a whole lot worse," "You'll find someone eventually," "It will happen when you least expect it." No one ever tells you to enjoy this time of being single or applauds you for doing what makes you happy. The emphasis is always on what you're missing from life.

These statements might be said with the best of intentions, but they imply that you can't fully believe you are happy or secure until you find this final puzzle piece. This kind of "single-shaming" is on the rise. A study conducted by Match.com, one of the world's leading dating sites, found that around 52 percent of single adults in the UK reported experiencing some level of single-shaming in the past few years.

These judgments and well-meaning questions from friends and distant family members about your dating life accumulate alongside the constant media messaging that single equals sad. All this takes its toll on your sense of self, leading you to make compromises in order to satisfy the requirement of being in a relationship.

Sometimes it's not shame but longing that makes us feel uncomfortable about being single. We can't help but notice and

crave the comfort and security of the people we see happily cou-
pled up. I don't think that's necessarily a bad thing; it doesn't
mean something is inherently wrong with us. We psychologically
crave what we don't have, due to the scientifically proven "grass
is greener" syndrome.

Everything looks better when we don't have it, because it's the
possibility that makes it so attractive. This can be explained by
the scarcity effect in psychology, mentioned earlier. When we feel
that something is desirable, worthwhile, or rare—such as a
relationship—our subconscious mind makes us want it more.

Women and Singlehood

We cannot talk about the stigma of singleness without examining the psychology behind gender and misogyny. The burden
that accompanies single-shaming is not felt equally. Think about
the words used to describe singleness past thirty: a woman is
called a "spinster," but a man is a "bachelor." Words are not
empty constructs! They contain an implied social message to dis-
parage women for their choices. Singleness is a curse for women,
but a period of freedom for men.

Women tend to endure the most shame or prejudice because
of the emphasis on marriage and child-rearing as part of female
identity. We can understand this by looking at gender schema
theory. Gender schema theory was introduced in the 1980s by
psychologist Sandra Bem. It suggests that the "differences" between men and women have become one of the basic organizational structures in human society: men are the breadwinners, the
moneymakers, the leaders, the powerful sex, while women are the

wives, the homemakers, the mothers. This way of organizing society impacts how individuals make decisions and see themselves.

As children, we learn about gender and begin to adopt this gendered schema based on observing how others behave, the media we consume, the words of our peers and adults, and the role of our mother versus our father in the home.

Stereotypically, girls are expected to behave with grace, kindness, empathy, and a nurturing spirit, whereas boys are expected to be leaders and are allowed to be rough, angry, and adventurous. When you act in line with that schema, your behavior is reinforced, you're praised, given attention, so you become conditioned to embrace a certain gender identity and expression. A big part of the female identity is being a wife and mother. We often construct the identity of a woman based on her relationship to others and her social role. And because of those very early, consistent influences, it feels like a natural duty to continue living up to your assigned gender expectations. Thus, when you are unable to "fulfill" that trope, you experience both external and internal discomfort. As a woman, who are you without a husband, without a mate, without a child?

The Alternative

Making the "best" of your circumstances seems to be the consolation prize for people who aren't in relationships. But being single can be incredibly rewarding. Some studies even suggest that the happiest and healthiest population subgroup in the world is women who never married and never had children. We may need some more evidence to support this, but it points to some of the benefits of singlehood that never seem to get the same attention as the downsides the media likes to flog.

To name a few more, singlehood means you get space to really know yourself, you build stronger friendships, you can be flexible and spontaneous because you don't need to constantly think about others' preferences or account for them in your life plans. Freedom of this kind seems to be the biggest upside. In 2020, a group of researchers asked a sample of 648 Americans their reasons for being single. One of the most common responses was, in their words, the desire to be "free to do whatever I want." There is something really significant about having the liberty to be your own person and discover what you want from your future. Your life becomes bigger than the need to find a relationship.

If your only focus is obtaining love, you won't care about what you need to sacrifice to get it, and so the relationship you have with yourself is no longer a priority. When the relationship you have with yourself suffers, so do all your other relationships, because you find yourself unable to articulate your boundaries or needs, or maintain a sense of stability over who you are. Finding the right partner is important, but before you can do that, you need to find yourself first.

There are a number of reasons I believe it is necessary to find yourself before you go out in search of love. First, when you aren't clear on the fundamentals of who you are, you can easily become swept into the story of who someone else wants you to be. This means you become more invested in keeping someone else happy than being happy yourself, which leads to a sense of personal detachment that bleeds into your sense of self and eventually into your mental and emotional well-being. Second, your identity is made up of so many elements that need to be equally prioritized. This includes your everyday personal experiences, hobbies, long-term goals, preferences, platonic and familial relationships, and work. Your relationship status is certainly an important facet, but when your entire identity exists in the pursuit of, absence of, or act of falling in love, you tend to neglect the elements that make you an interesting and interested individual.

Love is not the most interesting part of your story. If you believe it is, you might go through life never truly knowing who you are, because you never feel complete without someone else by your side.

Third, I think it's about reflecting back what you would want in a partner. Finally, knowing yourself means you see the value in your own company. Therefore, you don't fear being alone or stay in bad relationships because you are more terrified of the uncertainty and the shame of singleness than the very real possibility of spending your life with someone who isn't right for you.

Finding oneself is a rather broad idea that stems from a process of exploration and discovery. There are some things about us that we can't change, such as genetics, family, personality, and neurological wiring (even that is up for debate), but in almost everything else we have some kind of choice. This includes our beliefs, dreams for the future, sense of what would make us happy, environment, and relationships, among many other things. To find ourselves, we need to reflect on our values, beliefs, mission, and identity—and sometimes that requires being uncomfortable and being alone. When we are alone, we don't feel we need to be anything other than who we want to be, and through that process we reveal who we truly are. We create routines that suit us, we pursue our dreams without needing to accommodate someone else's, we stand for what we believe in, we are more focused on creating a life that is comfortable for us even if no one else tags along. We no longer fear a life alone, because we realize that romantic love is not the only love that exists. We receive love from our friends and families, from random strangers, and all of this can be equally fulfilling.

Finding yourself involves embracing your most authentic self—the version of you who acknowledges others' opinions, expectations, and wants, then chooses to prioritize your own. In this way, you make fewer compromises for love. Of course, this can get lonely, but that loneliness no longer has control over your decision-making, especially when you make prioritizing yourself a daily practice.

Loving Yourself First

When you're single, it might feel as though you're missing out on the love that others are experiencing. That's a form of FOMO, sure, but also a longing to be held, to be praised, to be comforted and seen. But being single doesn't mean an absence of love. Of course, we receive love from our friends and family, but we can also show it to ourselves and embrace the opportunity to date, love, and find ourselves.

Speaking your love languages to yourself is an excellent way to do this. Love languages represent the ways we like to give and receive love. They include words of affirmation, acts of service, physical touch, gift giving, and quality time. As conceived by Baptist pastor Gary Chapman, the core premise is that:

1. Each of us has a preferred love language.

2. People want to be shown love through their preferred love language.

3. Couples are happier when each person shows love
in the other's preferred love language and receives
it in theirs.

The notion of love languages has become increasingly popular in the last decade, notably with the rise of viral online quizzes.
The concept has made it easier for an entire generation of people
to express what they need from a relationship through a simple
metaphor and representation of one's core intimacy needs. It
definitely gets a few things wrong—most people tend to endorse
all five love languages as being important and they struggle to
choose only one. Plus, there are indeed more than just five ways
to give and receive love; factors like recognition, humor and
laughter, and emotional security are also important. The main
premise of love languages is that we need to receive them from
others, particularly a partner. The logic follows that, if you don't
have that special someone, your love language doesn't really matter or goes unfulfilled. But what if we spoke our love languages
to ourselves?

You can show yourself the love you feel you need from others.
If your love language is **words of affirmation**, be intentional in
speaking kindly to yourself and repeating positive statements
such as, "I am kind, I am lovable, I am generous, I am intelligent,
I am creative." If your love language is **acts of service,** make your
bed in the morning as a gift to your future self who's going to
appreciate coming home to a cozy, neat space. If it's **gift giving,**
buy yourself the nice things you're waiting for someone else to
get you. For **quality time,** carve out an evening each week to
spend alone, enjoying your own company, doing exactly what
you want to do. The hardest love language to fulfill on your own
might seem to be **physical touch.** This is where the power of the

self-embrace comes in, which is, quite literally, giving yourself a hug. This is known as "self-soothing touch." Research conducted during the COVID-19 pandemic, when touch from others was in short supply, seems to demonstrate that the act of wrapping yourself in a nice embrace, placing a hand over your heart, or making other gentle gestures reduces stress levels and has a similar soothing effect as a cuddle from someone else. There is no reason why you can't show yourself the same kind of physical affection you tend to receive from others.

Another amazing practice is to schedule date night with yourself and make it a part of your routine. I had a friend who would take themselves out to a new Italian restaurant once a month, solo. They'd bring along their journal, dress up because, of course, it's a date, and ask themselves the same five questions each time: What did you do today? What is making you feel proud of yourself? What are you looking forward to? What's been bothering you? What can you change in the next month? It sounds a lot like a relationship check-in, but with yourself. Make a ritual out of your self-love, something you can look forward to that you can come back to at any age, a deep pool of love for yourself that you can step back into. It doesn't have to be a solo date night; it could be cooking yourself a new dish once a week that you pour your love into, taking yourself to a movie, catching the sunrise once a week. All these things scream romance, but the kind of romance you don't need others for.

A final caveat. You don't need to entirely love yourself and know who you are before you open yourself up to love. There's a popular saying: "If you don't love yourself, how is anyone else meant to love you?" I get the message and in many ways I support the sentiment. But I don't think we ever really get to a place of knowing ourselves completely or being entirely free of insecurity, self-doubt, or the constant need to improve. That is a life-long process. We've focused a lot on loving yourself first as a way of ensuring you know what you want and have the space for someone else, but when you feel ready, there is a whole lot of healing that also comes from a relationship. It's this recognition that no one is perfect, that we each come to the table with small quirks, a complicated history, maybe trauma—and we embrace each other anyway. Once you have fallen in love with your solo life, the addition of someone else can only propel it further, if that's what you're after.

Love is not the most interesting part of your story. You are made to be so much more.

In a world that prioritizes partnership and places unrealistic expectations on love, choosing to date yourself and put yourself first is an act of radical self-compassion, even rebellion.

The relationship you have with yourself is your greatest investment. Cherish it and nourish it.

Romantic love should be the cherry on top of an already fulfilling life.

--- - - - - - - -

CHAPTER V

Unrequited Love and Situationships

CAN YOU BE in love with someone you never even dated? If there was no label, did the relationship even exist? Can heartbreak be one-sided? The answer to all these questions is a strong and affirmative YES. I know this firsthand, as I'm sure many of my fellow twenty-somethings do.

There's a unique type of relationship during this decade that causes us to ask many of these exact questions: the dreaded situationship. The not quite dating, not quite friends, exclusive but not committed affair that goes against everything we've been taught about love. It keeps you in a place of emotional purgatory for months, years even, as you wait for someone else to decide that you're good enough for them to commit. That person who you are unable to drag yourself away from, no matter how they treat you: nonchalantly one day and amazingly the next. The love that never feels big enough to hold you both, so one of you is always bound to fall harder, faster, cursed with all the terrible remains at the end.

You never thought this would be you, accepting less than you deserve, clinging to the promise of love like a small child. And yet here you are, begging for the bare minimum while someone else dismisses your emotional bids; trying your hardest to pretend it doesn't bother you when every part of you feels like it's been strung out to dry. It sounds dramatic if you've never been through it, but if you have, this might not even describe the whole picture. Let's talk about situationships in our twenties.

So ... What Are We?

Situationships are a unique type of psychological torture because of the Stockholm syndrome they create for the person inflicted with this emotional pain. We can't walk away, even though we know we should. At least that was my experience.

When I was twenty-one, straight out of my first "adult" long-term relationship, I met someone. He seemed unassuming, tame, nice enough, and made me feel less lonely. I was in no way pre-pared for a long-term relationship, but we always seem to fall the hardest when we are most unsuspecting. What followed was six months of incredible anxiety, a roller coaster of intense emo-tions, never feeling good enough. I never quite knew where we stood, and I wanted more, and he adamantly did not. I should have listened. The moment that really sums it up for me was a trip we took together in which I told him I was falling in love with him, and he responded by saying he had a date on Tuesday. It's embarrassing now to admit, because all the signs were there, but they were overridden by a deep desire for this person to one day love me back.

Situationships walk the line between committed relationship and a friends-with-benefits agreement. It seems that, for most people in their twenties, they are on the rise. They do not meet the traditional expectations and norms for a relationship; there is normally sex and emotional intimacy involved, even sometimes exclusivity, but no label or plans for the future. That's what makes them so confusing. We don't have a narrative or standard storyline for what is occurring.

Another defining characteristic of a situationship is that the relationship neither grows nor ends; it exists in this strange emotional and physical limbo where you never have a sense of security.

You also never get closure, because you can't break up with someone you never dated—even if you did all the things a couple would do—so these "relationships" always feel ambiguous and hard to process. Some people are able to navigate these types of relationships really successfully. They are okay with the lack of commitment and consistency and the innate convenience of these situations. People high in sociosexuality—a trait that increases our interest in casual, uncommitted sex—tend to be more receptive to this arrangement. You get the emotional connection but in a compartmentalized way so that you can still equally enjoy your freedom.

In our twenties, when the dating world has never been more expansive, some people may actually prefer these types of relationships. But when one person doesn't feel the same way as the other, stronger feelings of unrequited love emerge. We can also experience significant resentment, anger, even grief directed toward the other person in a situationship. We are frustrated at not getting what we want, but perhaps underneath that we are even more frustrated at ourselves for letting it get this far. So why do these kinds of pseudo-relationships emerge, why do they hurt so much, and how do we recover from this experience?

Why Am I Here?

Situationships remain fairly underresearched in the psychology space, perhaps because of the modernity of the term—which might be more psychobabble than measurable concept and theory. Despite that, ideas and suggestions have been offered for why twenty-somethings, like you and me, often encounter situationships during emerging adulthood. These explanations normally focus on avoidance of loneliness, commitment readiness (or unreadiness), emotional unavailability, and poor communication.

Many of us during our twenties face a struggle between intimacy and isolation. We don't like feeling lonely, or the fact that everyone else is having romantic experiences that we are not, and so we settle for situations that only partially fulfill our emotional needs because they fulfill a deeper social need to be seen, wanted, and loved. Some of us, myself included, are particularly sensitive to this fear of loneliness and the way it drives us to pursue relationships we know are shallow and unhealthy. When I was in my own situationship, I searched for explanations. I found the most significant factor is childhood emotional neglect, both in a family setting and by peers.

If our emotional need for connection was denied and dismissed in childhood, this can create adult dysfunction whereby we are constantly seeking the approval and admiration of others to prevent similar deprivation and feelings of unworthiness. Perhaps our parents weren't even aware of the emotional environment they were creating and were simply replicating how they were raised, but this form of passive neglect may mean that we now don't see our needs as important, so we struggle with identifying what we actually want and why we deserve to have these desires fulfilled.

Lonely children become adults who crave nothing more than acknowledgment and acceptance, even if what they're actually feeling is unrequited love.

The relationships we have with our peers and early romantic experiences also seem to influence this feeling. For example, childhood exclusion and social isolation seem to be correlated with a decline in self-esteem later in life, which, as a result, may exacerbate this experience of staying in or pursuing relationships where you don't feel entirely appreciated.

As a child, I always felt very left out and unseen by my classmates due to bullying. It didn't help that I was a bit of a late bloomer, and I will be the first to tell you I struggled to fit in. I wore leg warmers to school in 2014. Not exactly "cool." For years I always wanted to feel like I mattered and was important, and so when people would give me even a sliver of attention, it was addictive. I chose to ignore all the things I wasn't getting for that small prize I did receive.

I always thought that if I'd felt more accepted as a child and teenager, maybe I wouldn't be as needy when it came to emotional and physical intimacy. As the age-old saying goes, we always want what we can't have. In my experience, I wanted what I never got as a child and teenager, when I was most emotionally vulnerable, but always craved deep down in my heart.

Sunk Costs?

Beyond loneliness, it's also important to consider the concept of "commitment readiness," as individual differences in this trait may cause situationships to form. In psychology, commitment readiness is the idea that each of us has some level of preparedness, desire, or willingness to commit to a romantic relationship. We vary in commitment readiness throughout our lives.

For example, straight after a breakup, our commitment readiness is probably fairly low, but after a few years of being single and seeing all our friends enter long-term relationships, we might see ourselves climbing up the ladder of wanting and feeling ready for a relationship. **However, each person differs. Often the reason these ill-committed pseudo-relationships occur is because one person is high on the commitment-readiness scale and the other person is low.** The high-commitment person is ready and pushes for more, not realizing that the low-commitment person entered into this situation with a preconceived idea of what they wanted. This difference will shape how the relationship forms, leaving one person dissatisfied and the other person maintaining their desire to be free and nonexclusive. Both people can't be satisfied at the same time.

When you're really hungry to start dating again, sometimes you choose to ignore these red flags because you buy into the illusion that you can change the low-commitment person's mind. Unfortunately, that's often untrue. However, it's the possibility that keeps you hooked, along with the effect known as the "sunk-cost fallacy," borrowed from economics.

The sunk-cost fallacy occurs when we refuse to give up on something (or someone) because we have already put in so much time and energy. It's like a bad investment we keep putting money toward because we're hoping things will turn around. Giving up would mean we've lost all that we've already contributed.

I once bought a pair of boots that were the most expensive purchase I had ever made. These $300 boots (ridiculous, I know) broke after one wear, so I spent an additional $50 on fixing them. Then a few weeks later the sole tore—$100 to repair them again.

Of course I did it, because I'd already sunk $350 into these boots, so it would have been a waste not to. Really, I could have just taken that $100 and bought a whole new pair of boots, saving myself the inevitable future money I was going to spend on these poorly made shoes. It might sound like a silly analogy, but those boots are the situationship and that money is the continuous effort and time we put toward a dead-end relationship because we can't bear losing all the previous energy we have put in by walking away. **It's irrational, but so is human emotion.**

This combination of factors—high commitment readiness, loneliness, sunk-cost fallacy—might explain why we find ourselves in a pattern of situationships. This is especially the case when we start hearing what we want to hear from the other person. When they say, "I'm not ready for a relationship," we hear, "I just need time." When they say, "I don't see you in that way, I want to keep dating other people," we hear, "They just need me to convince them I'm worth it." But do you really want to be with someone long term who you had to persuade to take you seriously? I always imagine what it would be like to tell my future kids the story of how Dad and I got together—and I don't want that story to be that he spent months being unsure before I "wore him down." That doesn't sound like the kind of romance that causes relationships to last, or the example I'd want to set for my children.

The final reason we may find ourselves in a repetitive pattern of situationships has to do with emotional unavailability. We may think we want a relationship, but deep down we know we aren't ready, and so we continue to choose people who keep us at a distance in order to never have to commit. We never have to address our underlying fears or distance and can, instead, diffuse the blame onto the other person.

Maybe you are the emotionally unavailable one? You are afraid of getting too deep and getting hurt again, so you keep intimacy at arm's length. You love the chase, but acknowledging that doesn't align with what you consciously want, and so the cycle continues. It doesn't mean you don't still feel the hurt and pain during and after the relationship, or that you don't experience the stress of being on an emotional roller coaster. You just don't yet recognize your actions in getting to that point.

Why Can't I Quit You?

Why do situationships and unrequited love hurt so much? That's a question I've been asking myself for years, and I think I have some answers. The first is that they make us feel like a failure. We approach this situation with so many expectations and a deep vulnerability. Perhaps we start to tell people about this new person in our life, how excited we are, full of hope—we have an idea in our mind of a future with this person. When it doesn't work out, we feel like we weren't good enough.

Equally, we might feel quite silly for letting ourselves get wrapped up with someone who didn't deserve the time, energy, and love we were offering them. Our self-esteem is injured by this perceived rejection and, perhaps, by what others will think. It's hard not to take these situations extremely personally and ruminate on what you could have done differently to change the outcome. Did you come on too strong? Were you too available? Was there something about you they found unattractive or undesirable? The inability to take this relationship to the committed stage makes us feel like we are doing something wrong when it comes to dating, resulting in further injuries to our self-esteem.

Second, situationships lack certainty, leaving us in a constant state of confusion. When you never quite know where you stand with someone, this ambiguity can be really distressing, because you no longer have a script for what's transpiring. You can go from extreme emotional intensity one day—sharing everything, sleeping together, meeting their friends, revealing feelings—to nothing the next, and you're never sure what pattern it will follow.

Remember, the other person is still getting something from this situation—your attention, affection, sex, entertainment, all with the benefit of low to no commitment—and has an incentive to keep you invested and coming back, even if they have no intention to go further. This is known as "breadcrumbing": small actions and doses of attention that keep you hooked and coming back. They send you a "good morning" text one day, maybe they invite you to plans after a week of not talking, mention the future, reply to your Instagram story, but nothing has changed. They just want the validation of knowing you'll come back for more. It's enough to keep the hope alive, but not enough to bring it to fruition.

This confusion begins to bleed into all other areas of your life, because you're waiting for something concrete to happen: for them to either end things or take it to the next level. That waiting game can go on for months before you realize you need to give up on the fantasy that you can change them. You are left in a perpetual state of anticipation and anxiety, not wanting to let go but also fully aware that this relationship has become detrimental to your mental state. Eventually, you get stretched to a breaking point. For some, it takes months, but I've heard from people who were in this kind of situation for years. It's rare that situationships actually turn into fully committed relationships. This person already knows everything they need to know about themselves and, to an extent, about you. If they wanted a relationship, you would be in one. Ignore any fantasy or delusion that keeps drawing you back to the imaginary best-case scenario.

At some stage, something will finally stir you to take action or will convince the other person it's time to release you. For me, it was only when I realized I had lost myself completely in this other person—I had lost friends over him and had lost all confidence because of him—that I finally ended things. There were feelings I couldn't contain any longer for my own sanity, and after months of being strung along, I walked away. And then I spent the next year thinking about him. Even in situationships where there wasn't a formal commitment, you're still going to feel the loss of someone you sincerely connected with, who you shared intimate moments with, who you made memories with—good memories! No relationship is all bad—even the uncommitted kind—and it's those times when you felt hope for what the relationship could be that you keep replaying in your head. You are recovering from a unique syndrome: unrequited love.

Let's be honest: it feels nice to be wanted, so there is no need to shame yourself for believing in love. Shaming yourself for any feeling always backfires, because that shame just intensifies the emotional state you're in. You need to treat this situationship like a real breakup, one you would feel is worthy of all this suffering and grief. As they say, sometimes the only way out is through. This probably applies even more for unrequited love, when you're trying not only to get over someone but, simultaneously, to find the correct category and explanation for all your displaced feelings. There's no guidebook for heartbreak after a situationship. So I think we should bestow it with the same legitimacy as all other breakups and proceed accordingly.

You are not weak or silly for wanting more. You are only human.

There is someone who will want every part of you and who will be 100 percent in. Just because this person didn't, doesn't make you unworthy of love.

The grief you feel from a situationship or unrequited love is real grief! It's okay to mourn what could have been and process it in whatever way you need to move on.

CHAPTER VI

Heartbreak—Hurting,
Healing, and Thriving

I HAVE HAD three major heartbreaks that defined my twenties. The "first love" heartbreak, the end of my first long-term relationship, and the aforementioned situationship that occurred straight afterward (which arguably broke my heart even more). People often say it's the first heartbreak that hurts the most and, with each one, you become more "experienced" in coping with this world-shattering loss, as if breakups were a skill we could learn to improve. Maybe that's true for some people, but for me the last one was objectively the hardest. Of course, losing my first love still hurt, and immensely at that, because it was a whole new category of feelings and it gave me a whole new perspective on what it meant to be sad. Suddenly all those breakup songs made a lot more sense to me. But that final heartbreak was the sort that made the world stop spinning. It took away my appetite, made me a selfish friend, removed all the color out of the world, made me obsessive to the point where I was begging my brain to just stop thinking about this person, to let him go so I could find some peace and move on.

I'd been broken up with before, done the breaking up, experienced my fair share of unrequited love, but there was something about this experience that was different. I thought at the time it was because this person was "the one," because we were twin flames and soulmates. I thought the intensity of the grief was a sign that this relationship was more than we'd let it be and that we were meant to be together. It's funny how in those hard moments we always turn to grand illusions of fate and destiny to bring us comfort.

In hindsight, I can acknowledge how ridiculous that sounds and, equally, how so many of our thoughts during a breakup are deluded by our emotional state. With time, we can recognize these thoughts for what they are: our brain trying to find a way through the agony.

Heartbreak is, at its core, a psychological experience. The more you understand what is going on behind the scenes, in your unconscious mind, the more you can make sense of your grief and heal. Of course, anyone who has been heartbroken knows there is no simple equation; as annoying and clichéd as it sounds, time is really the best antidote. But I truly believe that, **while heartbreak is devastating, it is equally a transformative and sacred experience. It is one of the best opportunities to rediscover who you are, renew your focus on the future, reinvent yourself, raise your standards, and, of course, find someone better—even if that person is yourself.** So let's talk about the psychology of heartbreak.

Hurting

Whether you were the one who did the breaking up, you knew it was coming, or you were suddenly broken up with, the underlying changes that occur in the aftermath are pretty similar for all of us. If you've ever heard the idiom "love is a drug," understand that it's not just a silly saying; recent research shows that there is a lot more truth to it than we think, as explained by the addiction model of heartbreak.

This theory proposes that, throughout the course of a relationship, people essentially become addicted to another person: their company, the reactions they create in our brain, the memories, the fantasy of the future and their potential. When we fall in love with someone, we experience an intense rush of neurotransmitters and hormones such as dopamine, serotonin, and oxytocin, known colloquially as the "love hormone." This mix of neurotransmitters and hormones stimulates a neurobiological bond that creates that euphoric honeymoon period and "high" of young early love.

These chemicals are the same chemicals present and active when we gamble, take drugs, or do anything pleasurable. They are addictive because they feel so good, creating an emotional and physical dependence on the source. How could we not become addicted to this feeling of immense joy and happiness? That is why the end of a relationship is like withdrawal. When we no longer have access to a person regularly, as the love starts to fade and the connection between us is stretched and weakened, our brain has to cope with a literal chemical change. The source of all that dopamine and those happy hormones disappears, so we no longer have that regular fix. It creates physical pain and emotional withdrawal.

When researchers conducted studies to prove this initial theory, they used fMRI technology to take scans of those important pleasure centers inside the brain. They recruited some recently heartbroken individuals and subjected them to the cruelest thing imaginable in the days and weeks after a breakup: They showed them pictures of their ex. While in a laboratory setting. Attached to wires that would track exactly where their brain was lighting up in response. They then compared these scans to the brain scans of individuals who were addicted to substances like cocaine.

They found that the same brain regions fired when subjects were shown pictures of their ex as those activated in the brain of someone craving or addicted to substances like cocaine and nicotine. Many of these people were still drawn to these lost loves—that is to say, neurologically attached, even addicted.

A second part of their brains also showed increased activity: the frontal lobe. This region is responsible for a lot of our decision-making, emotional reactions, and behavior. The researchers concluded that this part of the brain goes into overdrive to stop us from doing something, quite frankly, idiotic in response to our pain. We've all had those experiences of being heartbroken and sending a message we regret, going on a dating app rampage, or cutting all our hair off. This part of our brain is trying to control these impulses, but it's trying to square our reality with the positive memories. The other parts of our brain are reacting like we're still in love, whereas this rational part is very aware of the reality of the breakup and trying to keep us sane and self-aware.

This theory explains why a lot of us continue to chase after our exes and find ways to get back in touch and revisit memories of them, like a bruise we can't stop pressing. Each time we do this, we receive those small spikes of dopamine that keep us addicted, attached, and unable to move forward. It's understandable why we think of our exes obsessively in the weeks and months after a breakup and continue to romanticize the good times, because our brain is demanding we do so, to lessen the withdrawal, to taper off our addiction.

There is another psychological aspect to the misery we feel in the throes of heartbreak. The pain of losing someone we felt deeply connected to threatens our sense of social safety, belonging, and community. Psychologists call this particular type of sensation "social pain," the agony of losing social connection or experiencing abandonment. This experience is quite literally painful and activates the same regions in our brain as when we get a scrape, break a limb, or bruise an elbow. From an evolutionary perspective, humans evolved as social creatures who need partners and company to survive and to create a sense of belonging and security. The loss of those connections could have amounted to a death sentence back in the day, and so our brains evolved to make sure we held on to those relationships. The brain does this by creating a negative feeling and reaction when those relationships disappear so as to motivate us to return. As such, a lot of our neural circuits associated with the experience of physical pain are also linked to the sensation of emotional pain. Another aspect I don't think is spoken about enough is the loss of friends that often accompanies a breakup, which further strips us of a sense of connection and acceptance, leaving us weak and vulnerable.

When I went through that catastrophic breakup at twenty-two, the thing that hurt equally as much as losing him was losing the people I had become friends with by association. I lost his friends as well. As soon as our relationship was over, they seemingly wanted nothing to do with me, despite my feeling as if we had a friendship irrespective of him. It was as if all the memories we had made independently—making dinner when he was out, going out for drinks, driving around, the revealing conversations about our childhoods—no longer mattered.

I remember trying to reach out to them a few times, getting incredibly bland responses, and still not taking the hint, because, quite honestly, I missed them just as much. It wasn't just him I was saying goodbye to; it was an entire network of people. This is hard because we can't expect people not to choose sides, and it usually works out that they do. And he had dibs. They had known him longer, they had regular contact with him, or maybe they just liked him more.

You're going to lose a lot more than just your person. It can leave you feeling remarkably stranded, especially when friendship is one of the only soothers to relationship grief. But it's also giving you a whole new blank canvas to work with. As you heal, you'll begin to realize just how much you may have missed out on if you'd ended up with the person you thought was "the one." Because let me tell you right now: They probably aren't.

Healing

When we are healing from a breakup, we often hear a lot of "rules" that are meant to determine the length, intensity, and severity of our pain. People will offer us seemingly helpful, innocent advice that we really just aren't in the right place to hear at that moment, because heartbreak is not a one-size-fits-all kind of deal. We don't need to hear about someone else's breakup from five years ago, because heartbreak is as unique as we are.

One of the most common "rules" of heartbreak is that it takes half the time of the relationship to get over someone. This is obviously false. If it was true, no one who got married at twenty and divorced at sixty would ever remarry. And yet they do. Those short, monthlong flings would only take a few weeks to recover from. And yet they don't. Certain studies have tried to put a magical number on how long it actually takes. A 2007 study looking at 155 undergraduates suggested eleven weeks as the turning point; another piece of research from two years later found that it took divorcees approximately seventeen months and twenty-six days to get over their former spouse. There really is not a one-size-fits-all to healing.

The other "rule" is that you can only grieve someone you were officially in a relationship with. Also incorrect. A label does nothing to either intensify or lessen our feelings, because our emotional brain doesn't care what word we used to describe this other person; it only cares about the bond and impression they left. It doesn't think in semantics.

The combination of these misconceptions leads to the final "rule" or expectation we have for heartbreak: the longer the relationship, the worse the heartbreak. For some people, this may be the case. But I've found that it's often those hot-and-heavy relationships that sting the longest, because you never get to take them to their final conclusion—you don't complete the entire journey of what the relationship could be. Because of this, the conclusion of your time together is so much more open-ended, and you have a lot more unfinished emotional business. What if we had a label? What if they'd told me how they were feeling? What if they'd given me a second chance? What if I'd acted differently?

Those hypotheticals are difficult to move past because, unfortunately, you will never find the answers. When questions linger, so does the pain. It's what I like to think of as emotional limbo or purgatory.

In contrast, at the end of a long-term relationship we often understand why it needed to end. We tried to work through problems and we looked past the red flags that were there all along. We are probably exhausted from the same fights on repeat, trying to fix the relationship so clearly broken. We have taken it to completion and know there is nothing left for us. In that way, sometimes there is less need for closure in longer relationships.

It's important to remember that **breaking up with someone involves mourning the person they were, the person you were with them, and the relationship in general.** It's comparable to the grief we experience when someone passes away. This person is no longer a part of our life, and all we have left are the memories. There is a lot of love that still exists, even if it no longer has a destination. We can't get rid of those memories, so we need to integrate the good times with our current pain and distress. Seeing heartbreak as a type of grief allows us to understand the "stages" we go through before we reach a point of acceptance. Let's talk about heartbreak and the stages of grief.

The Stages of Relationship Grief

In psychology, therapists like to talk about the five stages of grief, which originated in Elisabeth Kübler-Ross's groundbreaking 1969 book, *On Death and Dying,* one of the first works to systematically explore how people process loss. Though it has since been tested and revised, and has its fair share of doubters, I think the overall concept is still a valuable one.

In the weeks, months, and years after the death of a loved one, we cycle through five stages of grief: denial, anger, bargaining, depression, and acceptance. This process is not always linear and the timeline differs for everyone. It also is not exclusively applied to death: getting fired, losing friendships, and, of course, suffering a heartbreak all may follow a similar cycle and pattern of stages.

In the first stage, denial, we feel numb to what has just occurred. It almost feels as if the breakup is not real, that our beloved is just away for a few days on a trip. It's pretty common for us to say to our friends, "Yeah, I'm really fine, I'm already over it," when in fact what we are experiencing is our brain trying to compartmentalize the pain and delay our grief. This can last for a few minutes or months. When my first long-term relationship ended, I vividly remember not being able to cry for at least two months afterward. Then, one day, I learned my ex was dating someone else. That was the switch that needed to be flipped in order for it to sink in: we were not together anymore, he wasn't coming back, I needed to move on. What hit me next was a wave of anger.

Anger occurs when we feel a sense of unfairness or injustice. In the case of heartbreak, this can be anger at the other person for treating us badly, anger at them for moving on, or anger at ourselves for letting them go. Anger is also what we sometimes call a "secondary" emotion. Our anger often masks a more vulnerable feeling we're not ready to confront. It masks our fear, our hurt, our disappointment. If you've ever been so angry that you've cried, you'll know that feeling well. Sometimes anger is less complicated than the emotion we really want to express, and so we hide behind our rage. But as it wears off, it reveals what's at the root of our wrath: we are fragile and hurt. Our brains only have a finite amount of mental resources and stamina for such a heavy emotion, so eventually we exhaust ourselves and move on to bargaining.

Bargaining comes from a feeling of helplessness, normally

when we hit a point of stagnation in our healing process. It's when the what-ifs start to swirl rapidly in our minds and all the had-beens and could-have-beens come alive. In my experience, it's also the stage where we are most likely to try to win them back now that we've had a taste of what life is without them, making promises that we'll change or they will. Stop. Pause. This relationship ended for a reason. What you are experiencing is an emotional and social withdrawal. You have come so far. You can either be back where you are now in six months or keep pushing forward, keep working for a future where you will be okay and they will just be a loose, floating memory.

When the anger, the denial, and the bargaining subside, we are left with a deep sadness. The depression stage is where, I think, the heartbreak truly begins. All the things we typically associate with a breakup—the tears, the loneliness, the sleepless nights, the long car rides, the sad playlists, the torment—are clear signs we are deep in the depression stage. In this stage of the breakup, I think we start to feel the reality of loss a lot more acutely. We begin to contemplate questions like, Will I ever see this person again? Or, Who am I if they're not in my life? Will I ever experience love again? With all these really existential questions, our circumstances begin to become a lot clearer and our loss becomes a lot more unavoidable. And as that sadness grows, that's when the actual hard work and healing really begin.

It's important to note that the length and intensity of these stages are different for everyone, because we each have different, preexisting attachment styles, temperaments, and personalities. There are people out there who can disconnect from a relationship in an instant and who appear to move on really quickly. To me, that always indicates a prior and ongoing emotional unavailability that was probably already present during the relationship.

Moving on with someone new immediately afterward is also an avoidance technique, because the easiest way to distract yourself is with someone else.

If you're a sensitive person like me, sometimes that can be the hardest part: knowing that the other person has moved on while you're still grieving and trying to process your emotions. It's almost like a competition. Who can move on the fastest? When you're losing—when they seem fine and you've been crying so hard your eyes won't open—it just feels terrible. It really makes you question whether what you had was real. I promise you that it was. If someone appears to move on, especially straight into a new relationship, I promise you that this is an illusion, probably one they're subconsciously buying into as well. If you haven't taken the time to properly journey through the stages of grief, if you've skipped past that essential emotional work, you haven't accepted what's happened, and you haven't fully processed your emotions or what that relationship meant to you.

Getting to a stage of acceptance involves acknowledging the loss, knowing there's nothing you can do to change it, appreciating the good times, but also no longer resisting the pain that will occasionally flare up—because you and I both know you will be okay.

Your life does not begin or end with this person. To arrive at this point of acceptance, there are some things we can do in the prior stages to cement our dedication to healing. The trick to getting over someone you can't stop thinking about is to detach physically, mentally, socially, and emotionally—as much as you possibly can. You need to symbolically cut that line that is continuing to connect you to that person.

The most significant method to accomplish this is to go no-contact. You've probably heard this again and again. I'm sure your best friend has told you to block your ex more times than I can. But it can be difficult to apply that level of self-discipline, especially when you're in the habit of talking every day and keeping up with each other's lives.

The pain of going no-contact will be more immediate, but you also know, intrinsically, that severing your connection by removing contact, communication, and interaction—mainly online—will speed up the process of acceptance. There will be fewer reminders, fewer sources of that dopamine that keeps you addicted, fewer opportunities to compare how you are doing and to see if they've moved on, and a greater ability to recognize that your lives are now separate.

Some people argue that exes can be friends. In many ways, I think they can, but only after a period of complete disconnection. First, no-contact allows you to mentally demote your ex by removing the frequency and intensity of your interactions. Soon they are no longer the first person you think of in the morning, at night, every time something good happens in your life (or something bad, for that matter). Second, wanting to stay friends could just be an excuse to keep them in your life, when that might not be the wisest decision for your mental sanity or recovery. We con ourselves into believing this is possible, because unconsciously we aren't prepared to say goodbye. No-contact is so valuable because it forces us to detach from all these misconceptions and move forward without the distraction of possibility.

During that period of going no-contact, and in the months, even years, afterward, it's fairly commonplace to have what I call "memory flare-ups." It's been months since you last spoke and suddenly you can't stop thinking about your early dates. You're fighting the unexpected urge to reach out. These involuntary memory flare-ups are no more than "mind pops," the weird and only recently labeled phenomenon where our brain suddenly brings about memories and information that seem irrelevant in the moment. This involuntary memory recall often occurs when something in our environment triggers something from the past by acting as a cue for memory recall. Maybe it's a specific smell, a song lyric, a place, a food—and suddenly you're right back in that place and time, reminiscing years later on all that was good. If a memory is particularly emotionally loaded, this also increases how often we will recall it, because our brain sees it as significant. Sometimes it's just the result of plain old boredom. When our brain is relaxed, this reduces our inhibitions and conscious control over memories, causing them to suddenly reemerge like an unwelcome visitor.

The final explanation has to do with a concept known as the "anniversary effect." This term is often used in reference to individuals with PTSD, whereby the anniversary of a particular event triggers us to relive certain moments. Whether it's the anniversary of when you first met, or the breakup, or some other significant date, this may explain why you might feel you are completely over your heartbreak but still find yourself thinking about someone.

Don't fear these thoughts, and don't try to suppress them. They are nothing more than your brain deciding to fire in strange ways or doing what it does best: storing memories and recalling them when it thinks they may be useful. Just because you are thinking about an ex doesn't mean they were "the one"; it's not some spiritual sign you should get back together. It's just your brain short-circuiting, looking for that closure. Approach cautiously and with neutrality. Of course you miss them, you felt connected, they were a part of your life, maybe things ended in an unsatisfying way—all that can be true, but you don't need to remain emotionally invested in them.

It's also essential to question how you may be misinterpreting these memories, romanticizing parts of your relationship with your rose-colored glasses on. There's a reason why we only remember the good times. It's known as the "Pollyanna principle," the positive cognitive bias whereby we remember the good times more clearly than the bad, and therefore fixate on them. We romanticize the past to protect ourselves from negative memories, and in the process we engage in selective recall. When we think about an ex or some unrequited love, all we remember is what made them special; all the other things—the unanswered messages, the lack of effort, the unhappiness—are left out. It's no wonder we can't move on when we constantly remember someone incorrectly, despite our best intentions.

To counteract this, I like to use visualization techniques. Mentally project yourself into the future and imagine ending up with this person. Imagine spending the rest of your days with them, raising kids with them, celebrating every major event in your life with them—would that really have been fulfilling? Would they have given you what you deserved? Focus on all their irritating behaviors, the things you complained about to your friends, the attention they didn't give you, the love they didn't show you. Through visualization, you'll begin to realize that the end of this relationship was perhaps one of the biggest blessings you could have received, even if it feels like you're in the trenches right now.

Time will pass, and healing won't always be linear, but neurologically your brain cannot be in this much pain forever. It cannot sustain that kind of emotional burden, or it would exhaust itself. Everything is temporary in life, including this feeling.

Thriving

Moving from a point of acceptance to actually thriving is its own unique pilgrimage. You're in your twenties! You want to be having those incredible experiences you'll talk about for years rather than languishing in the aftermath of a heartbreak! You want to feel powerful and self-contained and independent and confident!

As I've said before, **love is not the most important part of your story; it's about the relationship you have with yourself.** In order to cultivate that, begin by finding that final piece of closure that you need. Closure occurs when our brains can create a structured narrative around why something ended and conclude a linear storyline of a relationship from beginning to ending. When we lack that closure, or sense of completion, our brain remains unsure of whether it's time to close that chapter, because it doesn't really have a place to put all those memories. It wants us to keep looking for answers and reaching back into the past for clues or some final, powerful understanding.

The biggest misbelief we tend to have about closure is that someone else needs to provide that closure for us. We believe that the answer to our grief lies in the same person who caused it and that there is something they can say or do that is going to make everything make sense. Unfortunately, this is rarely the case.

They may not even have the answers themselves—they may be just as confused as you are. There is rarely, if ever, going to be an answer that is fully satisfying. So you have to write the end of this story yourself—you have to provide your own closure.

Write this person a final letter, thanking them, being honest about how you've felt, and telling them why you need to move on now, why you are finally letting them go. Don't send it—that is crucial. Do not send this letter; this is an exercise simply for you to provide your own brain with the end to the story and let it rest. Burn it, throw it away, keep it in a box, time-capsule it. Know that every worry, fear, pain you still feel, any regrets or urge to go back—it's all left with that letter and it's time to move forward.

It's important to choose to prioritize what the end of this relationship has brought you, rather than what it may have cost you. For example, what are the upsides of no longer having this person in your life? Every time you miss them, think about how now you have more time to yourself, you always get to watch what you want on TV, you can make choices without considering their interests. Every time you think about those fond memories, think about all the new memories you're one day going to make with someone else, the quality time you'll have with your friends, the emotional clarity you're going to get from this experience.

Start investing in parts of yourself that they have no idea about. Sometimes the reason you find it so difficult to emotionally detach is that you feel as if a huge part of your identity for the past few months, years, whatever amount of time, has become intertwined with this other person. You need to start investing in a version of yourself that is untouched by this person—that includes new hobbies, new friends, new values, and new priorities. Refresh your environment, buy some new artwork, maybe even make it, try all the restaurants you never did with them, find some new music to listen and dance to, fill up that schedule. The end of this relationship is the beginning of your next chapter.

I got really into pottery after my first big breakup a few years back, pouring all my grief and pain into creating something special, running after the next one, and then, of course, my podcast. This was my meditation, my healing space, and I really believe we all need a version of this when we are trying to move on from someone we can't stop thinking about. Choosing to invest in yourself is a profound reclaiming of the self, a reclaiming of your independence—you are someone without this person, you are someone without their validation. You exist as a brilliant bright light, a beautiful person even if they aren't there to witness it. Remember to take what you need from the end of the relationship—whether that's a better understanding of what you want in the future, what you deserve, how you want to be loved. Spell out what you need and deserve, even if you don't feel ready for it yet.

Finally, to beat a dead horse, take your time before moving on. I think a lot of us have this intense instinct or urge to find a rebound as soon as our previous relationship is over, or if we've been left rejected or aimless. That is a short-term fix; it simply offers a distraction rather than a deeper solution. A group of researchers conducted a study on rebound relationships a few years ago punchily titled "Too Fast, Too Soon? An Empirical Investigation into Rebound Relationships." What they concluded was that rebound dating is reactive and done in response to the residual emotions from lost love. It is going to leave you more emotionally raw, and it may also trigger you to keep going back to the memories you have with your ex, because you'll be experiencing similar things—intimacy, going to the same date locations, being in the same environment, talking about the same things—just with a new person. You contain all that you need. Someone else will never be able to understand you better than you understand yourself, or heal you as much as you can.

It's not always going to feel like this. So just welcome the emotion and say goodbye to it. One day you'll look back at this moment and be grateful it ended when it did.

These emotions show just how deeply you feel. Imagine how amazing it's going to be when you give that love to the right person and receive it back.

Missing them doesn't mean it was meant to be.

Isn't it so exciting that the part of your story where you fall in love isn't over yet? You have so many more opportunities to find "the one."

- - - - - - - - - -

CHAPTER VII

Friendship—A Reason,
a Season, a Lifetime

OUR SOCIETY PUTS a premium on romantic love, placing it above everything else and positioning it as one of the ultimate pursuits of our twenties. **But in our twenties, our friendships are arguably more fundamental to the person we are becoming than our flings, romances, and dating stories.** If our parents were the defining relationship of our childhood and our partners are the main focus of our thirties, our twenties are devoted to our friends. They are normally the people we share the most intimate of things with, we hang out with the most, we laugh with, we suffer and thrive alongside. They're our emergency contacts, our platonic soulmates, our job references, our second family, and our confidants as we fall in love, get our hearts broken, get fired, complain about our jobs, and struggle with our families, mental health, money, and everything in between.

The quality (and at times quantity) of friends we have in our twenties can make or break many of the experiences we are having and, as such, it can become a real point of insecurity. This decade offers a challenge to find our people and hold on to them tight, even as we face the threat of distance, shifting identities, disconnection, friendship breakups, and major life transitions. It's also the time when we realize that not all friendships are forever, as the famous quote goes: they can be for a reason, a season, or a lifetime. Not everyone is meant to make it into the retirement home with you, but there are valuable lessons and memories along the way that touch you deeply and change the fabric of who you are and how you see the world.

The Importance of Friendships

There is no denying that quality friendships are vital for our mental well-being. There have been numerous studies detailing how people with close friends report greater life satisfaction and are less likely to suffer from depression. Naturally, our problems feel more manageable when they are shared. In contrast, people who are isolated or low in social connection repeatedly show poorer health outcomes, and not just when it comes to their emotional well-being.

In fact, one of the most noteworthy and widely cited findings from the past decade proposed that poor-quality friendships and social isolation are as dangerous to our health as smoking twenty cigarettes a day. These findings are often misinterpreted. Smoking and loneliness impact our health in very different ways—i.e., isolation may increase risk of suicide, while smoking may increase risk of lung cancer—and they also interact with our genetics and environment very differently. But the messaging remains important. While we are busy focusing on diet, exercise, medication, and medical interventions for improving our health, we should be adding friendship and community to that list for a more holistic approach. That's something that collectivist cultures have understood for millennia, but individualist Western cultures are only now catching up to.

Beyond our health, our friendships are also important for our identity and self-concept. Our self-concept is the image we have of ourselves: a combination of our beliefs, interests, history, deep dark secrets, and relationships. The saying goes that we are the sum of the five people closest to us. And in many ways, that is scientifically correct. More often than not, we end up liking the same music, movies, and clothes as our friends, living in the same cities, working in the same industry, watching the same TV shows. There's also been recent research into the capacity for our friendships to influence our voting decisions, when we have children, even the careers we choose. Those are pretty fundamental personal choices.

One view is that, of course, birds of a feather flock together— we seek out people who are similar and familiar to us. But scientists studying friendship are even beginning to notice surprising neurological similarities between close friends. Our brains start to look eerily alike as friend-group behaviors, attitudes, beliefs, and interactions cause us to shift and transform as individuals. Scientists studying friendship in 2018 came across a surprising finding when they began examining the fMRI data collected from friends viewing identical stimuli and videos: closer friends had more similar brain activity compared to individuals who are distanced. What does this say about the value of friendship in our twenties? Well, it says a lot.

The friendships we form and the friendships we keep in this decade will help shape our core belief systems, how we perceive ourselves, the world around us, and our overall outlook on life. Our friends from our twenties will likely be the people who walk alongside us for the rest of our lives, outlasting our relationships with our parents and even, at times, our boyfriends, girlfriends, and partners. So it is vital to choose the right people to take on this role in your life, as is understanding your responsibility as a friend.

The Difficulty of Making Friends in Our Twenties

While friendships reduce loneliness, create a sense of connection, and are undoubtedly critical for emotional flourishing—not just surviving—meeting people is not necessarily the easiest thing in the world to do, let alone shimmying your way into soulmate status. There is a significant emphasis on building a large network of friends in your twenties and being sure those are your people for life. But anyone who has tried to make new friends as an adult is under no delusion that this is an easy feat. I don't think it's revolutionary to state that making friends as an adult is hard.

Many of us remain comfortably in the friendships we've had for years, never branching out to meet new people. As humans, we crave what is comfortable and familiar, especially when it comes to something as precious as our community. But that means we never practice meeting new people, putting ourselves out there, expanding our horizons and opportunities for connection. So as our foundational friendships begin to shift, we may find ourselves feeling utterly lost and unable to flex the friendship-making muscle that, for many, was so strong during the childhood and teenage years.

For those of us who are yet to "lock down" a solid group of friends, these "in groups" or cliques make it incredibly difficult to break into new social circles. This might also come down to a lack of trust when meeting new people. In one 2020 study that identified six factors preventing people from making friends, the most significant one was lack of trust, followed by lack of time. In my mind, those two factors are linked. Trust is built through familiarity, and familiarity is built through repetition—spending time with someone frequently and consistently. The reason we feel so connected to the friends we make early in our lives, as teenagers or in university, is because those times in our lives afforded a lot of opportunities to interact and be around each other almost every day. That closeness, that time, is what built our trust. As adults, we don't have as much time to invest that level of commitment and energy into a new friendship. It takes roughly 50 hours of shared contact to become someone's friend, and an additional 150 hours to consider ourselves close friends with someone. But in the meantime, we have jobs to work, families to attend to, a house to clean, our health to take care of, bills to pay. It's hard enough to take care of ourselves, let alone a blossoming friendship.

The environments we operate in as twenty-somethings are also not particularly conducive to friendship-making. We flit between work and home, maybe stopping at the gym or the bar, going out for dinner along the way. The main opportunity we have to spend time with people is at work—it's no surprise that work is where most people make friends in adulthood—but we're really there to do a job, and there's not much bonding to be had, especially if you work remotely or independently, or you're stuffed into a cubicle.

This decade is a period of transition for all of us: career transition, mental transition, emotional transition, even physical transition as we move, scatter, and pursue different paths. Everyone is on their own journey at this moment, and we are all trying as hard as everyone else to just figure out what we want from life and how to actually achieve these things. As a result, our paths splinter. For the first eighteen or so years of our lives, we could assume most people our age were doing roughly the same things we were—going to school, playing sports, free on the weekends. We were living parallel lives because of the structure of childhood and adolescence. But in our twenties, that all changes. It's as if a life-path explosion takes place, destroying the friendship universe we were used to. Some of us are still living at home, while others of us have moved in with our boyfriends or girlfriends, who are now our priority. We're living abroad, some of us are still at university, some have gone completely off the radar. There's always the friend or old classmate who decided to have children while we're struggling to pick out an outfit in the morning.

It's at this point of upheaval, but also of significant growth, that we see the relationships around us change as well, and they will continue to do so for the remainder of our twenties, and throughout our lives. Often our twenties are when we are forced to shed some of our old relationships for people who better suit our lives, personalities, and priorities. You aren't who you were at eighteen, or even twenty-one or later. As you age, your values and priorities change, so it makes logical sense that your compatibility with some friends will wane as well. Friendships naturally fade and should be allowed to do so; it's not only extremely common but normal for this to happen. The bittersweet truth is that people grow apart.

Of course, you have a say in the matter as well. **Maintaining long-term friendships is a combination of effort, patience, opportunity, and managing expectations.**

Effort: Relationships don't just happen without some form of investment. Create plans, make each other part of your routine, through a weekly dinner, phone call, weekend market trips, or whatever takes your fancy; show up for your friends by keeping your finger on the pulse of their lives. I've found the best way to get a sense of this and to ensure you're still in the loop is to always be aware of the following three things: what they're looking forward to, what they're struggling with, and what they're focused on or interested in at the moment. Even if the friendship is long distance, small efforts like this show you care, and you're committed to maintaining your relationship.

Patience: People aren't always who we want them to be, especially when they're struggling with their own complex, internal lives. All good, long-lasting love involves a heavy dose of patience. This is especially true if a friend is sorting out their goals, trying to become a better friend after a period of ups and downs, struggling with their mental health, or stuck in a less-than-ideal relationship and neglecting their other crucial connections. The golden rule is to show your friends the grace that you would appreciate in their circumstances. I've been on the receiving end of this patience and know how much it counts; it was the only thing that saved a few friendships of mine. There was a time, two years back, when my mental health and a wave of depression made it hard to show up for my friends. As understanding as my friends were, not hearing from me for weeks, absorbing my sadness, and managing my mood, low energy, and forgetfulness also required patience on their behalf. Friendship is about seeing people through hard times, not just the pretty moments.

Opportunity: Effort is one thing, but sometimes there are just moments that take a friendship to the next level. We can't always plan or predict them because often the best moments in a relationship are unexpected, but when they come along, you'd better grab at the opportunity. This may be a particularly deep conversation, a weekend trip you unexpectedly take together, a concert . . .

or maybe they are the first person to pick up the phone after a breakup or during a time you really need someone. When you think about your closest friendships, my bet is that most of them have one of these pivotal moments that, in hindsight, made it possible for you to be the friends you are today.

Expectations: Finally, sometimes maintaining those lifelong friendships requires adjusting your expectations. People change over time, and loving them means letting them do so. Sure, maybe they aren't the first person you call with good news anymore, but just because the relationship has changed doesn't mean it's over and should be discarded. There is a saying: don't throw the baby out with the bathwater; and this applies to friendships. When we notice things beginning to shift, sometimes that can cause us to panic, and our instinct is to abandon the relationship before getting hurt or to move on with our lives. The alternative is this: try to readjust their position in what I call your "relationship galaxy." A relationship galaxy is a way of organizing where we sit in our relationships with different people so as to help us understand what we can expect from them and what they can expect from us.

Your galaxy has three main circles. The inner circle is your closest and longest relationships. This may include your siblings, your long-term partner, your childhood best friend who is destined to be an honorary aunt to your children. The inner circle is sacred and is reserved for those you could ask for anything and they'd give it—a kidney, a loan—and vice versa.

The second circle is those people you have an ongoing and close relationship with, even if it hasn't reached the intimacy of the inner circle. These are friends you see regularly; you rely on them for emotional support, shared experiences, and companionship. They might not be the people you turn to in a crisis, but they are the ones who enrich your daily life and provide you with a sense of community.

The outer circle consists of more distant relationships—acquaintances, colleagues, or friends you've grown apart from. These people are part of your life in a more peripheral way. They contribute to your social network but don't necessarily play a central role in your emotional world.

We could also include a fourth circle in the galaxy that contains people who have become strangers or who you have no desire to have a relationship with.

The outer circles typically evolve and shift through the years, whereas the inner circle should remain largely unchanged year after year. The further you move from the inner galaxy, the less you expect from someone and the less they can expect from you. You aren't as disappointed if they cancel plans, don't respond to your texts, or forget your birthday. Understanding where someone "lives" in your galaxy will help you manage your expectations, allowing people to shift between the outer circles and, when they do, adjusting your own behavior rather than letting your feelings toward the situation cause you to panic. Any minor shift between one circle and another qualifies as a friendship "fizzle"—a change in the platonic chemistry you have with someone. When someone abruptly jumps between, say, the inner circle and circle four, or from circle two to circle four, that is when you might have a friendship breakup on your hands.

Friendship Breakups

Sometimes the end of a friendship isn't always amicable, or might result from a slow descent into incompatibility. Some friendships just aren't meant to be, for more serious reasons. While no person is inherently "toxic" (this isn't a valid mental health diagnosis, nor a particularly helpful label), some people do create toxic situations for us or are a source of friction that can even undo the many benefits of our supportive friendships.

These characters could be jealous, overbearing, manipulative, exploitative, nasty . . . or maybe you have no idea what's gone wrong—one day you've just been left on read for one too many days and you realize you'll probably never hear from them again. Or you have a huge blowup that you know has been bubbling for months, maybe even years, an accumulation of resentment resulting from times when you should have said something or set a boundary. I really do believe that friendship breakups hurt as much as romantic breakups, because we never expect them. Friendships typically feel so permanent because these are people we choose to be in our lives, and the stakes feel lower than with our romantic partners. But in the pressure cooker that is our twenties, when our friendships take on a specific intensity, sometimes relationships are just destined to explode.

Friendship breakups are especially hard because they trigger what is known as "disenfranchised grief"—a loss that is not acknowledged as being "serious" or profound enough by society to warrant such extreme feelings. Our pain is seen as illegitimate. It's just a friendship; they are a dime a dozen. Actually, if the research I've mentioned proves anything, it is that they aren't. As with any romantic breakup, it is okay to grieve what was, to think about the friends you've lost, and to fight the urge to reach out. But it's also okay to recognize that, as with the end of a romantic relationship, this might have been for the best. Sometimes not only do we grow apart, but we begin to recognize how this person has caused friction in our lives. Maybe they have not respected our boundaries, our autonomy, maybe they took more energy from us than they gave, or maybe there was some event where suddenly you saw them in a new light.

I had a friend recently confide in me about a best friend she had for eight years. They were high school sweethearts in a way. As all their other friendships from their teenage years faded, they remained solid. They even had matching tattoos. (Word to the wise: This is never a good idea.) Then they went on their first vacation together and, throughout the trip, my friend slowly realized that this friendship needed to end, that when she returned it would have to be over. Her friend was cruel, would yell at her, would ignore her when other people were around, and wasn't willing to compromise. That isn't a good prescription for a healthy relationship. Sometimes we don't encounter those parts of someone until we see them in a new situation like a wedding, an engagement, the birth of a new baby, or a new relationship. In those situations, it's better to feel lonely than to be around someone who obviously doesn't have your best interests at heart. Friendships are fulfilling and protective only if they are healthy. Otherwise, they become a liability.

These situations feel terrible because they go against all our primal instincts for connection and belonging. However, I want to pose a hypothetical that may leave you feeling more sane. Imagine still being friends with every person you've known since kindergarten. Making time for them each week, having a meaningful relationship. It would overwhelm you and you would eventually become a pretty terrible friend.

In the 1990s, the psychologist Robin Dunbar came to the conclusion that, realistically, humans can cognitively handle 150 social relationships (including with friends, family, colleagues, and acquaintances), but we max out at around 15 good friends and

50 friends. If that sounds like an especially large number, think about how many people you meet in a year through work, through friends of friends, through family. Naturally we're forced to sometimes shrink our circles to expand them. I know it sounds callous, especially if you've been on the receiving end of this shrinkage. But life has the weird habit of surprising us with some of the best people when we really need them—but also when we have space for them, when we are at a point where we are searching for new connection rather than feeling comfortable in what is familiar.

Finding Connection

When you are struggling with friendship in your twenties, there are a number of strategies you can implement to find connection, to find community and hold on to it. The first is realizing that everyone is feeling this way.

I conducted a bit of a personal experiment recently. I started asking people close to me, even some of my more distant acquaintances, "Do you want more friends?" The answer was resoundingly yes. Not feeling connected to our friends by nature often means we don't talk about the very experience of wanting more and better friends, and so we experience this isolation on our own, unable to recognize how universal it is. But the fact that we are an increasingly lonely generation also means we have the capacity to be the most connected generation—because, to put it plainly, we want it the most.

People are more open, more willing, but what it requires is courage and an instigator. That can be you: the one who brings people together, runs the book club, hosts Sunday dinner club, signs up for social sports, creates the group chats. Choose one activity, once every two weeks, and commit to running it. Start small and ask people to bring a friend, invite people in, and the circle slowly grows. **All it takes is one person being interested to create a community by encouraging people to bring a friend, by staying consistent with your efforts like it's any other goal.** Or just go at it alone. The things you want to do, you can do by yourself and let your adrenaline and urgency help you talk to others.

Having the same routine is also really helpful. If you go to the same gym classes, cafés, bars, or book club meetings every week at the same time, the chances are that you will align with someone else's schedule. This provides the opportunity for unplanned interactions and proximity, two of the core ingredients for sparking friendships.

It's also important to be intentional. When you meet someone you really like, tell yourself and those around you, **"I'm going to be friends with this person."** Speak it into existence! This encourages you to make the efforts to create this reality because you've already committed to it in your mind. It prevents you from being passive about new connections and letting them pass you by. The words you speak to yourself about a situation often become your reality because they implicitly influence how you behave. One of the reasons manifestation techniques can prove so powerful, rather than channeling some unspeakable power, is merely that they influence your expectations and create a self-fulfilling prophecy.

This person WILL become your friend. Show interest; be open and excited by other people. This doesn't need to feel artificial; instead, when you can see someone is especially excited or engaged by something, you file it away for a later date. It might sound clinical, but sometimes friendship-making in adulthood has to be, compared to the nonchalant approach many of us had as children and teenagers. I'll happily present myself as a case study of this working. Two of my longest friends, Kate and Phoebe, will gleefully tell you about how, minutes after we first met, I declared: "We're going to be friends. Did you know that?" Lo and behold, seven years later we still are.

Do not lose hope. Every single one of us, in our lifetime, will encounter at least a few people we're compatible with and who want to be our friend. Connection is something we're hardwired to value and collect. Think about your parents—have they known all their friends since childhood? Have they made new friends in the last ten or twenty years? Or your older coworker who is doing double dates with the forty-three-year-old woman she met on vacation last year, and now they're the best of pals. If you want an even nicer story, two years ago my grandparents moved to a unit in a new city at the ages of eighty-eight and ninety. They called me up the other day to tell me about the group of best friends they have over for tea at least twice a week, including a thirty-year-old comedian, a forty-five-year-old university lecturer, and their seventy-year-old next-door neighbor widow with two Pomeranian puppies.

Your window for friendship-making doesn't suddenly close the day you turn thirty, or forty, or even fifty. Social connection is a lifelong investment, and a lifelong pleasure.

Our twenties can feel particularly isolating and lonely. If it's any consolation, we're all in the same boat—we're just not willing to talk about it, which would reduce the stigma that comes with acknowledging our isolation and loneliness. Whether it's because you're struggling to make new friends, are injured and vulnerable because of a recent friendship breakup, or are realizing that your life path has split from the people you were once close to, know that this feeling is temporary. Just because a friendship isn't forever doesn't mean it's not valuable. The same can be said about the disconnection we experience in our twenties. It's not forever—but it does teach us something important about the need for quality friendships, and the joy of finding them.

Society places a premium on romantic love, but it's your platonic relationships that matter the most in your twenties.

It's normal for your friendships to change as you get older and evolve. Not all relationships are destined to last forever.

If you are yet to meet your people, you have time. The window for friendship does not close at thirty, or any age.

Work in Progress

Maybe it's because it's the physical place where most adults spend the majority of their time, but work feels a lot bigger than just a source of income: it becomes our home away from home, our place for socializing. Work is what helps us feel meaningful, and important. The further we get into this decade, the more our careers begin to sculpt our identity. After all, it's one of the first questions we ask a stranger or acquaintance: What do you do for work? Your answer to this question can tell people about your values, interests, daily routine, strengths, even your income and education level. That's a lot of pressure to put on a job title, and you definitely feel that pressure in your twenties to get it right and pick the correct path.

If work dominates so much of our days, we want to do something we actually enjoy or that elevates our lives in some way. That kind of job can be hard to find during a decade when we're still getting to know ourselves! That's probably why this period of emerging adulthood is when we experience the greatest level of career anxiety, imposter syndrome, and burnout as we try our hardest to find the perfect job, that perfect career path, and also balance the parts of us that exist beyond the workplace.

The thing is, work is just one aspect of who you are. And yet, when you feel like you're off track or falling behind, work can quickly take up a lot of your precious mental space. I want to talk about why that is and how to adjust your thinking about work so that it's an addition to your identity and life—not the whole cake. Work is also intrinsically linked to some other crucial components that define this decade: most prominently your finances, but also, on a psychological level, your self-esteem and sense of purpose.

Let's talk about why your twenties are the time to experiment and be flexible about your career, but also establish the boundaries and kind of relationship with your job that will put you ahead for the future.

CHAPTER 1

Imposter Syndrome and Self-Sabotage

THERE IS AN imposter living in the brain of every twenty-something. This imposter is a tame and lazy visitor most of the time; it likes to eat the food out of our fridge, help itself to our clothes, and putter around the house all day, not doing too much. But this imposter becomes nasty when a new guest arrives. This new guest represents our growing success and confidence, the skills we are building, the new jobs we are offered, and the opportunities that come our way—all of which disturb the imposter's peace.

The imposter lurks in the shadow of our achievements, a silent antagonist, telling this new part of us that we are a fraud and undeserving. It tells us we aren't smart or good enough, and the whole world is about to discover what the imposter already knows is true: we are actually the imposter. We have somehow gotten away with the biggest deception or scam in modern history. We have made others believe what we don't even believe ourselves, which is that we deserve to be here. We deserve to take up space. We deserve our success. This imposter is wrong, and if we are not careful, it can end up taking over our entire lives. It's best to evict or make friends with it early, before that happens.

Who Is the Imposter?

Imposter syndrome comes with the territory of being an accomplished twenty-something. It is described as a persistent self-doubt toward one's abilities, skills, talents, and accomplishments. The easiest way to identify your imposter syndrome is by taking note of some of its favorite sayings and excuses:

- This happened by mistake.
- You are just lucky.
- You don't belong here.
- Everyone else is smarter/better than you.
- You have to work harder to prove yourself.
- When they see you're a fraud, your whole life will be over.
- What gives you the right to be here?

This pattern of thinking keeps you unable to enjoy your accomplishments, because you are constantly worried about when the jig will be up. It creates a self-fulfilling prophecy whereby the more you believe you are an imposter, the more you act in a way that confirms this belief. You become less assertive and more anxious about your performance. You overthink your decisions, procrastinate, and speak poorly about yourself, worried that any small misstep will be the undoing of your mass deception. In some of the worst cases, imposter syndrome contributes to what is known as the "Jonah complex." This is when you fear success so much that it stops you from living out your potential.

There are a few reasons why this is particularly common in our twenties. For many of us, this decade is the first time we experience what it means to be truly good at something and, simultaneously, to experience the praise and accomplishment we had always reserved in our minds for the truly exceptional people in the world. We begin to receive promotions, or new jobs that we feel underqualified for; people listen to us; we find surprising talents that create entire new careers, and successful ones as well. Many of us have spent a great deal of the last twenty-some years working up to this point where we have some level of skill, mainly through the pursuit of higher education. That, combined with general life experience, means that we are beginning to be recognized as independently quite talented, or an asset, or successful. When you have always been the one admiring others, watching the lives of strangers or friends accomplishing incredible things, it is strange to experience this rapid role reversal.

That is the best-case scenario: doing so well that you can't keep up with your own success. But this is also when some people will experience their first serious failure, which can leave them feeling dejected and insecure. A work blunder, a career letdown, a missed job opportunity or embarrassment equally contribute to shaky self-confidence. Am I as good as I thought? Or has everyone been lying to me all this time? When you don't get in front of these irrational and incorrect beliefs, they can become persistent aspects of your self-concept fairly quickly.

Imposter Syndrome and Self-Esteem

Of course, it's impossible to discuss imposter syndrome without discussing self-esteem: the way we value and perceive ourselves. It is no surprise that these two things are a package deal. The opposite of feeling like an imposter is feeling deserving. Acknowledging that you just may deserve the success coming your way involves acknowledging that you contributed to this outcome through your hard work and personal attributes. That means an acknowledgment that you have value and worth.

However, if you have poor self-esteem, these statements of self-recognition oppose how you see yourself. They are incredibly hard to accept. If you have spent your life being told you are not good enough, or smart enough, or attractive enough, or hardworking enough, this is not automatically undone by a few experiences of accomplishment. Because it feels unnatural to take credit for your successes, you negate your efforts by seeking out a more "probable" explanation, such as "I am just lucky," "This must have been a mistake," or "I am a fraud and everyone will see that soon." This seems more in alignment with your self-concept and self-esteem.

A study conducted by KPMG found, unsurprisingly, that imposter syndrome predominantly affects women. In fact, the initial research on imposter syndrome, conducted by psychologists Pauline Rose Clance and Suzanne Imes in 1978, focused exclusively on the experiences of high-achieving women. They observed 150 women who had earned PhDs, were respected professionals, or had achieved exceptional academic excellence, and they found that very few of them felt an internal sense of success. One woman who had two master's degrees, a PhD, and numerous academic publications concluded that it must have been an "administrative error" that she was in her current teaching curriculum. It's hard to imagine a man saying those words.

For women in particular, this kind of self-doubt in a professional setting comes a lot easier than a sense of confidence and pride in our abilities. Women and young girls are socially conditioned to downplay our intelligence, talent, and achievements in order to appear polite and inoffensive to those around us. This continual and repetitive internal and external disparagement becomes part of our belief system, resulting in women having considerably less confidence in their abilities. As a result, when success comes our way, we attribute it to a more "stable" or believable cause, such as luck.

In a more general sense, early childhood and family history can also be a contributor. In the same research paper, Clance and Imes identified two types of dynamics that tend to give rise to the imposter. In the first case, you may have had a sibling who was identified as the "gifted" one. They are constantly put forth as the example of excellence, talent, and intelligence, creating a sense of competition and motivation for you to prove yourself through academic achievement. However, nothing you do can dislodge the belief in your family's minds that your sibling is still the brightest of stars, resulting in the conclusion that your family might be correct and you are an imposter.

On the other hand, maybe you are the exceptional child. You are continuously told how incredible you are, that you are going to be a huge success, that you have everything in you to achieve your wildest dreams. But as you enter your late teen years and twenties, you are faced with those moments when you can't do everything. There are people who are smarter, harder working, more beautiful, or more talented than you are. Your parents never told you about them! You begin to doubt what you have been told and feel like your "raw ability" your parents always applauded is not genuine. You are a fraud.

It certainly doesn't help that, in many cultures, people are scolded for celebrating their success, leading to excessive self-deprecation and a downplay of their achievements. In Australia, we have a term for this phenomenon: tall poppy syndrome. The tallest flowers are always the first to be cut down and made into a lovely bouquet. The people who choose to stand out and talk openly about their success are deemed arrogant or smug and face backlash for their openness. In the Philippines, this is called the "crab mentality"; in Japan, it's the idea that the nail that sticks up gets hammered down. Across the world, there is this pattern of people hiding what they are truly good at for the sake of "modesty." When we don't have open and honest conversations about our accomplishments, and the strange, confusing emotional reactions that come with them, we begin to feel as if we are the only ones feeling this sense of deception and self-doubt.

Self-Sabotage

When my podcast first began to receive listens, I imagined that this was about as good as it got. I was twenty-three and had somehow stumbled upon this whole new career and audience, and it was something I genuinely loved doing. However, for months I was waiting for it all to fall apart, waiting for people to realize they had made a mistake, to stop listening and cast me out. I kept imagining what amazing karma I must have received in a past life to have this much luck. But if something is based on luck, it's impossible to sustain, hard to take credit for, and even harder to predict when it will end. It paralyzed me. My nights were spent in terror, my days filled by telling myself, "Don't get too used to this, don't get too comfortable." Some small part of me wanted to just stop making the show altogether. I would spend hours putting off a new episode or overworking to prove I deserved this. My self-doubt had spiraled into self-sabotage.

When we don't feel like we deserve what we have, we will search for ways to prove that we are right. It's easier for us to undermine our own success than wait for someone else to do it for us. That is why we see so many twenty-somethings engaging in the types of behaviors that seem contradictory to their larger goals.

Self-sabotage is a pattern of habits, actions, and unconscious decisions that are innately harmful and undermine our goals and well-being. These behaviors can be driven by unresolved emotional pain, low self-esteem, or a sense of unworthiness from as early as childhood. In 1991, a group of researchers decided to investigate the correlation between childhood rejection and neglect and later self-destructive behaviors. Their report suggested that many adults who engage in self-destructive behavior have childhood histories of trauma and disrupted attachment styles. They also concluded that childhood trauma—whether stemming from significant abuse, bullying, divorce, low school performance, childhood illness, or emotional neglect—contributes to the initiation of self-destructive behavior.

Unresolved emotional trauma injures our core beliefs and identity and can result in internalized guilt and self-blame, including negative core beliefs such as "I am unlovable," "I don't deserve good things," and "I am unworthy." Then we act accordingly. This comes out in many forms, including procrastination, impulse buying, indecision, poor dating choices, starting conflict, isolating oneself, overworking, and even more serious habits like substance abuse. But at their very core, all of these behaviors stem from the negative assumptions we hold about ourselves, feeling we don't deserve the good things in life, so we choose to sabotage ourselves before they occur. That makes a lot of sense in the context of imposter syndrome. If you are so scared others will discover your status as a "fraud," you may as well reveal yourself before they have the chance.

Freud was one of the first clinicians to identify these behaviors. He posited that they derived from what he labeled the "death drive," whereby all humans innately want to be free of responsibility and expectations—as if "dead" to the world—and so engage in self-destructive behaviors that provide a catharsis and relief from all this self-doubt. Ruining one's life means being free from ordinary stressors and responsibilities, and while that may inevitably come back to haunt us, for just a second we feel liberated. Freud conceptualized this part of the self motivated toward self-destruction as the "anti-self," the part of our subconscious that creates obstacles for us in order to realize our deep-seated and worst beliefs about ourselves.

For example, you may want to treat your body better by eating healthier and being more active. But you find yourself inexplicably always missing your workouts, eating foods you know won't make you feel good, and drinking soft drinks instead of water. This is because your logical, conscious mind, responsible for goal-driven behavior, is being undermined by this anti-self. And this anti-self, this unconscious impulse, stems from a belief you don't deserve this version of yourself, you aren't worth the effort, you have already failed.

Self-sabotage and the "anti-self" interact with imposter syndrome to produce a few key behaviors:

- **Procrastinating:** Putting off important tasks to the last minute because you can't face the fact that something might not be perfect or you cannot find the motivation. Deliberately setting yourself up for a poor outcome so you can say, "I knew it. I'm not meant to be here."

- **Minimizing yourself in front of others:** Refusing to accept credit for your hard work, playing down your skills and abilities, pretending to be less intelligent than you are. Comments like "I'm so stupid" or "It really wasn't that hard; anyone could have done it."

- **Negative self-talk:** Letting your inner critic talk over your inner cheerleader. Scolding yourself for small mistakes, telling yourself you will always fail, you are undeserving, you make too many mistakes, no one likes you.

- **Walking away when things get hard:** Refusing to believe in your ability to push through hard times and persevere. Not giving yourself an opportunity to prove yourself or commit to your growth, even if that means making mistakes or not doing everything right the first time.

Silencing Self-Doubt

Undermining your own success is a bad habit you need to break in your twenties so that it doesn't carry into your later years. You do deserve your accomplishments. What other people see in you is accurate. You are intelligent, you are hardworking, you are creative. It is not arrogant to appreciate the times when you succeed and to take credit for that outcome. Breaking the cycle of imposter syndrome and self-sabotage begins by identifying the origins of this tendency. Begin with some autobiographical digging: Can you remember a specific instance when you first encountered self-doubt, or has it been around since before your active memories? In the latter case, the root could be childhood. Is it primarily attached to your academic or work performance, but absent in other areas of your life? Is it reactive—i.e., felt in response to praise—or constant, even when others have nothing positive or negative to say?

Four questions help guide this exercise:

- What is my earliest memory of self-doubt?
- What do I mainly feel self-doubt around—my intelligence, looks, creativity, productivity, success?
- What situations trigger this sense of inadequacy?
- How do I usually respond—by withdrawing, by self-sabotaging—and where did I learn this tendency?

Working backward, dipping into the past, often has the opposite effect, of pushing you forward into a more self-aware future self. I like to think of it as a tangled ball of yarn. When the yarn is snagged on itself, you can only pull the piece you want to use so far. That's your potential. You are limited by the knots. But when you go back into the mess and start working through the knots, untangling piece by piece, you can go so much further, and your capacity to make something—of yourself or out of the "yarn"—expands.

Once you have a basic knowledge about what your self-doubts are actually based on and brought on by, you can verbally address them. Talk to your negative beliefs and self-doubt as if they are an unwelcome guest or bad friend. Visualize your imposter sitting in front of you, nasty and cruel, sneering at you while it tries to tell you you're not good enough, you're a fraud, you're just a liar. Interrupt your imposter. Don't react, don't get angry, but respectfully tell it to wait until you've spoken first, because you don't want to hear it anymore. If a friend was saying these things to you, you wouldn't tolerate it. If someone was saying these things to your best friend, or your partner or siblings, you would be furious and you would defend them to the end. So why are you letting this little part of your brain speak to **you** this way?

Visualize yourself telling the imposter that you're done talking and you most certainly are done listening. Get up from the table and leave it behind. You are choosing not to believe its lies. This is an excellent way to challenge your negative beliefs, by treating them as an external nuisance rather than an internal truth that you need to listen to. Every time you hear that voice in your head, pause and deliberately choose to replace it with a belief that is more positive and more accurate.

> "I don't deserve to be here." ⇢ "Yes, I do, and I'm going to embrace this opportunity."

> "I'm going to fail." ⇢ "I'm going to try my best and at least I'll get to learn."

> "They're going to realize I'm a fraud." ⇢ "I'm not a fraud. I got here honestly and by my own merit."

> "This was a mistake." ⇢ "This was not a mistake. It's just something new, and I'm growing into this successful version of myself. It just feels different."

> "This will all fall apart." ⇢ "Then I'll get to try something new."

The more you repeat these positive affirmations and reinforce accurate beliefs about your self-worth, the more they will become automatic and begin to outweigh the negative inner critic.

To avoid reverting to self-destructive behaviors in the face of change and accomplishment or challenge, build healthy coping strategies that you can leverage instead. Replace the need to impulse buy, overwork, or go out drinking with activities that promote self-care, such as exercise, an art class, journaling, or hobbies that bring you happiness. By providing an outlet for negative emotions, you are also proving to yourself that you are willing to invest in your well-being, because you are deserving of good things and healthy coping.

Finally, write out all your doubts, all your fears, all your delusions—get them out of your mind and onto the page. This is an effective way of processing self-doubt, by making it tangible and articulating exactly why you feel the way you do. I always find that a problem written down is a problem halved, and the same logic applies here.

> Your imposter syndrome is a voice, not a verdict. You don't have to listen to what it tells you.

> Every person you admire has felt like an imposter at some stage. If they had believed this nasty inner critic, everyone else would have missed out. Don't deprive the world of what you have to bring to the table.

> Everybody feels this way. We can't all be faking it.

> You are deserving of every opportunity that comes your way. Call it luck, call it fate, call it a fluke, but your accomplishments are a testament to your skill, dedication, and ability.

CHAPTER 11

Career Anxiety and
the Myth of the Dream Job

Do WHAT YOU love, and you'll never work a day in your life. That quote has been attributed to about every famously wise person in history, from Marc Anthony to Mark Twain, Steve Jobs, Confucius, and Oprah. It's the kind of bold, inspiring statement you see printed on a flimsy poster in your career counselor's office at college and don't think anything of. It's why I don't feel bad for admitting that I hate that saying, with a vengeance.

As twenty-somethings, we are always being impressed with this idea that what we do for work is an incredibly profound and life-changing decision, and in many ways it is. We spend about a third of our lives at work, and this idea that we can enjoy that time—rather than see it as stressful, pointless, or a black hole of wasted hours—seems quite revolutionary and attractive. The idea is beautiful in theory, but it hinges on one essential assumption: that we actually know what we'd love to be doing.

Yet many of us don't have a clue, and even when we do, it's hard to imagine making a career out of it and still loving it the same way. Even then, our ideas about our "dream job" tend to shift as we mature and change as people. **There is no perfect job for each of us, no single calling that will make us complete.** However, during a period of career anxiety and uncertainty, this appeal of a straightforward solution is hard to turn down. I hate to burst your bubble, but finding the perfect career is going to involve a few setbacks and quite a bit of trial and error and re-starts. But if you are guided by a sense of purpose, rather than perfection or status or a need for certainty, you open yourself up to so many more opportunities for fulfillment in your career.

In Flux

Having no idea what you want to do in life is the norm, not the exception. I think we all need a reminder of that. You are just like 80 percent of other twenty-somethings if you still picture your future and draw a blank. Despite that, we tend to buy into the delusion that everyone around us has it figured out and we are the ones falling behind. This is largely because we are more aware of our own inner insecurities and doubts than those around us are, because we spend more time thinking about ourselves than about how others may have it.

This can leave us feeling like failures, assuming that we're not disciplined or passionate or motivated enough to have a dream and make it a reality, compared to everybody else. It can feel as if everyone else is zooming ahead while we are still taking baby steps. A lot of this comes down to the rise of what I call the "wunderkind society."

"Wunderkind" is a German term for someone who achieves significant success at an abnormally young age. Think the child chess prodigies or millennial business moguls, the teenage tennis stars, or the twenty-year-old entrepreneur giving a TED Talk that has been viewed millions of times. These people are incredible and talented, and deserve their accolades and reputation. But they are not the norm. We have been conditioned to compare ourselves to what is exceptional because of how much we, and society, idolize and publicize success, when these individuals only make up 0.001 percent of the population but close to 100 percent of adoring headlines.

It also comes down to the fact that this generation is so competitive. Spots at good universities, coveted internships, or high-paying jobs, even jobs that pay a livable wage, feel more limited. There is an increasing emphasis on not just being well educated and successful in your community, but having impact and influence on a broader, sometimes even global level. There are more opportunities for social comparison, and therefore self-doubt, than ever before. There will always be someone doing better than you online, an old classmate announcing their promotion on LinkedIn, another person posting about their PhD thesis or new-found business success. We used to be able to block that out and focus on ourselves and our journey. That is becoming a lot harder now. When our models for success are increasingly spectacular, it makes us feel increasingly average and, consequently, like we are falling behind.

Here's your reminder that you can take the scenic route through life rather than speeding onto the highway straight out of the gate, zooming through your career milestones and achievements. You can take your time to discover what you love, stop for a swim in the ocean, pause at that random roadside town for an hour, watch those other cars going a hundred miles an hour, and know you're still going to end up in the same place. You're just giving yourself a chance to enjoy each step, rather than constantly thinking, "What's next?"

Figuring out what you want to do with your life (and how to make it meaningful) is also difficult because of our changing environmental context as emerging adults. For the first few decades of life, we had the structure of school to contain our ambitions. We knew what we were working toward: that common goal of graduation. All our efforts, all our energy, all our concentration was focused on this singular thing that we needed to achieve before "real life" began. After high school, we might then move into the structure of university or college, where, again, the main goal is quite clear: walk across the stage and graduate. But after that, the goalposts we were so used to basing our life around suddenly disappear, and we are left without a natural next step or milestone. **The loss of that structure creates a significant amount of uncertainty, combined with a newfound sense of agency.** That agency is quite liberating, especially if you've spent the first two decades of your life in a classroom. But with great power also comes great responsibility: now that you are in charge of your days, you are also in charge of deciding what you want from life. You may have had some practice leading up to it and some sense of a plan, but it's just as common to feel completely directionless. It's at this stage that the next thirty or forty years of working life don't feel exciting but daunting.

It certainly doesn't help that the questions suddenly turn from "How is school?" to "What do you want to do with your life?," "What's next?," or "What's the five-year plan?"—as if you're not asking yourself the exact same things. Discovering the answers to such questions might take a few iterations and wrong turns as you search for the mythical "dream job" that will be the final destination. But you have time. You have time to fail, to start over, to quit dead-end jobs and take career breaks, to struggle with terrible bosses and doubt your future while searching for the answers.

The "Dream" Job

The dream job is society's solution to combining passion and money. The concept of the "dream job" surely rose in popularity in the twentieth century as education levels increased and incomes expanded. People were no longer resigned to work the jobs their fathers and mothers had worked, or to go searching in the local newspaper ads for whatever was available. After World War II, many Western countries saw a massive rise in wealth and, with that, the opportunity for many people to be able to pick a job they enjoyed rather than one that simply kept them out of poverty. Thus the idea of the dream job was born. It's become a lot more common in our generation, especially as we've seen entirely new industries emerge in recent decades with the invention of the internet and expansions in technology, essentially creating a shift from seeing work as a chore or necessity to something that can be enjoyable.

Nowadays, there seems to be a greater emphasis on work as a part of our identity and an expression of our authenticity. In 2019, a team of researchers in Melbourne, Australia, observed that young adults faced a high level of anticipatory anxiety when choosing their degrees, not just because they wanted to secure future jobs, but because they wanted to do something with meaning, even if it was seen as self-indulgent.

Job security and career stability are no longer the most important aspects; happiness is also an important factor impacting our decision-making. We begin to adopt this philosophy of finding "our calling" from a young age. Think back to when you were a child. Without ever working a day in your life, you probably already had some concept or fantasy for your career. We dreamed of being ballerinas, doctors, teachers, marine biologists, fashion designers—you name it. Back then, it all seemed equally possible before the concept of bills and adult responsibilities had pierced our childhood innocence.

We are also conditioned from a young age to see jobs as governed by a hierarchy in which some jobs are filled with joy and passion while other jobs just need to be done. I suspect a lot more children want to be an author or zookeeper than a tax officer or maintenance person, even though all these jobs have an important place in society. Part of that is because some jobs are idealized and made to seem amazing or like a dream, while others barely get a mention. This contributes to an overwhelming sense that there are some jobs you can be happy in and some you can't. Take that a step further and you begin to believe there is one career that is best for you, and you're bound to be miserable if you don't find it. Spoiler alert: I don't think that's true.

The dream job is a myth for a number of reasons:

- **People can be happy doing many things.** Humans are not puzzle pieces that can only slot into one place; they are adaptable and flexible, filled with multiple interests and passions, but also commitments, that they get genuine satisfaction from fulfilling. Your job might not be doing what you absolutely love, but you could be contributing to your desire to travel, invest in your future, or support your family, which brings you equal gratification.

- **It's not always what you expect.** You may spend years working toward your dream job, only to realize it is a huge letdown and it really isn't what you had imagined. My friend Liz spent almost ten years training to become a doctor, only to start her first residency and realize she absolutely hated it. Her whole family had been in the medical field, her siblings were both general practitioners, and she saw it as her calling. But the hours were heinously long, she felt incredibly stressed, and she didn't have the impact she wanted. She realized she had been doing it for the wrong reasons all along. She started her own tutoring business a year later, and is now training to be a teacher. We can get so wrapped up in the fantasy of our dream job—the prestige, how amazing it's going to feel when we get there, what others expect from us—that we begin to treat it like the golden key to our happiness, therefore ignoring reality.

- **As you change, so do your interests.** The person you were at eighteen when you decided you wanted to become a nurse, a hairdresser, a politician, a lawyer—whatever it was—is not who you are at twenty-five or thirty. As you change and mature as a person, so does your conception of what you find fulfilling in a career. When we are too rigid, we don't let ourselves accept the new version of us who will come into existence the moment we let go of our old, outdated dreams. There is also the factor of practicality. You may dream of becoming an athlete, but as you age, your body can't keep up with the needed level of effort. We typically have different dreams at different stages of life.

- **Your career and your identity can be separate.** The idea of a "dream job" requires a huge personality and identity investment, which can be pretty hard during our twenties, when our identity is still forming. You are allowed to pursue a career you are not 100 percent invested in on a personal level. A job can just be that: a job. It can provide a paycheck for you to actually do the things you love that you can't make money from, and that is okay. That is no less valid than the people who have found their calling and absolutely adore what they do for work.

Don't worry if you still don't have a clue about what you want to do in the future, if you're still experimenting, working dead-end jobs, struggling to really get into your work, especially if you've yet to find the elusive "dream job." I think this pursuit often backfires and leaves you feeling even more closed off and stuck than you were before. When you get too invested in the concept of the "dream job," you can struggle making even minor choices about your future career, because they feel so much more significant. When you assume every step needs to be perfect, your decisions require a lot more thought, which can cause you to get stuck in the contemplation phase, overthinking every small detail and eventually not doing anything at all. This can contribute to a pattern of chronic indecisiveness whereby the possibility of making the wrong choice paralyzes you into believing that if you just give yourself more time to think through the options and predict every possible outcome, you can better set yourself up for success. The fallacy behind this thinking quickly becomes apparent when you realize you spend more time fantasizing and worrying than doing. Instead of striving to find your "dream job," you are better off recognizing that there are many things aligned with your purpose that can make you satisfied in your career.

Purpose Over Perfection

If you aren't striving for your "dream job," what are you meant to be striving for? The short answer is: purpose. Aiming to find purpose is much less restrictive, because purpose comes in many forms and can be fulfilled in a myriad of ways. Once you find what motivates you on a professional and personal level, more doors open not just in your environment but in your mind.

In Japanese, there is a term for this, *ikigai,* which basically translates to "the reason for living." Your ikigai is made up of four components, and where they overlap at the center is your purpose or reason for being:

- What you love.
- What you are good at.
- What the world needs.
- What you can be paid for.

When choosing a job that will be enriching, try to choose something at the intersection. You may love talking to others. You're good at talking to others. The world needs more people who are open and empathetic, and you can get paid to talk to others. Fulfilling all four components fulfills your ikigai, but this concept goes to show that there are multiple ways you can do that: you can become a therapist, an emergency call center operator, a public speaker, maybe even a podcaster if that's up your alley.

Purpose is driven by multiple things and can be realized in multiple professions and roles, not just one. Additionally, one thing may not match all four categories. You could love watching movies and be very good at analyzing the themes and the plot, but that's not necessarily something you can get paid for or that the world needs. Watching movies is a difficult way to make a living. So instead you work as a nurse, because it's something that the world needs that you can get paid for, and you still watch and analyze movies to realize all core components of your reason for being.

For their book *Ikigai,* authors Héctor García and Francesc Miralles, who popularized the term in the West, traveled to Ogimi, the "village of longevity" in Okinawa, Japan. Okinawa is part of an exclusive club of five "blue zones": areas where, researchers claim, people are the happiest and healthiest in the world, outliving all the rest of us. Though these claims have been hard to substantiate due to limited control studies, when García and Miralles interviewed a hundred elderly residents, they all seemed to have one thing in common: ikigai, a reason for being. Almost all participants had hobbies that they engaged in regularly, something they were good at and gave back to the community, like gardening or a skill or trade, something the world needed. A lot of them were also living on old-age pension, so in essence were getting paid to pursue what brought them joy and meaning.

We can take a lot from this small village and apply it to our own lives and careers in our twenties. Finding and pursuing something you love in any capacity is highly protective for your mental and emotional well-being. You don't have to be paid for that thing to fulfill your ikigai, but if you can be, this only expands your job options. When you are led by purpose and a deep sense of your mission or reason for being on this planet, finding the "dream job" is no longer the ambition. It's about finding what is unique to you, what you want from your profession or vocation, what you can provide the world and others, in full recognition that there are unlimited ways to do so.

This may take some time. You may not know what you really love because you haven't come across it yet. That doesn't mean it's not out there. The beautiful thing about being in your twenties is that what you lack in experience, you make up for in time. Don't hesitate to try new things, to apply for jobs that seem out of your comfort zone, to invest in your passions and hobbies in a way that could transform into a career. Don't be afraid to make a career change at twenty-nine, even if you think it will put you "behind." The questions you should ask yourself are: "Behind what?" "Behind who?"

What is this invisible standard you are falling short of? Who exactly are you comparing yourself to, and why does their success and accomplishment diminish your own? This isn't school; we are not all being graded on our progress or ranked based on our résumés or experience or life "scores." It can feel intimidating to start again when we have been conditioned to think about life and, to a big extent, our careers as a competition. But that mindset leaves little space for true discovery, which, at times, involves feeling uncomfortable and uncertain and not having all the answers quite yet. A few months or years of ambiguity and unpredictability is a lot better, in my mind at least, than a lifetime of passivity and duty.

Maximizers vs. Satisficers

When you find yourself getting overwhelmed by making the right decision for your future self and pushing forward your career when faced with multiple paths, it might help to think about the distinction between maximizers and satisficers. This concept was introduced by the economist and psychologist Herbert A. Simon back in the 1950s. Simon observed how particular consumers made decisions when it came to big purchases like a car or a home. What he found was that there is a group of people who always seemed to be more concerned with making the "correct" choice and took more time to decide, but who, despite all their careful planning, still displayed more regret after the fact.

These people were known as **maximizers.** They need to choose the thing that is going to provide them with the highest possible benefit, or else they won't choose at all. They weigh all their choices extremely carefully to make sure they are selecting the perfect one, but still feel that, no matter what they choose, something could have turned out better.

You may have three career paths calling to you that you idealize equally—teacher, journalist, author. Teachers have more job security, but journalists have more diversity in what they do each day; authors have more creative freedom. You go back and forth trying to decide what path to choose, and then consider what steps would be best—go to graduate school, do some unpaid internships, start volunteering or networking, just write a manuscript or articles and put them out into the world. You go back and forth about what is going to give you maximum returns, but the problem is that the information you need to be conclusive is never going to be available. Not unless you can predict the future.

Whatever you choose, you are always going to be ruminating on what could have been, whether that's choosing a job or an ice cream flavor. Studies have shown that maximizers are more prone to perfectionism, regret, and self-blame.

In contrast, **satisficers** are okay with whatever satisfies their basic requirements. They consider all the available situations and what they can gain from each choice, much like maximizers, but they are more concerned with what will make them happy, even if they are not the happiest person alive. If they want a job that pays the bills and gives back, they'll choose to pursue teaching, even if they think one day being an author could pay off. If they're not as worried about money but really like a sense of creative freedom and expression, they'll get started on their debut novel. It's no surprise that satisficers tend to be quicker at making decisions, but they also seem to be happier in the long run. While maximizers may do better, they feel worse. So even if they have maximized all the potential benefits and payoffs, do they really have the chance to enjoy them?

All of this goes to show that, when it comes to our careers, there will never be a perfect choice. The more you look for it, the denser the maze becomes. Hopefully this lets you breathe a sigh of relief. Everyone you admire, everyone you see as a picture of success, has been at the same crossroads as you and has had to close doors to open others, has had to face the uncertainty that comes with so much during this decade.

Life Beyond Work

The triumph of finally getting a secure job—one you actually enjoy, which can pay your bills and is aligned with what you want to do—is one of the greatest feelings, and it's something to celebrate. Thinking about my first full-time job out of university, I remember the sensation of peace and certainty that I finally had it all together. That degree hadn't been for waste; I had a place to go each day, duties and responsibilities, a way to start paying back my loans. It can feel like you've finally made it, but it's also an adjustment.

The older we get, the more it seems that work dominates our lives in almost every capacity. It overtakes our days, our waking hours. Soon it seems that all our conversations come back to

"How's work?" It determines the friends we make, how much time we spend with family, doing the things we love, our lifestyle. Work can also influence the expression of our personality.

A recent longitudinal study in the United States has delivered preliminary insights that suggest our work environment determines our confidence, levels of extroversion, and proactiveness when it comes to out-of-work activities. When we spend eight hours or more a day working toward the same goal, often doing the same activities in the same environment, it can eventually feel quite limiting. This experience has a name, Groundhog Day syndrome, named after the well-known movie in which the protagonist, played by Bill Murray, is forced to relive the same day again and again, trapped, bored, and hopeless.

What we're really experiencing is habituation: the more we encounter a stimulus or an environment, the less we respond to it. What was once exciting and new becomes tame and boring with repeated exposure. The free snacks in the office kitchen, the commute that was once exciting, your new work outfits, the learning curve—they all lose their sparkle. When you think about it that way, it feels pretty bleak. The irony isn't lost on me that we spend so much time wanting the stability of a good job with a good income and some kind of purpose, but end up finding the very thing we dreamed of to be restrictive and stifling after a while.

You can counteract this in a few ways. It doesn't all come down to job choice or work environment. The solution is not quitting, spontaneously changing professions, or going in search of your next career challenge without a plan while somehow expecting everything to be different at your next job. These options may be instantaneous and rapidly resolve your boredom, but they're not necessarily realistic or long-lasting. **Instead, it comes** down to how you continue to be intentional in the life you lead beyond work. Yes, work takes up a significant portion of your hours, but you get to choose how you spend all the rest of your time. If you get to the weekend and choose to lounge around, it might feel restful and rejuvenating, but you're not filling your cup and satisfying your deeper need for stimulation, learning, growth, and entertainment.

There is a formula to staying fulfilled in your "real life" and fighting off your lingering Groundhog Day symptoms. Every day, try to do one thing that fulfills each of these buckets:

- **Something joyful and personal:** Do something each day that is just for you and no one else, something that may seem silly but brings a smile or sense of peace to your life. This could be as simple as listening to your favorite podcast on your way to work, doing your daily crossword, journaling about your day, praying, or dancing for a few minutes before you start cooking dinner. The only condition is that it can't feel like a chore.

- **Something productive:** Do something practical that makes you feel purposeful and will hopefully help out your future self. It can be as minor as throwing your covers back on the bed or quickly cleaning your nightstand in the morning, paying your bills, organizing your calendar, or ticking anything off your to-do list that has been lingering for too long. This helps you regain a sense of control over all the little things that slip through the cracks when you are engulfed by work.

- **Something cognitive:** Maybe you feel cognitively or mentally stimulated by your job. That doesn't mean you need to stop pursuing knowledge or interests outside of work. Subscribe to a newspaper or online journal like *The Atlantic, The Guardian,* or *The New York Times* and spend ten minutes each morning reading an article or story that fascinates you. Play *Words with Friends* throughout the day, turn on a science or history podcast, or watch a documentary rather than your favorite comfort TV show one night a week. These small choices and practices will keep your brain active and learning, rather than falling into the procedural and automatic nature of work.

- **Something physical:** It's very easy to become sedentary or in-active when you begin full-time work, especially if you work in an office. You don't even realize how little you move your body until it comes time to go for a run or get outdoors and you really know how much your fitness has tanked. Physical activity reduces stress and has established mental health ben-efits everyone can seek to gain from. You don't need to train for a marathon or intensely work out, but you do need to find a way to move your body. When I was in the trenches at my consultancy job, I would walk to work instead of catching the train, even though it took an extra thirty minutes—but by nine a.m. I had already done some form of movement. Even stretching in front of the TV, going for a run on your lunch break, or doing a class with a friend instead of going out for dinner and drinks—physical activity of all kinds has impor-tant benefits for your health.

- **Something social:** Our friends help activate the parts of us that we normally have to switch off at our jobs. They let us feel uninhibited and seen; they are the people we get to share life with. Sometimes they slip off our list of priorities the fur-ther we get into our twenties—I implore you to not let that happen. You might not always have time to see them, to keep up-to-date with everything going on in their lives, but once a day find time to reconnect. Whether that is having a quick phone call on your commute home, playing video games to unwind, sharing a funny video, or meeting up for lunch. Keep in touch with your social side, regardless of profession or aspiration.

This might seem like a simple formula to some; to others it may sound impossible to squeeze it all into one day. But **how you live your days is how you live your life.** Be intentional about how you treat your time outside work so that your job doesn't consume your entire life.

No one has it figured out, even those who seem like they do.

In a society that is increasingly competitive, it is okay to take your time and enjoy the scenic route.

There is no one dream job for any of us. Be led by purpose, rather than a specific ambition.

Focus on creating meaning beyond work so that your career doesn't become your entire identity.

- - - - - - - - - -

CHAPTER III

Burnt-Out or Still Burning?

BURNOUT IS THE epidemic of this generation. In 2020, the American Psychological Association noted that around 79 percent of employees they surveyed had experienced some form of burnout, and nearly all of them reported negative impacts as a result. It also seems that the people most at risk are women, but also workers under thirty—i.e., twenty-somethings like you and me. That shouldn't come as a surprise. We are new to the workplace, trying to find our footing, and eager to please but not yet aware of (or able to express) our limits and boundaries. We are the foot soldiers of the working world and expected to pay our dues while also navigating an economic and social context that is increasingly challenging.

Anyone who claims that this generation has it easy has not lived a day in our shoes, trying to make it in the world we have inherited from our parents: one that expects more from us than ever and is increasingly expensive, with the future uncertain and our careers demanding greater sacrifices and even less work-life balance. Being busy has become a status symbol—the more you can push yourself, the more packed your schedule, the fewer hours you sleep, the more you paint yourself as hardworking, successful, and deserving of praise, even if your life is falling apart. This has caused a lot of twenty-somethings to face the kind of chronic stress that is not expected at this age. It can be hard to say no and learn your limits when you are junior, fresh to the workforce and to adulthood.

But it's essential that we find a way to protect ourselves from burnout and being the "yes" person before it becomes entrenched and part of our identity, in the workplace and beyond. We must resist always being the "busy" one, the overworked one, the one who will give everything and leave themselves nothing.

Why Burnout, Why Now?

In recent years, hustle culture has become the norm: the notion that we always need to be "making moves" or working toward some next big achievement, accolade, promotion, or success. Our hours and calendars should be booked up; a five a.m. wakeup followed by a workout and working overtime is normal. We're expected to always be looking to climb the ladder, posting on LinkedIn, looking to make more money or give more to our jobs. This leaves little time for a fulfilling private life.

When I was working my corporate job as a consultant, it was so easy to find myself accepting this as my reality, especially when everyone around me was also participating. Hustle culture glorifies overworking as a badge of honor. I watched people stay into the late hours of the night, even when they had nothing to do, just to prove to our bosses and colleagues that they were willing to go the extra mile. I watched people miss important personal milestones for professional kudos. It often sets up an environment of fear, guilt, and shame, as if you're always one step behind the person ahead of you. Hustle culture is a social structure that has power only because we buy into it. Its power comes from our participation. And as more and more of us feel forced to partake, it's leading to collective burnout among twenty-somethings.

What's worse is that you don't need to buy into the rise-and-grind culture to experience burnout. There's also the ongoing expectation to have it all outside the workplace: a huge group of friends, hobbies, time for yourself, a regular exercise routine, a loving partner and relationship, good mental health, and a side hustle, all while constantly growing and challenging yourself and keeping everything else in your life organized and tidy. If that sounds impossible to you, you are not the only one.

Burnout is this generation's professional and personal hazard, born from an increasing pressure to be exceptional and have more demanding careers and lifestyles. In fact, the World Health Organization lists burnout on its International Classification of Diseases as an occupational hazard. Whatever happened to just wanting a slow life or a job to just pay the bills without requiring you to sell your soul? It seems quite radical in this day and age to just want what you have, to not be chasing some big win, to not make your career your whole life. We have glorified "having it all," which has resulted in so many of us struggling to grasp this ideal life without hitting a point of complete physical, emotional, mental, and social exhaustion. At that point, we are forced to take a break, shut down, stop replying to messages, sacrifice some part of our routine, or take a big chunk of sick days until we feel like we're just about ready to climb out of the burnout hole, only to repeat the same thing three months later. We find ourselves in this vicious cycle of guilt for not working hard enough or not having it all, but then extreme burnout when we do.

The Basics of Burnout

So what exactly is burnout? The term was coined in the 1970s by the American psychologist Herbert Freudenberger to describe clients he was seeing who had reached a point beyond exhaustion. These people were often in what we'd call "helping" professions, such as psychologists, teachers, and doctors, whose jobs demanded a greater personal commitment or sacrifice due to their connection with the people they helped.

Nowadays, we know that burnout can occur in any profession. The causes are normally the same: unreasonable hours, unmanageable workload, little professional reward, an overbearing or demanding boss, not taking breaks or vacations, feeling like you have no control over your work, and a high-pressure environment. We spend eight or more hours of our days working, as much as or more than we spend sleeping. That is equivalent to approximately a third of our lives, so it's no surprise it has such a significant impact on our mental state. Freudenberger saw burnout occurring in twelve stages:

Stage One: Ambition and the need to prove oneself.
Stage Two: Pushing oneself.
Stage Three: Sacrifice.
Stage Four: Displacement of conflict.
Stage Five: Buried under work.
Stage Six: Denial.
Stage Seven: Withdrawal.
Stage Eight: Behavioral changes.
Stage Nine: Depersonalization.
Stage Ten: Emptiness.
Stage Eleven: Depression.

Stage Twelve is where we arrive at the point of burnout—when we reach our tipping point. Our jobs have sucked us dry, everything just feels too much, and life's demands have piled up too high. Symptoms typically include the following:

- Loss of interest in work and the activities you used to enjoy.
- Trouble concentrating.
- Extreme fatigue or insomnia.
- Feeling highly irritable or short-tempered.
- Getting sick more often.
- Cynicism toward your work and life.
- Decreased productivity and motivation.
- Persistent feelings of worry and tension.

Shame and Burnout

Unfortunately, once we begin to notice these stages of burnout, we are probably already at a place of emotional, physical, mental, and social shutdown. At this stage, it takes a lot more than a good night's sleep or a weekend away to recover. Some people have talked about the months of chronic exhaustion that follow, constant fatigue, a complete lack of passion for the things they once adored, finding they have no option other than to quit their job, a total work-life reset. Or you could just push on. That's what a lot of us believe we should be doing. We think, "This is just a temporary stressor. It will get better when everything slows down in a few weeks"—then it's a few months, the rest of the year. All the while you are still actively burning out, slowly watching your life, your mental health, your relationships go up in flames but justifying your commitment because you always think there is an end in sight. There will come a reason to slow down.

I remember being at my corporate job after weeks of not logging off before nine p.m., compulsively checking my work emails before bed, worrying about deadlines, and sometimes fantasizing about getting in a car accident just severe enough to give me a few weeks off or getting a cancer diagnosis so I would have a reason to not be at work.

It was at this point that my therapist rightfully told me that if you're daydreaming about a tragedy in order to avoid work, that is not healthy. It was alarming that I needed someone else to tell me that. The most terrible part of burnout's pathology is that it bleeds into every aspect of our lives—not just who we are at work, but who we are and what we need in our personal lives. It is hard to be a good friend when you have no energy to talk to people at the end of the day. It's hard to be a good partner when all your irritation and frustration from work get displaced onto the person you love. It's hard to be kind to yourself when all you want to do is shut down and sleep. Burnout is such a total body experience that it consumes us from the inside out.

We can recognize all of these consequences and many more. Yet we still feel so much shame at the idea of coming out and saying, "I need a break. I need to step back." We have trouble acknowledging that we just aren't coping, because we implicitly associate this need for rest as a sign of laziness. For a generation raised to be exceptional, it feels embarrassing to not be keeping up with our peers or on some timeline set by the powers that be.

Additionally, I believe that the rise of hustle culture has caused us to associate our worth with our output. Our self-esteem becomes tightly linked to how productive we are, how many things we can impossibly juggle, while people watch on and ask, "How do you do it?"

This praise works as a form of external validation and reinforcement, causing us to feel that the reward of pushing ourselves to our limit is justified. This is especially the case for overachievers. Chronic high achievers have a relentless drive to excel at all costs, because their identity is tied to their material accomplishments. Often they have been conditioned to believe that they will be celebrated, validated, or seen as "worthy" only if they prove themselves through excellent grades, long hours, accolades, and everything in between.

It might stem from a place of inadequacy, from being labeled a "gifted" or golden child when you were younger, from the expectations placed on you by family or mentors. What it results in is a substantial imbalance in our lives whereby we incorrectly assume we can do more than others. We aren't the kind of person who gets burnout. We need to work through it. Once again, it's the shame associated with rest and slowing down that creates this internalized, hostile attitude toward striking a balance between work and real living.

Rest is not a bad thing. It is one of our primary psychological and physical needs as humans. When we neglect it, when we overwork or overcommit, we think we're being more productive, but we usually perform worse. To demonstrate this, I love to give the example of the legendary gymnast Simone Biles, who took two years off from the sport to tend to her mental health and well-being. So many of her critics belittled her decision and suggested that she would never return to her previous level, that she had "wasted" her talent by taking care of herself. Three years later, she returned to the Paris Olympics to become the most decorated U.S. Olympian ever, claiming four gold medals. Sometimes rest is the missing ingredient we need to perform at our best.

Rest is a practice and you can introduce it slowly. Try to schedule regular periods I like to call "reset weekends." I know it feels difficult to not be constantly doing things, but these weekends are about **doing nothing.** That's your task and your objective for those two days. Maybe it feels uncomfortable at first: there is an internal drive to be productive that isn't easy to switch off, but focus that feeling onto just doing things that take limited mental effort, that genuinely give you the space to process how you're feeling, how you're doing, and what you need.

Our rejection of rest from a place of shame is one thing. On the other hand, sometimes we feel we just have no other option but to keep forcing ourselves past our mental and physical limits. Societal levels of financial anxiety are increasing as we battle the costs of living, inflation, and the looming possibility of recession. These are all environmental factors that have a very real impact on our mental well-being. A job offers security against our fear of going broke, having to move back in with our parents, or being unable to afford our bills or financial responsibilities. And if our job demands that we work overtime without pay, that we come in on weekends, that we burn out, we are going to do what we need to do from a place of survival in an increasingly expensive world. All of these factors create the perfect burnout storm for twenty-somethings, a storm we feel we will inevitably be sucked into. However, I don't think that needs to be the case. There has to be another option. **We want to prevent burnout before it occurs, rather than find ourselves at the point of shutting down and trying to fight our way out.**

Boundaries, Boundaries, Boundaries

Preventing burnout requires three things: reflection, boundaries, and the courage to enforce those boundaries. Here are three questions you can ask yourself to reflect on the cost of burnout, and what the alternative might be:

- What is burnout taking from me?

- Is the sacrifice really, truly worth it?

- What needs to change to make my life more enjoyable?

Often what needs to change is a rethink about our personal and professional boundaries. We tend to think of boundaries as explicitly personal. They are reserved for the relationships we have with our family, our partners, or our friends. However, boundaries are powerful in many contexts and the workplace is one place where they are an absolute necessity. Each of us has some conception of what we need in order to feel secure and healthy, what is required for us to achieve that ideal work-life balance. That is a reality we can achieve if we are willing to identify and verbalize our nonnegotiables when it comes to our work's intrusion on our personal lives.

Remember: workplace boundaries do not make you demanding or difficult to deal with. They actually create a more positive environment, because you are essentially saying, "I care enough about this career or job that I want to keep it. I care enough about staying with this company that I want to feel like I can stay on without giving up the things I require to live a fulfilling life."

Some examples of workplace boundaries include: I will not answer emails after hours. I will not work weekends. I will not provide a justification for when I take sick leave. I will not come in on my days off. I will not take on the duties of my colleagues. Beyond that, it's also about communicating when you begin to notice the beginning stages of burnout, preferably before you get to Stage Six, Denial.

Boundaries also need to be enforced rather than just verbalized. It's the threat of enforcement that lets people know you're serious about your limits. What will be the consequence or cost to your boss, your company, your manager if your boundaries are repeatedly crossed? Have this in mind upon setting the boundary. Will it be that for each additional eight hours of work, you take off a day when it's most convenient to you? Will it be a complaint to HR? Will it mean that you take drastic actions and quit? Make sure this is clear both in your mind and to others in order to guarantee obedience and respect of your needs.

If people at your job are not willing to listen and accommodate your boundaries, I want you to remember: it is just a job. No matter how close you are with your colleagues, no matter what they've done for you, it is a business and they are in it to make money. It is a transaction: you provide a service; they pay you for it. **Just because they pay you doesn't mean they are entitled to your entire personhood.** If you were no longer useful to them, they wouldn't think a second about letting you go.

I have a story that confirms just that. When we were both twenty-four, my friend Amelia was working at a PR agency. Her boss hired her as a junior but asked her to perform a more senior role while paying her thousands of dollars less than her colleagues who had a more advanced title. Her boss was demanding, would deny her leave requests, criticized her work in front of others, constantly demeaned her to the point of making her cry, and then would ask if there was "something going on at home."

It got so bad that it was making her sick and break out in hives, yet she kept trying to prove herself and go that extra mile. As soon as the agency lost a major client, they fired her. The only explanation was "We just don't have any use for your services anymore." That is fair enough. But here she was, treating this job like it was the center of her life, showing commitment, a willingness to grow, tolerating behavior she would never tolerate from her friends or family, all because she thought it would mean something to her bosses. But as soon as she wasn't useful to them, she didn't matter. It is just a job. Treat it like the transaction it is.

This experience showed me something else. No job, no sense of success, no achievement is worth your health. Your health is your most precious asset, and the chronic stress you endure from burnout has real, long-lasting impacts on your health. You can't always get that back. Ask for rest when you need it, delegate tasks you can't manage, take the leave, set your boundaries. Spending hours pushing yourself might be romanticized by our society, but at the end of the day (at the end of your life) those hours are not the ones you will remember.

Hustle culture wants you to believe that your self-worth is tied to your output. It is not. Being productive is not the only thing you're good for.

Your health is your most precious asset. Prioritize it above all else.

When you're young, it can be hard to set professional boundaries. But boundaries come from a place of respect: respect for yourself, respect for those around you, and respect for your work. Learn the skill early, practice often.

- - - - - - - -

CHAPTER IV

Money, Money, Money

IF I COULD come back as any person in the world, I would like to come back as a twenty-something who never had to worry about money. Quite honestly, I think everything else in my life would become a lot easier if I never had to think about where my next paycheck was coming from or worry about my long-term financial security. Who hasn't fantasized about what they would do if they won the lottery, how much more liberated and free they would be, all the places they would travel, the doors that would suddenly fly open? It is one of the given facts of this decade: no one ever feels like they have enough money. Even when we do, we don't know how to manage it and it never feels like it will last.

Money Is a Huge Source of Stress

This generation is experiencing significant levels of financial anxiety as the goalposts for what constitutes "financial security," a good wage, and a livable income keep moving. We can't afford the kinds of lives our parents had, or their parents before them, because of inflation, the rising costs of living, and overall economic insecurity. Money determines so much about our lives: where we live, how we socialize and date, the opportunities we have, our future decisions, and just the everyday sacrifices we have to make. This takes its toll on our mental health. We can become fixated on our financial situation and feel like it is at the center of our world, clouding all the defining experiences of this decade. It turns out money is not just material; it's psychological, and it has a lot of hidden implications for our relationships, our mental well-being, and how our twenties pan out.

When I was twenty, I worked in a steak restaurant in Canberra, serving $100 steaks and vintage wines to politicians, lawyers, business executives, and sometimes their children (otherwise known as my classmates). I was dead broke. I would skip breakfast, ride my bike to work on the weekends, and eat the extra potatoes left over at the end of the service, then pay $5 for my staff meal and save it for the next day. I was living in a three-bedroom house that I shared with four people, someone squeezed into the living room. Sometimes the pipes in the back would get blocked and flood our backyard with sewage. We wouldn't switch on our portable heaters in the middle of winter to save money, and we could see our breath in the air when we woke up. Like I said—really broke. But there was also a deep sense of camaraderie that we were all going through the same experience.

During that time, I thought about money every day, often multiple times a day. It seemed like my life stretched only as far as my money did. Money took on an emotional role in my life. And even though I knew I was luckier than most—the government took on my university loan for me, I had a job, I had family who could help me if I was truly desperate—I still found myself checking my bank account obsessively, thinking about what I was going to do if the balance hit zero, and becoming super stingy when it came to groceries and other necessities. It would keep me up at night, that's for sure. What I was experiencing, and what many of us experience in our twenties, is a kind of "financial phobia," a term used to describe how seemingly well-adjusted individuals become seized by anxiety, panic, and guilt when it comes time to manage their money.

In a pioneering study conducted in the early 2000s, Cambridge University sociology professor Brendan Burchell polled one thousand adults and found that a fifth of them experienced psychological and physiological symptoms of distress when talking or thinking about money. More than half of them experienced significant apprehension or a racing heart, accompanied by feelings of dizziness or paralysis. Just the thought of money could have a physical impact on people. The groups impacted the most? Women and respondents under the age of twenty-four. This makes a lot of sense. Women have traditionally been deprived of a lot of the financial literacy men have had access to, and women still face pay discrimination. And people in their early twenties typically earn very little, often stretching what they do make from paycheck to paycheck. Here's the interesting thing, though: even as we start to earn more, that anxiety and insecurity about our finances don't seem to go away. That's because our early perceptions and feelings about money impact our psyche a lot more than we think.

There is this misconception that how much you have in your bank account will determine whether you experience financial distress and anxiety. Obviously, there will be a difference between a person with zero savings and a millionaire, but how we think about money comes down to three factors: knowledge, values or importance, and emotion.

Having good financial literacy will inevitably determine your level of anxiety and stress about your finances. Furthermore, how you spend or save will also be determined by your values and what you see as important. These two factors seem well understood. However, the emotional aspects of money play a significant role in determining how spontaneous versus cautious we are with our finances in our twenties, and a lot of these emotional reactions come down to our early perceptions and experiences with money, especially in our childhood.

Our Money Story

Each of us has a "money story" that we inherit from our early experiences, which shapes how we relate to our finances. In each of our money stories, we are the main character and money plays the role of a villain, a god, someone we want to protect, or just another passerby. The role money takes on determines your money script. In 2011, researchers in Kansas developed four scripts based on the money stories and beliefs of 422 people. They were:

Money Avoidance: People with money avoidance avoid money because they believe it is bad or will corrupt them in some way. They think that it is difficult to be wealthy and a good person, or that money will alienate them from those they love, so they want to get rid of their wealth.

Money Worship: This is the extreme opposite of money avoidance. Money plays a huge role in these people's lives and in determining their happiness levels. They believe life would be better with more money and they can never have enough. However, they also assume someone is always "out to get" their wealth and so become quite possessive.

Money Status: People who follow a money status script take it one step further. Money isn't just valuable; it determines what kind of person you are. They believe that if you are wealthy, you have no reason to be unhappy. They project a lot of value onto material status symbols: the Ferrari, the brand-new house, the Hermès bag. Interestingly, researchers also found that people who adopt a money status script are more likely to lie about their income, exaggerating it to impress others.

Money Vigilance: People with money vigilance see money as something that should be saved and not spent. They look for the best deals, are financially cautious, and turn away from extravagance. They also believe that finances are a private affair: you should not ask others how much they make or disclose that about yourself.

Each of us will identify more with one of these money scripts than the others, and your money script determines the mental role money plays in your life. Your money script is typically unconscious, based on your context and, importantly, inherited during childhood. If you didn't grow up with much money and watched your parents struggle with bills, this is likely to contribute to a money vigilance script. In your twenties, you're frugal with money and, to conserve it, you go to great lengths to save that final penny just in case you need it tomorrow. Unexpected bills or expenses can be extremely stressful and cause you to latch on to a worst-case scenario, because money is not just a piece of paper—it is an emotional trigger for all those times you went without, how awful and scary that felt, the feeling of taking on financial anxieties of your parents. You know what it feels like to go without, so money takes on a whole new meaning for you.

We can also see the opposite occur. In 2013, a group of researchers wanted to see whether scarcity in childhood determined whether adults were more likely to save or spend. What they found was the opposite of the above scenario. When people who grew up lower income eventually did have money, they were more impulsive, took more risks, and approached temptations more quickly. While the initial inclination may be to covet and save, you also never learned any emotional regulation when it came to money, because you didn't need to. You had what you had; there was no room for luxury or overspending. But as an adult who is now in control of your own finances, perhaps with a bit of extra coin in your back pocket, it's harder to feel in control. All those things you once wanted but couldn't have—the new clothes, the treats, the vacations—can be yours now. It's hard not to give in, having wanted them for so long. Spending money also provides the illusion that you have control over your money, because why would you spend what you don't have and if you weren't comfortable?

This leads to a difficult emotional cycle whereby you fulfill this very deep urge or desire to satisfy your wants, but then are pulled back into your financial anxiety, unsure how you're going to budget your way out of this, counting down the days to the next paycheck. Even if you did grow up with money, you are probably in a similar boat; you just got there a different way. If everything was available to you and you never had to worry about finances, when you are suddenly in control of your finances, you're not used to the concept of budgeting or putting off purchases, so you equally overspend.

At the end of the day, so much about how we treat money is psychological. It's not about the bills or the number in our bank account; it's about what money means for our sense of agency, our sense of independence, our sense of security, alleviating childhood scarcity and securing the life we want.

How to Emotionally Manage Your Money

Knowing the psychology of money is one thing; knowing how to manage it is another. But if the theories are correct, we can change a lot of our impulses, poor financial choices, financial anxiety, and everything in between by understanding how our emotions impact our spending and saving. This is especially important in our twenties, when our long-term financial habits are taking shape. Let's talk through four ways our emotions impact how we treat money and how we can correct these patterns of behavior.

Avoidance

As the saying goes, out of sight, out of mind—and often that's how we end up treating our money. A lot of us have this mindset in our twenties, when facing our dwindling bank account or our overspending can be overwhelming. If thinking about money triggers financial anxiety, not thinking about it brings a sense of peace, at least temporarily. It also reduces feelings of shame or panic around our inability to manage our money and upcoming bills, expenses, or current debts.

We might avoid checking our bank balance, not open our bills, or put off paying back our friends or an invoice until the very last moment, all to delay that inevitable sense of doom.

Avoidance is a type of maladaptive coping mechanism whereby we unconsciously ignore a situation or stressor in order to minimize an uncomfortable emotional reaction. If we avoid it long enough, we form a **habit loop:** a neurological pattern that governs our behavior. It consists of a trigger (or cue), a behavior, and an outcome. In the case of financial avoidance, anytime we get an alert for an overdue bill or check our account and see it in the negative (the trigger), we may push the feeling down by immediately calling a friend, rushing to switch on the TV, or dismissing the alert (the behavior). This creates the same outcome, time and time again. The situation just gets worse, but because we are not addressing the culprit behavior (the avoidance), we maintain the habit. However, this will inevitably come back to bite us, because by not having oversight over our spending, we don't have discipline, and when we do eventually face the financial consequences, we are even less equipped to deal with them.

To counteract this, remember the **number one rule: the sooner you address a problem, the sooner it is solved.** The sooner you check your bank account, the sooner you're going to curb your spending in response. The sooner you pay that bill (if you can), the sooner it's off your desk. The sooner you contact your credit card company or your bank and say, "I can't pay this off," the sooner you can work out a plan of attack.

Become aware of what is at the root of your avoidance: Is it because you are ashamed of your finances? Because you want to keep up with your friends and don't want the reminder that you sometimes can't? Because your parents always struggled with money and you don't want to be like them? Or simply because you just don't want to take on the mental strain of having to deal with your finances? When you come to your own conclusion, pose a hypothetical to yourself: Does avoidance or awareness help me more in this situation? In almost every situation where you have adopted avoidance, knowing more would probably help you, but you just are too scared to operate in this way because of the stress it could cause. Test yourself by taking the next month to put your spending and finances under a microscope, even if it feels uncomfortable. Notice how your anxiety lessens as you are able to make more informed decisions.

Penny-pinching

Another way we respond to our financial anxiety is by becoming excessively cautious with our finances. If a lack of money keeps you up at night, making sure that will never happen—or at least providing yourself with that illusion—is a great antidote. There is great discipline in being frugal and a lot of benefits in finding the best deal, setting up an emergency fund, and not overspending.

However, penny-pinching can also become unbalanced when we refuse to buy things we actually need or deny ourselves some of the experiences and adventures that define our twenties. There are so many opportunities at this age that become harder as we get older, as we become less flexible due to family, partners, and careers. Travel, for instance, is especially romanticized and emphasized during this decade. But travel also requires sacrifice and, of course, money. If you find that your money is better suited for saving rather than spending, it can feel like you're missing out as those around you decide to throw financial caution to the wind.

There is this lingering question a lot of us face in our twenties: Do I prioritize wealth or experiences? What we are really asking is: How good is money if I can't actually spend it? What is it really worth? For many people who are disciplined savers, the answer is that money is worth a sense of security. It's worth the knowledge that you will never have to be without the necessities, that you can always provide for yourself. This comes down to not just your money scripts, but your values. Do you value stability or adventure?

It turns out you can actually have both. But this begins with having a clear understanding of two things: what your financial values and financial goals are. **Your financial values are the core**

principles and beliefs you have about money. Money scripts are one aspect of this, but on a deeper level your financial values also reflect what you see as important in your life. If you value spontaneity, experiences, or thrill-seeking, you will use your money more liberally to bring about these things. But if you value permanence, long-term wealth, and stability, you will use your money to provide you with security by saving for a home or making long-term investments. Acting in accordance with these values will minimize your sense of financial guilt—the feeling that you are spending or using your money incorrectly—and, as a result, your financial anxiety.

Be clear on your financial goals and what it is you're working toward. There is no point in excessively saving without a purpose, whether that is an emergency fund or safety net, a house deposit, paying off a debt, or something smaller. There is a level of money you need to meet your goals and sustain yourself, but money is also made to be exchanged—not just for items, but for experiences and the kinds of memories you make in your twenties that only increase in value as you grow older, eventually becoming priceless.

So, if you find yourself overwhelmed by the prospect of spending money, remember that you can spend without being risky or indulgent, as long as you accommodate experiences as part of your budget. That is money just for your enjoyment. By applying this budgetary rule, you minimize your cognitive dissonance and discomfort about spending money. Previously, anything you deemed nonessential spending may have created a sense of internal inconsistency: you believed one thing—that money is meant to be saved—and when you would pay for drinks on a night out or for a weekend away, that created a discrepancy between your belief and actions, resulting in distress. But experiences are an essential part of your twenties, and therefore an essential part of how you spend money during this decade. You need to make space for them.

Impulse spending

If penny-pinching and financial hypervigilance are on one end of the spectrum, impulsive spending sits on the other end. Impulse buying occurs when we make an unplanned purchase. Often it's something we don't need and can't afford, which leads to buyer's remorse and feelings of regret and panic. If it causes such a negative reaction, why can't we stop? Why do we keep waking up to packages we don't need, extra grocery items and gadgets we won't use, or clothes we'll wear once and then inevitably forget about until six months later when we no longer like them? These kinds of irrational behaviors have been studied by researchers for years, and the answer comes down to a combination of internal and external factors.

"Retail therapy" might sound like a buzz phrase, but it has important psychological roots that explain why we impulse buy. Sometimes the thrill of buying something is more alluring than the item itself and provides the instant gratification we are after. The act of purchasing something fulfills a strong emotional desire that overwhelms the logical part of our brain. In the moments during and immediately after the purchase, we experience a flood of happy chemicals and pleasure, but these sharply decline when we get home and realize we really didn't need this. The item was a proxy for some deeper psychological desire: a sense of empowerment, of control, confidence, excitement when we otherwise find life quite boring, or of course a sense of happiness when we're having a rough week, or maybe a rough year.

To put it simply, acquiring things makes us happy. It makes us feel empowered. But after a while the buzz wears off and we are just left with this shallow object that brings us nothing but clutter. It's not all our fault, though. Companies have learned how to use mental triggers to exploit our emotions and get us to impulse buy. One way they do that is through a good old-fashioned sale.

A big sign that says 50% OFF elevates the value of the product because we feel like we are saving money, and therefore making money in a sense. It also creates a sense of loss aversion. Humans don't like feeling that they have lost out on something, such as a great bargain or an item that will never be restocked, and so we act irrationally. Psychologists will tell you that the pain of losing something (like a good deal) is twice as powerful as the pleasure of gaining something. Put the two together and you have the perfect conditions for an impulse purchase.

So how do you gain control over your financial impulses? You do this by interrogating your motivations and cognitions behind a purchase. Ask yourself these four questions:

- Does this purchase fulfill a need I had before today?

- If I waited a few days, would this have a big impact on my daily life?

- Am I buying this because of an emotional urge or for a practical need?

- What will I have to give up or sacrifice by buying this thing— i.e., can I afford it?

Once you pause and consider, the emotional cloud tends to clear and you minimize the likelihood of buyer's remorse. It's also useful to purchase from places with a return policy, so you can change your mind once the pleasure has worn off. And give yourself a forty-eight-hour window to reconsider before buying something. Yes, the big 50% OFF sale might be over, but you could end up saving yourself more money than if you had impulsively overspent during that window.

Lifestyle creep

At some point in our twenties, we are going to experience a raise, a bonus, or a fancy new job title with its own fancy salary increase. All those years of pinching pennies and worrying about our $5 coffee seem far behind us, and we start to see a lifestyle change. We go out to eat more, we buy nicer clothes, we catch more Ubers, we buy the name-brand grocery products—and slowly but surely our spending begins to match our income. As we reap the rewards of our hard work, one thing that doesn't increase is how much we save!

Typically, we become more interested in enjoying our newfound financial freedom through spending, because we suddenly can afford the nicer things, without actually thinking about how the rest of our financial habits are scaling. Let's be super transparent for a moment. When I started at my first full-time job, I was making $65,000 AUD, and in my second year I got a pay increase to $75,000 AUD. In my first year at work, I was catching the train to work, which cost me about $8 a day. In my second year, I started catching Ubers more regularly, costing me $25 a day. My income increased 15 percent, but my daily travel expenses increased by almost 200 percent. In my mind, I could now afford to make my life a bit easier, but my savings definitely weren't increasing at that excessive rate, so I was actually being more financially irresponsible without realizing it.

This bias is particularly common in our twenties because there is a big jump from minimum wage to livable income, followed by an income that allows a few luxuries. Additionally, when we are finally released from a deprivation mindset into an abundant one, we don't always have the self-control to match. As we watch our friends' incomes also expand, there is a pressure to keep up and be able to participate, even if it's relatively more expensive for us than for them. This can hinder our progression toward our short- and long-term financial goals (whatever those may be).

To combat this kind of lifestyle inflation, **be mindful of the emotional temptation to upgrade your lifestyle beyond what you can afford, and continue to differentiate between your needs and wants.** Scale your budget with your income and make sure you don't get swept up in other people's spending habits. Sometimes you can't afford the same restaurants, trips, stores, or expenses as your friends. Addressing this disparity doesn't require you to reveal your income, but instead set financial boundaries with those around you, the same way you would set emotional boundaries: "Sorry, I can't spend that much right now, I'm focused on saving at the moment." "I probably can't pay you back immediately, so please keep that in mind before making financial choices with me." "Can we go somewhere cheaper?" Offering alternatives can also be more comfortable—that way, you won't feel like you're shutting down an opportunity to hang out or spend time together just because of money, but instead finding something that works for you.

Remember, each of us has a different relationship to money, one that is deeply emotional and psychological, stemming from our unique childhood and early experiences. Money can be a tense subject, not just with others but with ourselves. It can be easier to avoid than to confront head-on, especially in our twenties, when it feels acceptable to have a nonchalant attitude to our finances. But when we take the opportunity to learn our money script and the habits and cognitions that create financial anxiety and guilt, we feel like money dictates less about our lives.

Money is not just a material subject but a psychological one. It can greatly impact your everyday emotional state and mental well-being.

How you see your parents treat money will normally create your own narrative toward the subject. It might feel irreversible, but you can unlearn it.

Addressing your financial concerns early is always the best strategy.

Spend your money according to your values, not in response to your emotions or what others are doing! You get to choose what is important to you in life, and in your finances.

Everybody Is Healing from Something

Our twenties are when our adult lives are just beginning, but already we are starting to show the scars and weathering of being human. By the time we reach our twenties, we already have two decades of memories, many of them beautiful moments, but also things we would rather forget. Those years leave an impression, and no one escapes them without a few psychological, emotional, and, at times, even physical scars.

This period of emerging adulthood is when we first begin to peel back the curtain on our childhood and teenage years with the self-awareness and budding maturity of someone with the distance needed to see experiences more clearly. What we find in those memories and moments can reveal a lot about why we are the way we are, and what we may need to heal from in order to find a deeper peace within ourselves. Finding a way to incorporate those early and formative experiences without letting them define us (or cause more damage than they already have, as difficult as that might be) is one of the biggest tasks of this decade. Undoing and understanding the damage we didn't cause is, for many of us, one of the hardest things we ever do. But avoiding this undertaking doesn't make it go away. Instead, it just lets it fester and create patterns and behaviors that continue to unconsciously influence us, or the next generation.

Everyone is healing from something, even if you think your "something" is small in comparison to the big, bad things others have been through. Perhaps it is childhood trauma, difficult family relationships, bullying, or negative body image—it all deserves your attention and the gentle touch of the adult version of you who knows better. The past can also leave its mark on the present. We are the loneliest generation in history, some may even say the saddest and the most anxious. But we also now have the language and the awareness to name those things, validate them, be open about our experiences, and find the strategies and the knowledge to help. Let's talk about how to heal those parts of yourself that feel more dark than light—and why, as with most things in your twenties, you're never alone in even the hardest and most isolating experiences.

CHAPTER I

Family Ties

OUR TWENTIES ARE filled with a lot of complicated experiences and relationships, but none as complex as the one we have with our family, our parents in particular. There's a famous quote by the author Philip Larkin that's stuck with me for years: "They fuck you up, your mum and dad. / They may not mean to, but they do. / They fill you with the faults they had, / And add some extra, just for you." It might be one of the most profound pieces of poetry for the simple fact that nearly every person on this earth can relate to it.

Wherever you are in the world, whoever you may be, however picture-perfect your relationship with your parents is nowadays, the further you get into adulthood and your twenties, the more you realize that so much about who you are came from the way your parents chose to raise you. Their personalities, anxieties, faults, mistakes, best intentions, and past get swirled around, mixed in with some of your own life experiences, and help create the person you are now. For better or for worse.

As you gain greater self-awareness in your twenties and struggle to figure out exactly who you are and who you are becoming, one of your biggest battles lies in redefining your relationship with your parents and finding a way to engage with them as an adult, rather than as the child you are always going to be in their

eyes. It involves working through a lot of blame and resentment, having empathy for why they chose to raise you as they did, coming to terms with the fact they are human, just like you, perhaps undoing some of their mistakes, and, eventually, deciding what parts of them you want to take with you into the future and which memories or experiences you want to leave behind.

There's a statistic suggesting that, by the time we reach age twenty, we've already spent up to 90 percent of our time with our parents. We didn't necessarily have control over that chunk of time, because we were bound to our caregivers by the need for security, safety, a roof over our head, food on the table, someone to cry to, to help us with our problems. The final 10 percent is when the relationship changes the most, because we get to set our own terms. That is the period when we are searching for a natural separation and independence, when we strike out on our own, and when we have to come to terms with who we are because of them or despite them while we still have the chance. How do we redefine our relationship in the face of all this baggage, perhaps anger, hurt, or confusion? That's what we're going to find out.

I'm Just Like You

Our parents get a lot of blame for the things we don't like about ourselves, and not a lot of credit for the things we do. At least, in my experience, it's easy to pin all the things I wish I could change about myself on my mum or dad: my athletic inability, for one, my fun tendency for disastrous thinking, my insecurity. But when it comes to the things I like, such as my creativity, my intelligence, my work ethic, that's all me.

Fair enough, science might say—parents actually deserve it, because during the most formative periods of our lives, they are the ones in control. Our parents get to decide what values to implant in us, where we grow up, what religion we practice, what school we go to, how we are disciplined, how we are loved, how we think about the world, and how we think about ourselves. Then there are things they don't always get to decide, but which are inevitably influential: our socioeconomic status, the mental health disorders we are more prone to, the opportunities we have available to us, the social, cultural, or political environment we are raised in. Likewise, the absence of our parents is formative, as anyone who has sadly lost a parent, become estranged, or been abandoned will tell you.

In that way, parents have the privilege (or maybe the burden) of determining almost all the experiences we have in our most formative periods of development. That is the nurture side of things. On the nature side of the equation, every bit of our DNA comes from either our mum or our dad, as much as we may want to fight the implications of that. There are some pretty important things contained in our DNA that determine the person we become. Of course, there's the predisposition to certain diseases, how we look, our blood type or eye color. But then there is also our personality.

Recent estimates tell us that about 30 to 60 percent of our personality traits are inherited from our parents, meaning no matter how hard you try, there are elements of you that are hard-wired to mimic your parents. This includes your level of openness to new experiences; whether you are extroverted versus introverted; how anxious (or neurotic) you are; how agreeable you are; and your sense of duty, responsibility, or conscientiousness. Anyone who has ever done an online personality quiz will be familiar with these traits, as they make up what are famously known as the "Big Five." The Big Five are as ominous and important as they sound: our five most important characteristics on which we can measure and articulate our personality and, importantly, what makes us each unique. And it seems we have Mum and Dad to thank.

Let's talk about how this mixture of nature and nurture shows up in our adult selves and the true impact our parents can have on our identity, behavior, and everything else in between.

Morals and Behavior

Our morals are what make us good humans. Kindness toward others, generosity, honesty, and respect all make someone a positive member of society and, to be frank, someone who's actually nice to be around. Our ethics are not something we're born with, though. We do not fall out of the womb knowing right or wrong; we learn a lot through observation.

When we are children, our parents are the center of our universe, and so we pay special attention to how they act in a certain situation to guide our own behavioral responses and attitudes. In one of psychology's most groundbreaking and famous studies, the psychologist Albert Bandura observed how children learn certain behaviors and moral standpoints by mimicking what they see adults do. The types of behaviors he was most fascinated by had to do with violence, specifically the reasons and ways we learn to express violence toward others. Bandura exposed children to aggressive behaviors by letting them watch an adult assault an inflatable doll, known as a "Bobo doll." This poor doll experienced a torrent of abuse. The adults would kick, punch, and throw the doll around as the children observed from behind one-way glass. Eventually it was the children's turn to play with the toy. As Bandura and his colleagues watched from the sidelines, he saw the children copy exactly what they had seen the adults do, lashing out at the doll and behaving violently. In particular, he observed that the child's level of aggression increased when the adult seemed powerful, competent, and similar to themselves. Our parents are the most capable and powerful people in our lives as children, so it makes sense that their example is going to be the most salient and, therefore, impactful.

This study is an extreme example of how children inherit certain morals and values through observation learning. On a more general note, it reminds us how our parents are our very first teachers and get to imbue us with all their ideas and views of the world. That's the special part about having a child: you get to mold them to be everything you like about humanity, and exclude all the stuff you don't agree with. From the violence example, though, it's scary to think how much of our parents' less than ideal behaviors bleed into our own sense of personhood, even by accident.

Naturally, the values that parents prioritize in their own lives shape the values they emphasize to their children, because these values are the ones they believe in. For example, if your parents value altruism, they may encourage you to give back, volunteer for those less fortunate, or make sure you are aware of your privilege. If they value success and power, they may push you to pursue competitive sports or an elite, esteemed career pathway, putting you into accelerated programs or pushing you to be assertive and dominant.

Our parents set these values or moral standards and reinforce them through praise and positive reinforcement, showing us love, affection, and reward when we perform according to their values, and scolding us when we don't. As a result, we become their Mini-Me's because we want their approval and to be seen as good and deserving. The older we get, though, the more we tend to form our own ideas of right and wrong, meaning we naturally begin to assert our own individuality and push back against the norm set by our parents.

Beliefs

As children, we think that our parents are gods. They protect us, tell us right from wrong, provide for us, and show us what we should believe in. In this way, their guidance takes on an almost spiritual or religious overtone of importance, because they act as our guides through the complexities of life. Our beliefs about the world are a direct result of what our parents chose to expose us to, and what they thought they needed to shield us from, and how we were taught to interpret the world around us: the things and people we should celebrate and value, and in contrast the things that were bad and evil, and should be avoided. So our mental stance toward life's big questions is primarily derived from what our parents saw as worthwhile and important.

As we get older, we may question their philosophy toward life, but that doesn't mean their beliefs don't still have an influence. For example, most people tend to follow the religion their parents believed in, apply their moral judgments on things like sex, relationships, and money, and see the world the way their parents taught them to.

Where this becomes most apparent is our voting decisions. Research on voting shows that our choices are largely formed in our early life. Not only do our parents' voting behaviors determine whether we're going to show up to the polls and vote, but also who we vote for. A 2005 survey showed that about 71 percent of young adults in the United States have roughly the same social and political ideology as their parents. That means most of us are the political clones of our parents. Of course, there are other influences, like your friends, your education level, where you live, what you do for work, your own moral values, and so forth. But if this sounds unbelievable, just think about how many of your opinions align with your parents', why voting patterns take generations to shift, and why so often your gateway into political engagement or membership is through your parents.

On a psychological level, this might not seem very important, but your worldview shapes so much else about who you are below the surface, like who you choose to hang out with, the kind of news you read, what kind of career you might want, whether you are motivated by money or purpose (or both), where you want to live, whether you want children, and how you want to raise those children. **The more you start to notice parental influence on your life, the harder it is to not link everything back to how you were raised.** That can cause you to experience a crisis of identity.

Have I ever had an original thought or ambition, or am I just a clone, a reiteration, of my parents? This thought can be somewhat distressing, especially in our twenties, when we are going through an extreme period of identity formation. We might overcorrect in a panic and end up going to a whole different extreme out of this innate need to prove our uniqueness. Pause for a second before taking charge. Just because it's a life your parents wanted for you, does it make it a bad life? How many of your choices have truly been your own, without the influence of friends, or circumstances, or a chance encounter, or your environment, or context? Each of us is a reflection of our experience, but you still make your own decisions within that space; you just have to be able to discern what your motivation is. Are you making decisions for yourself, or to satisfy someone else—your parents? There is a distinction between being influenced and totally living for others.

How You See Yourself

Our values and beliefs are important parts of who we are. But we don't spend a lot of time thinking about them, and they only really come to the surface at important moments, or when we are at a crossroads. But we do spend a lot of time thinking about ourselves: what kind of person we are, what other people think of us, our flaws, our mistakes, whether we're doing everything right or disappointing ourselves and those around us. This disembodied view of who we are is expressed in our self-concept. If you think you are a bad, lazy, mean, and unintelligent person, you will have quite a negative self-concept. If you see yourself as kind, generous, resilient, strong, smart, and capable, you have a positive self-concept. It all comes down to how you speak to yourself.

Each of us has a little voice in our head that either scolds or celebrates us. What's remarkable is how much that voice ends up sounding a lot like our parents. A friend once asked me: "That voice in your head, does it sound more like your mother or your father?" It stopped me in my tracks because I knew the answer immediately. Ask yourself that very question now: When you are belittling or criticizing yourself, is it your voice you're hearing, or

your mother's? When you find yourself getting angry and wanting to scream or lash out, is that your impulse or your father's?
One is often going to be louder, and what our parents say to us
as children usually ends up becoming our inner voice as adults.

If you only ever heard criticism, you will become the adult
who is always self-deprecating or tearing themselves down. If
you never heard praise, you're going to spend your adult life trying to impress someone before you realize this will become your
undoing. If you were constantly pitted against your siblings, that
rivalry doesn't go away the older you get. If your parents never
stepped up or intervened when you had a problem at school or in
life, your inner voice will constantly tell you, "You're on your
own"—meaning you may push others away and become hyperindependent the older you get. But if you heard how lovable you
were, how proud you made those around you, how cherished and
special you were, those words become part of your deep inner
truth.

On an even deeper level, we tend to absorb the ways our parents spoke about themselves. An area where that becomes really
apparent is body confidence and positivity. A lot of people can
relate to having a parent—particularly a mother—who was constantly speaking negatively about their own body, always on
some fad diet, and, consequently, introduced this belief system
of unhealthy dieting or eating habits to their children. For many
of us, the reason we learned to hate our bodies is because our
mothers hated theirs. We saw how they looked at themselves in
the mirror, how they grabbed at their skin, the times they would
throw out all the sugar in the house, call themselves fat, declare
we all needed to eat healthier to lose a few pounds after the holidays . . . And those thoughts, opinions, and attitudes became our

own. That's a burden we now carry that we need to unlearn or risk passing it on to our own children, or letting it influence how we see ourselves for the rest of our lives.

If you're still working on changing that voice, that's okay. The very fact that you are conscious of it means you've done about 95 percent of the work, because once you know that voice isn't your own, you can start to question it more, silence it, and replace it with new thoughts and beliefs, a kindness that is your own. That is how you heal: by choosing a better path for yourself even when it's difficult. By separating yourself from the inner critic in your mind, detaching yourself from the voice.

Trauma

Childhood may be the period of innocence, but that doesn't mean we don't encounter incredibly difficult things—even if at the time we don't have the cognitive ability to understand what is going on, and sometimes, unfortunately, at the hands of our parents. In childhood, we are particularly sensitive to emotionally charged and traumatic events that threaten our sense of safety and belonging, because we are such vulnerable little creatures. And when that safety is threatened by our own family, we have nowhere else to turn. We are stranded in our circumstances, and that powerlessness is a trauma in itself.

Trauma is a tricky concept because it is so subjective: what others might brush off and never think about again may be the biggest event of someone else's existence and shape them for years to come. When we think about trauma, our mind tends to go to extremes. We think about car accidents, the death of a parent, terrorism, war. But emotional neglect, constant criticism, humiliation, witnessing violence between our parents, chronic illness and injury, parental substance abuse or mental illness— these might not make headlines the way a serious accident or war would, but they still have a very real psychological impact. There is no single truth when it comes to defining trauma other than that it is deeply distressing and influential to the individual experiencing it.

Abuse of any sort has the capacity to change us on a molecular level. This is because abuse is what is known as an "epigenetic factor," an aspect of our environment that has the capacity to influence how our genes work. In other words, even if our genetic blueprint is set up one way, certain events can quite literally change how our body reads that DNA sequence, meaning we become a different person. In a series of studies conducted by McGill University researchers, the brains of adults who had been abused as children showed observable differences in their cortisol receptors and how active they were. Cortisol is the hormone primarily responsible for stress, meaning that suffering from abuse makes people less able to handle stress or causes them to become overwhelmed when it does occur. If we struggle to handle stress, we also tend to struggle in relationships when things get tough, we struggle in school and in the workplace. What might seem "small" to some people in fact has a domino effect.

When I was in my first year out of university, I saw this firsthand. I interviewed people as part of Australia's first ever Child Maltreatment Study. Hours and hours of calling people across the country and asking them to reveal some of the darkest parts of their lives. I quit before the findings came out, but I didn't need the experts to tell me what I was already hearing from people every day. Although so many of them didn't even realize what they had experienced was abusive, onetime abuse victims were much more likely to report that they struggled with mental health disorders and risky behaviors such as binge drinking, smoking, or drug use. The effects of hardship and abuse can be invisible—even for the person who experienced it—but they still shape people into who they are becoming, particularly through their ways of coping.

When we encounter something emotionally painful, our brain needs to find a way to process this experience and manage our distress before it becomes overwhelming, so it adopts a number of defensive or survival strategies to help us cope. These strategies range from being productive and healthy to being entirely unproductive and unhealthy. Proactive coping mechanisms include things such as establishing boundaries, seeking out the support of friends, removing yourself from a toxic or dangerous situation, or channeling the experience into something beautiful or useful. We all want to be able to harness proactive coping mechanisms, but what's something else you notice about these behaviors? None of them are things we can do as children. Children don't know what it means to set boundaries—what would that even sound like? Our friends are also children and so aren't going to offer the mature support we're after; we can't just run away—or we can, but surely with even greater consequences. And so we are forced to turn to things we can control, like escaping through daydreaming, risky behaviors, lashing out, turning to substances or alcohol, emotional eating, isolating ourselves, pushing people away.

The coping mechanisms we needed to survive our childhood experiences follow us into adulthood and become our vices, our way of dealing with complex emotions, our self-destructive patterns. Despite their initial protective purpose, despite the fact they helped us survive, they ultimately hinder our ability to heal, grow, and form healthy connections with ourselves and others. So where do we go from here? Are our twenties and beyond ultimately defined by our childhood experiences? The answer is no, they are not. Humans have a deep, natural capacity to heal from their past as long as they can find a way to make those memories make sense. We need a story for what happened to us that allows us to find closure in these experiences and accept them as part of our past—not the defining determinant of our future.

One option is to conclude that you deserved this all along because you were a bad child and a horrible person. The other option is to recognize that you didn't deserve any of the bad things that happened to you. They were not your fault. You are not to blame for your own suffering. What you experienced was a product of, perhaps, generational trauma—a cycle of pain and dysfunction that has been passed down through your family, shaping your environment and influencing the behaviors and beliefs of those around you. It stemmed from your parents' inability to provide the care and love you needed because of their own history and issues. Most of our parents' behaviors come from **unconscious** efforts to relieve their own **anxiety**, their own experiences and distress, not from calculated attempts to irreversibly damage us. They were operating at the ceiling of what they thought was possible based on their own childhood experiences, and that was not what you deserved. Recognizing this pattern can be a powerful step toward breaking free from the cycle of blame and self-shame, allowing you to shift the focus away from personal guilt, away from anger for your family, and toward a broader approach of intergenerational healing. Meaning the cycle stops with you.

Redefining the Relationship

Some people think we become adults when we are allowed to drink, when we start driving, when we make independent decisions, when we start having sex, when we move out of the home. **Personally, I think we become adults the moment we realize that our parents are just people and that, like you and me, they don't always get everything right.** Our childlike innocence toward the world is broken at that moment, because when our parents are no longer untouchable, we truly realize that we are on our own and we allow ourselves to acknowledge what our parents perhaps did incorrectly. I think some level of resentment is natural in the aftermath, but so are the assertion of our independence and wanting to redefine the relationship on our terms.

Redefining that relationship shows up in different ways: getting frustrated at your parents, arguing with them more, wanting distance from them, visiting them less on holidays, finding they keep coming up in therapy, creating your own chosen family among friends, or rebelling more and more against the beliefs and values your parents instilled in you.

For me, the kicker was thinking about all the ways I was going to raise my children differently. To name a few: I would get my kids to talk about their feelings more. I would never use the phrase "because I said so." I would be stricter with them about routines. I would never bring up clothing sizes or have them weigh themselves on the little bathroom scale. I think we can all come up with our own list of what we would do differently. I've never heard anyone say, "Everything was perfect. I would do it exactly the same." That's because part of establishing our own independence and our own viewpoints, values, and beliefs involves questioning what our parents could have done better, then coming to terms with some of the wounds they unintentionally left behind.

At this point, you basically have two choices: you let it go and never address any of your concerns ever again—you bury the so-called hatchet—or you work through the past and, during the process, learn more about why you are the way you are because of your childhood, taking stock of what you want to change.

Not everyone needs to engage their family in this process, for a number of reasons. First, they may not be around or alive for you to speak to. Second, engaging with them could be dangerous or unhealthy, and the need for closure or answers isn't worth that risk. And so, third, it may be better for everyone that you remain apart and heal on your own. Our parents aren't always going to be responsive to our need for accountability or recognition. Coming out and saying things like "I never feel like I'm good enough because of you," "You taught me to hate my body," or "You never protected me when I needed you to" may not be met with the response you want. In most cases, you'll probably be met with a lot of shock and denial.

What is occurring in those moments is a great deal of cognitive dissonance from your family member or parent, because they see themselves one way—probably as a decent, nice, kind, well-intentioned person—while you are telling them their actions and behaviors contradict this self-perception they have. This challenges their ego, and in order to overcome the discomfort, either they have to choose to believe that what you are saying is true—and therefore must accept their faults and wrongdoings—or they can deny your experience and therefore maintain their self-concept and identity as a good person. Which do you think is more likely?

When we are just coming to terms with appreciating and unpacking our own experiences, this denial is unhelpful and can just reopen old wounds. There's also the fact that when we end up arguing with our parents or disagreeing, we tend to emotionally regress. We revert back to how we would have behaved as a child or teenager in this situation—insecure, unregulated, flighty, aggressive—because this is the only way we've ever related to our parents during these times of tension and conflict. In that moment the child-parent dynamic returns in full force, pulling us right back into that previously hurt and vulnerable version of ourselves. Subsequently, it can undo a lot of the healing and maturity we've gained since we left our parents' orbit and control. All of this to say, **we can't always look to the person who shaped us or hurt us to heal us.**

Healing on Your Own

Appreciating how your upbringing has shaped you is hard work, but the very fact you are considering it shows you are prepared. Approaching the past comes in waves, but there are four principles you should be guided by:

• It doesn't have to be black-and-white.

You can acknowledge your parents' mistakes and still love them. You can be aware of where things went wrong and still really value the relationship. You can be self-aware without looking for someone to blame. Not having a perfect childhood doesn't mean it was all horrible. It's also important to note that understanding parental influence isn't about protecting their ego or needing to go scorched earth; it's about finding answers for yourself about why you are the way you are and whether that's something you're okay with or not.

It's also possible to still accept the parts of you inherited from your parents—the parts you really like. Your tenacity, creativity, spontaneity, humor, intelligence, taste in music, whatever it is. If we are an amalgamation of our parents and our environment, disliking and dismissing every part of them also involves dismissing a large part of who you are. There is a lot we can still feel grateful for.

- You know your truth better than anyone.

Your memories and your experiences are fully trademarked, by you. No one can take away what you have experienced, or your interpretation of these moments and memories, even if they see things differently. Everyone's memories about the past are different, because we interpret them through our own unique perspective, influenced by our individual emotions, beliefs, and values. It can be difficult not receiving an acknowledgment of your experiences or recognition from your family of what you went through, maybe even at their hands. But what would them accepting responsibility actually change? It certainly helps in getting closure, it helps us feel that they are working on themselves, and it can make us feel safer in their presence. But when it comes to healing from the past, sometimes what we need most is our own approval. *Yes, this did happen, and it has impacted me. Yes, my memory of this is correct. Yes, my anger is justified even if my parents believe they did the best they could.* That doesn't mean you still don't have your own personal interpretation of your childhood to work through and settle. Trust your gut, trust your emotions, and stand firmly behind your truth. Taking up their denial and making it your own typically only delays your eventual epiphany moments and compounds the trauma.

- Forgiveness is powerful, but only when you are prepared.

In a lot of the literature on redefining our relationship with our parents as adults, forgiveness seems to be at the center. Forgiveness is a really powerful healer, not just to absolve others of their wrongdoing, but also to bring about peace for yourself. It means you have completed the cycle of recognition, anger, understanding, acceptance, and release. You get to let go of your resentment and move forward. It's incredibly empowering, because you get the final say. You realize there is power in choosing to forgive, and there is no response that can match your act of grace and, ultimately, liberation from the experience. It's also not for everyone. Yes, forgiveness is painted as this miracle antidote to all our childhood pain, but if you're not ready to forgive, don't force yourself into believing you can. Those emotions will still continue to bubble up, and when they do, you may feel like you no longer have the right to express them because you prematurely closed that chapter. **Only when you, and you alone, are ready is it time,** even if that's never.

- Find comfort in community.

When I first started talking about childhood resentment, it was rather quietly. I didn't want people to think I wasn't grateful for everything my parents and my family had done, all the happy memories, or that I was exaggerating my experiences. I think this comes from the long-standing beliefs we all have to respect our elders or to keep private matters private. But a problem spoken about is a problem halved. The more I began speaking about it with friends and those around me, the more people began revealing their own stories. A lot of us don't know how to talk about these things, because there is no right way, no guidebook, no standard. But when we open ourselves up to community and we share our experiences in whatever way we know how, the truth becomes easier—and so does a sense of closure. You'll begin to realize how many others have a story just like yours, that you are not the only one conflicted, or home to complex emotions. You are not the only one trying to break generational curses and fix two relationships at once: the one you have with yourself and the one you have with your parents. So don't carry the weight alone.

Challenge the notion of perfection in parenting and acknowledge that parents, like everyone else, are fallible. Recognizing their mistakes doesn't diminish their love or your gratitude; it simply allows for a more honest and authentic relationship.

Take control of your inner narrative by examining the voices that shape your self-concept. Recognize that the critical or nurturing voices in your head may echo those of your parents, but ultimately you have the power to shape your own self-perception.

Trauma doesn't need to be sensational to matter. Only you alone understand your experience.

People go through their entire lives never considering why they are the way they are. Unhealed wounds are inheritable wounds for future generations.

CHAPTER 11

Healing Your Inner Child

WHO WERE YOU as a child? What was your favorite outfit? Your favorite things to do, favorite TV shows, favorite snacks? What do you remember from that time? Seriously ask yourself, are all those memories as magical as they are made out to be? Do you still feel as if that version of you exists somewhere, even if your physical form has changed? If this is the case, your intuition is correct.

The idea of our "inner child" has gained new popularity as we begin to better understand how many of our current emotional wounds, reactions, attachment styles, and patterns of behavior have their roots in childhood. The logic follows that, by healing that childhood version of ourselves, we will heal the present-day version too.

Understanding this relationship between the past and current version of myself—the child and the adult—has been a significant part of my healing. For a long time, the memories from my childhood seemed to be tinged by this sense of pessimism, along with an unmet desire for acceptance. There was something contained in those memories that I could not let go of, a part of me that had to grow up too soon that wanted to be a child again. I don't think that's an isolated experience. Things like childhood bullying, parental neglect, divorce, even geographical dislocation and frequent moving, can disturb the security that we crave and innately need as children.

The term "inner-child healing" might sound like the kind of alluring pseudoscience that would attract someone looking for answers in their twenties. But there is some important science and psychology behind this concept that is neglected in modern-day interpretations. This form of healing has its roots in the work of Carl Jung—one of the most well-known psychiatrists of the twentieth century and a founder of modern psychology. Through his work with patients at psychiatric hospitals and his research on the contents of the human psyche, Jung established this idea that each of us possesses an inner version of ourselves that has existed since the moment we entered this world kicking and screaming. Who you were as an infant, as a child, as a teenager does not disappear but remains within you, in the shadows of your unconscious, impacting your actions and decisions.

Our Childhood: The Source of All Problems

Our inner child is the keeper of all our early experiences. Those experiences will impact the type of "inner child" each of us has. Some of us have a wounded inner child archetype, or an innocent inner child, an abandoned or divine or vulnerable inner child.

The theories suggest that many of our adult dysfunctions and problems and quirks and trauma come from our childhood experiences. When we peel back the layers we have built up to protect ourselves, we will find at our core an innocent, injured version of ourselves who just needs to be loved. **By loving this version of us** unconditionally—by deliberately healing them, giving them what we perhaps did not have as children—we can address the things we most want to change about our adult selves.

Our childhood is the most crucial developmental period of our lives, not just physically but also emotionally and cognitively. We begin to learn our most basic emotions within the first year of life, and we learn who to trust within a matter of months after being born. By one year old, we have begun to form our attachment style, and by five years, most of us have unique personalities and ways of relating to others that predict our behavior well into adulthood.

In psychology, as in parallel disciplines like philosophy, there is this idea that children are born as a "blank canvas" on which their experiences slowly build up, image after image, layer after layer, until the canvas begins to fill up and it becomes harder to paint over or start again. Those layers of paint are our memories and the network of neurons that forms in response to our experiences. The inner child represents the part of your subconscious that has been there for all those moments, that has seen it all. Our inner child holds emotions, memories, and beliefs from the past, as well as hopes and dreams for the future.

Our inner child is the one who remembers what it felt like to giggle uncontrollably on the playground.

Our inner child is the one who remembers falling asleep in our parents' arms and being tucked into bed.

Our inner child remembers what it felt like to be excluded and bullied.

Our inner child remembers what it felt like to be yelled at when we were just trying to be good.

Our inner child remembers what it felt like to be abandoned or lonely.

Our inner child remembers what it was like to play for hours, what it was like to feel scared of the ocean, what it was like to fall down, hurt yourself, and call out for your mum, to eat warm cookies. They remember what it felt like the first time you failed, the first time you didn't belong, what it felt like to start a new school and to be scared.

The good and the bad intermix and form the unconscious mental scaffolding for how you perceive the world. Your childhood wounds begin to emerge when those dark memories overwhelm your joyful memories. Identifying when your inner child may be injured or wounded is the first step to healing an abundance of issues in adulthood.

I remember in university being triggered by events where I perceived people to be rejecting me, even if they weren't. I reacted irrationally and from a place of fear. After years of bullying, that same question I'd had so often as a child—"Do they actually like me?"—was still there. It hadn't disappeared with time. That was when I realized just how many of my behaviors might have an unhelpful origin—the toxic relationships, the strong self-criticism, the inability to say no to parties or social events even when I was exhausted.

There are some critical signs that you may have a wounded inner child. These are:

- Difficulty trusting others.
- Emotional unavailability.
- Feeling guilty or undeserving of nice things, including nice emotions like love and generosity.
- Having a strong inner critic.
- People-pleasing tendencies.

- Abandonment issues.

- Feeling you need to collect people or friendships.

- Suppressing hard emotions.

These experiences impact all of us differently, and there are certainly more signs than appear on this list. Remember: just as we each perceive our reality differently as adults, we also did as children. Much of the literature on inner-child healing suggests that these reactions and emotional habits are indicative that, at some stage in your childhood, you experienced something that altered your ability to relate to yourself and others in a healthy and sustainable way.

Often these reactions stem from what some therapists and psychologists call "childhood wounds."

There are four typical wounds that psychologists talk about concerning inner-child trauma: the guilt wound, the abandonment wound, the betrayal wound, and the neglect wound. Each has its own origins and unique manifestations. Depending on which, if any, of these you relate to, the way you move forward with your inner child will be different.

Guilt Wound

The guilt wound often comes from childhood experiences in which you were tasked with caring for others the way they should have cared for you. You may have experienced way more responsibility at a young age than should have been acceptable. Maybe you were responsible for a parent or sibling, or mediating conflict in your household. You may have been made to feel guilty for asking for your needs to be met and, as a result, continue to feel undeserving of basic emotional and physical necessities. As a child, you may have responded to this by trying your absolute hardest to be good, being highly susceptible to guilt-tripping, especially by those close to you, or feeling responsible for bad things that happened in your life or the lives of those closest to you.

How does this manifest in adulthood? An unaddressed wound of this nature may result in severe people-pleasing tendencies, needing to constantly apologize, feeling guilty for establishing personal boundaries, such as saying no to social events or activities you don't want to go to, or feeling guilty saying no to favors others ask of you. When unaddressed, it can also result in your adopting the same guilt-tripping tactics that were used against you as a child.

Healing this wound requires setting healthy boundaries—you don't want to find yourself in situations you'd rather avoid because your guilt dragged you there. Some people benefit from creating a set of commitments to themselves based on their ideal boundaries. These include statements such as "I will put myself first in this situation," "I will speak honestly about my opinion," "I won't try to anticipate others' needs," and "I won't stay somewhere I'm not comfortable." You can then review them each morning before stepping out the door.

Healing this wound may also involve exercises to release subconscious guilt that potentially clouds your judgment and ability to practice forgiveness with yourself. Somatic therapy, in particular, recognizes how unresolved guilt can register in our bodies. By providing a release for these emotions through movement or bodily awareness—noticing which muscles and areas of our body hold emotional tension—we begin to channel our emotions through our bodies, rather than just our minds, because there is only so much thinking we can do.

It can also be as simple but life-changing as journaling every time you feel guilty for the past, for a mistake, for letting someone down, for letting yourself down. Just finish each page by writing, "I forgive you." It sounds simple, but it will give you permission to release the guilt you believe others are holding over you by providing forgiveness to yourself.

Abandonment Wound

The abandonment wound is perhaps the childhood wound that receives the most acknowledgment. This type of hurt stems from feeling that you were abandoned by someone who was meant to care for you. It's most often associated with people whose parents went through a difficult divorce or separation, who had a parent pass away, or whose parents were very distant.

As a result, you have deep fears of being left on your own, and you can become very fixated on people and anxious when you perceive even the slightest indicator that they are withdrawing. Recent literature has acknowledged the increased feelings of shame among these children because they blame themselves for the abandonment, finding themselves defective and undeserving of love. Because we are not yet aware of the complexity of adult relationships, generational trauma, substance abuse, or emotional unavailability, our childhood self cannot understand why someone walked out on them. And so the child is left to deal with this absence alone, often concluding that there must be something wrong with them. A child's rational thinking skills are not developed enough to understand the complexities and nuances of human relationships.

As an adult, you may fear loneliness and rejection, because these moments imitate your childhood experience of abandonment. You learn from that pain and find ways to avoid it in any and all future relationships, becoming hypervigilant to any cues from partners or friends that they may be preparing to pull away. If this reminds you of an anxious attachment style, you would be correct in assuming that these experiences are linked. Individuals with an abandonment wound will often find themselves in highly codependent relationships or have trouble trusting people, specifically romantic partners, because they have been primed to expect that one day everyone will suddenly leave.

To heal from this, you first need to heal your fear of history repeating itself. Just because the past exists doesn't mean it's going to be repeated, and you must acknowledge the ways your coping and defense mechanisms may create a self-fulfilling prophecy through avoidance and self-abandonment. Here is your reminder that you do deserve love, the right people DO stay, and your worth is not valued by others' decisions.

Betrayal Wound

The third wound is the betrayal wound. As a child, you may have found that you could not trust your caregivers, they failed to fulfill their promises to you, they never showed up when you expected they would, they would gaslight you, they put you in situations of potential harm, or they didn't stand up for you when you needed it. You may have also developed a unique form of trauma called "betrayal trauma." This concept, introduced by

Jennifer Freyd of the University of Oregon in 1991, describes a situation in which a child who has experienced betrayal has to continue interacting with the betraying person due to a social dependency, despite feeling like they can no longer trust them.

When you exit the orbit of this individual as an adult, you may develop a hyperindependence and an inability to trust others. Hyperindependence is more than just trusting your own instincts, liking your alone time, or wanting to do things on your own. It also extends to social withdrawal, perfectionism, needing to maintain control over your life by doing things perfectly and without fault, refusing help even when it's deeply needed, being highly secretive or self-contained about your feelings or mental state, and refusing to be vulnerable.

Hyperindependence can create a lot of additional suffering, because it keeps you disconnected from community and the people who want to help you—the people who believe you are deserving of unconditional kindness and love, the people who won't let you down. Of course, when, due to your history of betrayal, you've come to expect that people won't follow through on their commitments, it can be hard to trust people without questioning their true intentions. Isolation goes hand in hand with the betrayal wound.

To heal this wound, build inner trust by keeping promises and commitments to yourself first. What is a simple goal you want to achieve? Maybe that is drinking more water, avoiding your phone fifteen minutes after waking up, eating at least one piece of fruit a day. Select a goal that is easy to achieve and show yourself how you can display follow-through and, thus, can expect the same follow-through from others. Healing the betrayal wound may also involve a kind of exposure therapy to trusting others: create a ladder of activities that start small ("confiding in others about my daily frustrations"), growing to medium ("relying on others for advice"), and then big ("allowing someone to pick me up from the hospital" or "sharing big fears or insecurities"). This process can take years, but at the root of the betrayal wound is fear of being hurt again, and this exercise helps you overcome that fear in small, incremental steps that build up to larger healing and surrender.

Neglect Wound

Finally, we have the neglect wound. As children, we so want to be seen. From infancy, children strive to maintain social contact with the intention of gaining attention, feedback, comfort, connection. It gives kids that special sense of belonging and importance that stays with them all the way into adulthood. When a child is ignored, disregarded, or told to sit down and be quiet, the neglect wound emerges. Someone with a neglect wound may recall memories of being overlooked as a child, treated as an afterthought, being unsupported, or not receiving their emotional, physical, and social needs. This can come from parents and family, but I've heard from people who felt they were overlooked and disregarded by teachers and mentors, leading them to believe their work, their efforts, their achievements weren't enough.

An old colleague of mine from my corporate days had a brother who was a highly successful child star, appearing in movies, commercials, and TV shows. Her parents later confessed they never put her up for any roles or thought to promote her in the same way because she didn't have the "face or personality" for it like her brother. This asymmetrical dynamic in the apparent talent and success between her brother and her resulted in her parents giving preferential treatment to him. He got all the attention; they would travel with him to shoots while she stayed home with an aunt. While they may have seen it as supporting their son's dream, the unintended consequence was the neglect of their daughter and an unconscious favoritism. These situations can be super nuanced and different for everyone, but often this childhood wound results in low self-worth, a pessimistic outlook on life, repressing and suppressing true feelings, and having low standards for friends and romantic partners. If you never received the level of love you needed, it's hard to feel deserving of any more love than what is offered.

Healing a neglect wound is about putting yourself first. Intentionally promote and celebrate your innate worth, as well as your achievements, small wins, and setbacks, and all the emotional highs and lows in between. They may have gone unacknowledged in the past, but you won't let that be the case anymore. You may have been overlooked by those who were meant to nurture you, but now you are the main adult in your life, and that inner child won't go overlooked anymore. This starts with the big stuff, of course: celebrate your wins vibrantly and out loud. You got promoted? Tell people, grab a cake, put some candles on it even if it's just you. Buy yourself the flowers. It also extends to the seemingly smaller things. You feel scared, lonely, or insecure? Don't suppress those feelings, don't hide them from yourself, don't self-silence just yet. Instead, offer yourself comfort. This can be physical comfort, by setting up a cozy safe space with your comfort food, a warm shower, and your favorite TV show, or it can be emotional comfort, by repeating reassuring statements to yourself. Your only task now is to make your inner child feel as seen as possible, by staying present and being attentive to your current self and experiences.

Healing Your Inner Child

The basis for inner-child healing is known as "reparenting." As you become the main adult in your life, you also become the parent to your inner child. It is your responsibility to create a safe space where your inner child is allowed to lead, whether you had a healthy example of what that should be like or not. By creating the space, you give yourself permission to explore significant events that are perhaps uncomfortable or unpleasant, to get in touch with your true feelings and parts of you that may have been rejected and labeled by others as "inappropriate," "unlovable," or "too much."

To nurture your inner child, you need to honor and express your feelings, as ugly and dangerous as you think they are. You can practice this through a method known as "shameless release." Similar to what I've said about childhood guilt wounds, deep and powerful emotions sit in the body, creating tension. The longer you suppress them, the more uncontrollable they become and the more damage they cause, both physical and mental. Shameless release creates the conditions for the kind of catharsis you need to surrender your hurt, fear, shame, and anger. That may involve therapeutic exercises like boxing, screaming at the top of your lungs in nature, singing and yelling the lyrics to a cathartic song, or creating art that allows you to bring your emotions to the surface, make them tangible and known.

Children who have experienced neglect, betrayal, or abandonment are used to hearing "no" when they ask for something that will meet their needs. So, as an adult who is now responsible for this child version of yourself, you have to let yourself say "yes" to your needs and wants. Maybe that involves saying yes to the food you want to eat, buying something because it makes you happy even if it's impractical, saying yes to fun things like nights out with friends, or going to the movies just because you want to. You're the parent now—you have to look after your inner child and treat them with the love and generosity you deserved but maybe did not receive.

It's also about accountability.

When we embark on the journey of reparenting, we recognize that caring for our inner child isn't just being goofy and silly and giving in to all our whims, but also making the hard decisions. We wouldn't allow an actual child to eat junk food all day. We wouldn't say yes to everything to the point where they were exhausted, or allow them to stay friends with people who brought them down and encroached on their boundaries. So you can't allow your inner child and, with that, your present-day self to accept that treatment either. It's just as much about responsibility as compassion and love; it still involves boundaries and discipline.

I think it's worth mentioning that these specific categories or wounds all seem, on a surface level, to be rooted in extreme trauma. But neglect, abandonment, betrayal, and guilt can all occur on a micro scale as well, even in ways that we don't always recognize, because of the subconscious nature of our inner child. You don't need to have objectively, or even subjectively, experienced trauma to incorporate inner-child healing as part of your daily practices. Inner-child healing doesn't just resolve problematic habits or behaviors rooted in your childhood; it can also help you tap into the joy and silliness most of us lose as we get older. We become hardened by adulthood and obligations and "duty." But giving yourself space to release those constraints is truly magical.

A great place to start is to reconnect with things that remind you of the childhood version of yourself. Take note of how exposure to these things makes you feel. For example, the other day I rewatched the *Hannah Montana* movie. That movie was released when I was nine years old and I was obsessed with it. I loved that movie, I memorized all the songs, the dances, I bought clothes just like Miley Cyrus wore in the movie . . . I saw it in the cinema probably three times. Rewatching that movie at twenty-three made me so incredibly emotional, but also so aware of my innocence and vulnerability during those moments. That positive reaction reminded me that she, my inner child, did actually exist, because those emotions I was experiencing were derived from memories of that time, the memories that I had made as a child.

If you're feeling detached from your inner child, try to recreate moments and memories from childhood to reunite your current, conscious version of you with your former, subconscious versions of you. That can be aided by sensations like smell, sound, and sight, or activities such as watching a classic movie, cooking your favorite childhood meal, or reading your favorite childhood book, because our memories are strongest when they are tied to multiple senses. You'll be amazed how much your mind and body will respond to these experiences from a reflexive and unconscious place.

To further that daily practice of reconnection and remembering, change your phone background to a childhood photo of you, or place a picture on your mirror, somewhere you look every day. I have a photo of me from the fourth grade next to my computer at home, so any time I'm getting stressed by work, I look to my left and I am reminded that everything I'm putting myself through, everything I'm doing, I'm also doing to her. And would she be proud of me for that? Is this what her dream was? Would she be happy with where we are now? Is she receiving what she deserves? It really puts your decisions and treatment of yourself into perspective, and I've found that it's made me a lot more gentle in my self-judgment.

Do something creative: When we are young, we have art class and time to do things that are creative. The older we get, the harder it is to find time to do that. Life drawing, pottery, knitting, coloring in books. A study published in 2019 found that art improves health and well-being, promoting resilience, coping skills, and overall happiness levels.

Be messy: Mess is acceptable in childhood, not so much in adulthood. Find a way to let yourself step outside of the constraints that growing up places on our freedoms. Cook with rash abandon, repot some plants, get your hands dirty. It's good for your neurons, it's good for your synaptic connections and growth, it's good for your happiness. You can clean up later, but for now your inner child will feel a sense of relief.

Hug yourself: The feeling of being touched releases oxytocin. We can release that ourselves because our brains can't always tell the difference between someone else's and, well, our own loving arms. I know it sounds silly, but do it now: put your arms around yourself and hold them there, squeeze yourself in. It will immediately make you feel better—a great way to practice self-love.

Play: Nothing says childhood quite like play. Engaging in play unlocks something deep within you that is curious, joyful, uninhibited. Go and play tag occasionally. Again, sounds silly, but the bliss and excitement you experience as a result are so pure and wonderful, you can ignore your "adult responsibilities." Pull out those Monopoly or Uno cards, make yourself a big chocolate sundae, buy yourself some ridiculous fluffy toy just because you want to. Pretend you are taking the little version of you out for the best day ever and give them all the experiences they could have wanted, more of those positive memories.

Being aware of your inner child is one thing; being in touch with them—you—and giving yourself the space to be vulnerable and nurture them is another. The biggest impact this relationship journey has brought to my adult life is the way I now speak to myself and the way I honor my emotions. We all tend to be very hard on ourselves, saying things to ourselves that we would never imagine saying to someone else. Mean things, hurtful things. That is terrible for our self-worth and identity, but also a hard habit to break. Being in touch with your inner child is incredibly useful for that.

When you've failed, when you've been rejected, when you feel unhappy with yourself, take note of your inner dialogue and imagine that your five-year-old self is sitting in front of you right now and you are speaking those things to them.

You wouldn't yell at this five-year-old version of you.

You wouldn't tell them they're fat.

You wouldn't tell them they're useless.

Or worthless.

Or stupid.

So why would you say those things to yourself now?

The same goes for how you let others treat you. If you wouldn't let someone treat a child the way your friends or your partner or your parents or your colleagues treat you, then a boundary needs to be put in place. Obviously, we have more emotional maturity in our twenties than we do as children, so someone offering you constructive criticism or asking you to do your job or to be independent may seem intense for a child but acceptable for an adult. I think it goes without saying that healing your inner child is not about regressing to that version of you. It's about being better at acknowledging how people and situations make you feel, where that reaction may have come from, and how you can properly respond from a place of growth and maturity, while still honoring the childhood version of you that needs love, respect, and safety.

> Your inner child remembers and projects what your adult self needs to heal. Be the person this version of you always needed.

> Appreciate your innate vulnerability, innocence, and playfulness and find a place for these parts of yourself in your adult life.

> Healing your inner child requires you to be gentle, but also honest and forthright, both with yourself and others.

- - - - - - - - - -

CHAPTER III

Healing Your Inner Teen

HEALING OUR INNER child is one thing; healing our inner teenager is a lot more precarious. It is very easy to channel, and advocate for, the version of us who is naive, innocent, and lovable. How could someone so vulnerable do any harm? But our teenage selves are a lot harder to forgive and a lot easier to blame. They are filled with rage and confusion, hormones and insecurity, still young enough to be finding their footing but old enough to take on some responsibility.

You may also be asking: Why is a book about our twenties talking about my teen years? The reason: They are deeply connected. We may have left that time of our lives behind, but that doesn't mean a brick wall has been erected between who we were then and who we are now. That version still exists within us. Tending to the person you were as a teenager—your memories, experiences, and beliefs—creates a great deal of self-awareness and release. Our teenage years were a period of significant emotional, physical, and social transition that none of us exits unscarred—if you want to understand where your rage comes from, your battered sense of self-worth, your insecurities, perhaps it's contained in those weird years surrounding puberty.

When I reflect on my teenage years, it is with an overtone of cringe. Why did I wear leg warmers to school for six months?

Why did I treat my parents so badly? Why did I waste that valuable time with my siblings by hiding in my room? Why did I hate the world so much? Why did I love that boy so much more? It's easy to disregard the experiences of our teenage years because of how messy they are and how in flux that whole period feels.

This version of us reflects all the failures, mistakes, and pain we had to go through to become this current version of ourselves, so we naturally want to look away. However, just because that person is a bit messier and complicated doesn't mean they don't deserve the same kind of deliberate love we give our inner child. In fact, they may need it more because of how misunderstood they are.

Wounded Teen vs. Wounded Child

The wounded teenager looks very different from the wounded child. While the inner child is your emotional core—the vulnerable, innocent, often needy part of you—your inner teen is a lot more chaotic. They are angry, isolated, insecure, and very quick to reject your help. Some indicators that you have a wounded teen, or that your inner teenager is in control, include:

- High rejection sensitivity.
- Uncontrollable anger and outbursts of rage for no apparent reason.
- Self-sabotaging behaviors like procrastination, overspending, emotional eating, and substance abuse.
- Replicating early romantic partners or experiences.
- Regression to adolescent habits and coping mechanisms.

As teenagers, we were intellectually and emotionally developed enough to be able to rationalize what we were experiencing, but not to process it fully. The nature of inner-teen experiences is going to be very different from that of inner-child ones, more aligned with the milestones we go through during this turbulent period. That is why approaching inner-child healing and inner-teen healing separately is so valuable.

The primary distinction between teenage wounds and childhood wounds lies in the age you were when they occurred. However, in developmental psychology, the distinction between childhood and adolescence is more than just age. Yes, we tend to see teenagers as those between the ages of thirteen and nineteen, but during that time we are also undergoing a rapid level of emotional and social development that distinguishes us from children. Specifically, this is the time when we begin to figure out our identity and where we sit in the world.

The psychoanalyst Erik Erikson described this stage as reflecting the conflict between identity and role confusion. During this stage, adolescents search for a sense of self and personal identity, through an intense exploration of personal values, beliefs, and goals, often rebelling against our parents or broader societal norms. This includes our sexual identity, our relational identity—where we stand in relation to our parents and our peers—and also our personal identity: Who do we want to be? It's natural during adolescence to try on a few different characters or costumes before settling on an identity that will inevitably change once more when we reach our twenties, and a few more times after that. What Erikson concluded was that if we don't successfully move through this stage, resolving this conflict between who we think we are, who society thinks we are, and our true self, then we begin to see emotional and social wounds most characteristic of our inner teen.

At the same time we're experiencing greater emotional, personal, and social independence, we're also seeing a major biological shift in the form of puberty. This exacerbates a lot of the experiences that we ultimately need to resolve. Beginning at puberty, the brain is quite literally being reshaped through a process known as synaptic or neural "pruning." The brain starts to remove connections it no longer needs, resulting in the estimated loss of some 50 percent of synaptic connections as it makes room for new pathways to be formed with our new adult experiences.

As we are experiencing this rapid pruning, our bodies are being pumped with an enormous amount of adrenal stress hormones, growth hormones, and sex hormones like testosterone and estrogen. All of these greatly impact things like mood and impulse control, even mental health. Some recent studies have suggested that higher rates of estrogen impact the availability of serotonin. Serotonin is one of the primary neurotransmitters responsible for happiness. Therefore, less availability equals less chemical happiness. It may explain why women, in particular teenage girls, have significantly higher rates of anxiety and depression, due to this hormonal shift as girls become women.

These developmental shifts create the mental and biological backdrop for a number of simultaneous social and emotional transitions, but also universal adolescent experiences that can create a great deal of pain and frustration, reflected in our teenage wounds. These include the battle for independence, feeling misunderstood, social exclusion, first sexual experiences, and feelings of shame. These experiences can produce the wounds we see in adulthood, and each of us is likely to have undergone at least one.

Social Rejection and Exclusion

Teenagers can be mean. Really mean. The exclusion and social toxicity we see between the ages of thirteen and nineteen are really like nothing else we will experience in our lives. When I was a teenager, I went to a progressive arts-based high school. Everyone was really cool, or at least trying to appear to be cool, with their trendy-but-not-quite-trendy clothes, alternative music, and "fuck you" attitudes. I was not cool. I could never dress the part or act the part. I was sensitive and academic whereas everyone else appeared focused on something else I couldn't quite figure out. My inability to fit in with the in-group led to a lot of exclusion, both active and passive. Group chats made behind my back, parties that I'd hear about on a Monday hosted by the people I thought were my friends, comments about my outfits. I remember being so lonely. The more people pushed me away, the more I craved their validation, and if I couldn't get it from them, I would get it from teachers and my parents by being studious and a good girl.

In that way I felt I missed out on a lot of the teenage experience because a) I was always preoccupied with what others thought of me (but then again, what teenager isn't?), and b) I was deeply committed to being good and taking on the responsibilities that would get me out of that high school and somewhere else entirely. After high school, I left that city behind, but as I entered college, I completely regressed and began to live out the teenage life I hadn't allowed myself. I got tattoos, I dyed my hair, I smoked cigarettes behind my college, I missed classes. Because my inner teen had missed out on so much and always felt lacking, I was trying to make up for lost time.

Being ostracized or bullied as a teenager creates many lasting psychological scars, particularly around our sense of self-worth and whether we are deserving of love. Each of us has an innate need to belong and to be accepted by the social groups around us. According to Maslow's Hierarchy of Needs, belonging comes just after our need for food, shelter, and safety. It is also a requirement if we want to discover our identity and reach a point of self-actualization.

Therefore, when we are deprived of a sense of belonging due to social exclusion or bullying, we are unable to undergo some of that self-discovery and establish an important foundation of self-love and confidence. This will influence our ability to make and sustain friendships as adults. We have learned just how painful it is to not belong; therefore, when we sense the slightest bit of hesitancy or doubt from our relationships, or feel as if people are pulling away or just aren't interested in us, that lonely and hurt teenage version of us is triggered. Once they are in control, they act from a place of teenage anger and insecurity, perhaps isolating us further as a protective mechanism. How can I be hurt by this, if I pull away first or make it impossible for them to leave me?

We see this need to belong in so many ways: codependency, clinginess, feeling intense anger at even the slightest sense of rejection—all indicators of a deeper emotional origin for our behavior. One way in particular that I've noticed in my own behavior is the need to hoard or collect friends, and sometimes even take on different identities with different people or groups in order to ensure I'll win their affection and friendship.

Another hidden indicator of this is the need to fill up our social calendar or circle with so many people that we find it impossible to maintain all these relationships at once. This may seem like we are protecting ourselves, or are "healing," but it's actually an unconscious defense mechanism against past hurt. If we collect friends, have dozens of acquaintances and connections, we'll never have to feel alone again, we'll never have to feel rejected, because there will always be someone there for us. The inner teen is still wounded.

Fighting for Independence

Independence as a teenager is about wanting to seem older while also not really understanding how young we truly are. We are in such a rush to grow up, push the limits, appear mature, move beyond the scope and control of the family, that we sometimes don't appreciate the season we're in, or we rush into experiences that we are unprepared for. This period of "flying the nest" is a natural part of human development, perhaps the most crucial milestone to becoming an adult. As we reduce our reliance on our parents, our friends usually become our main source of support. We start to put ourselves in situations that we see as "adult," seeking employment, drinking, pursuing romantic partners. Sex, in particular, is for many of us the point where we go from children to adults. What's more adult than this kind of illicit intimacy reserved for our parents and the cooler, older kids?

People lose their virginities at all ages. Not everyone will have sex in their teenage years or even in their twenties. We are all entitled to take our own time. What we may not realize is how much these early sexual experiences we seek out in our fight for independence have long-term psychological impacts that we don't really come to terms with until much later in life. Recent studies have begun to suggest that the age of a person's first sexual experience can determine romantic outcomes later in life. One 2013 study suggests this is particularly profound for women and their later sexual desire, because sex is such a powerful learning experience in our teenage years. This especially relates to the development of our attachment style and self-concept. There is so much pressure on the first time that we often don't acknowledge the insane level of trust, intimacy, and potential for trauma within that. We are actually still very much children—that's how the legal system, the voting system, the health system all see us. And yet we're beginning to have these very adult experiences.

That search for independence is normal, whether it's through relationships or otherwise. But sometimes our parents are not willing to give us the freedom we need, in which case we rebel and push against their boundaries and rules. This is where a lot of our rage and anger can come from, feeling like our emerging adult selves are being oppressed. The same goes for strict parents who may have contained our identity, not allowing us to pass through that role-confusion stage or explore and make mistakes and test our limits. This may develop into a hatred for authority, to such an extent that you may struggle in your twenties, and beyond, with people in higher positions, such as your boss telling you what to do and your acting in defiance because it's triggering that teenage version of you who felt misunderstood. Narcissistic parents and the environment they created—where teens are forced to maintain a certain image for their benefit—are also major contributors to an inner-teen wound, one of perhaps future rebellion or anger.

And then there are instances when we are deprived of our independence because we are taking on the role of caregiver within our family. This is known as "parentification." Parentification occurs when we experience a role reversal with our parents or caregivers in which we have to provide them with the emotional support we actually need from them, often acting as a confidant or mediator. We become the parents. This role reversal disrupts the natural process of maturing because we are required to take on responsibilities as adolescents well beyond what our years should require. We are denied that chance to be a bit helpless, to have someone help us and to make mistakes. The consequences of this accelerated maturity may show up later in life when we act out or do impulsive, risky things in the name of reclaiming the teenage lives we lost to being our parents' caregivers. We may also be highly emotionally reactive, particularly when we feel a sense of restriction or responsibility, because our inner teen is, once again, in control. Those unhealed wounds are telling us to act in a certain way based on our past experiences.

Shame

The experience of shame represents a crucial emotional shift from childhood to adolescence. When we begin to worry about how other people perceive our behavior, this indicates that we have entered a new emotional chapter in which we are aware of other people's internal lives and how they influence our own. If you imagine your childhood self, you really didn't have those concerns: you were happy to play and run around without fear of what others would think. If you've ever spoken to a seven- or eight-year-old child, you know they often say the wildest things with absolutely no impulse control. At that age we would wear whatever we wanted, everybody could be our best friend, we were not self-conscious about our bodies. When did that stop? When was the first time you realized that maybe you didn't fit in, or you became aware of the expectations and opinions of others, and how is that impacting you now? When was the first time you felt like you were a bad person? And in what ways is that teenage version of you still seeking out others' approval as an adult in order to avoid that shame?

Shame is a powerful psychological tool that is used to enforce conformity and an obedience to the status quo. In doing so, it asks us to deny our true selves, or deny our experiences because they may be difficult for others to hear. Shame in that way often manifests as an extreme form of self-rejection.

As adults and twenty-somethings, it's hard to accept those parts of us we felt embarrassed by as teenagers, because shame is something we instinctively conceal, or perhaps try increasingly hard to disprove. This results in extreme efforts to win others' approval in adulthood, but also a continual battle between who we know we are and who we wish we were.

I had a friend who was always criticized as a child for being disruptive, being too loud, not being able to focus. She tells of a distinct time she was scolded by a teacher in front of the class-room and, for the first time, knew what it meant for someone to really hate her. As she grew into a teenager, her inability to con-centrate and her hyperactivity continued. The shame she felt at being unable to control her behavior and the animosity she expe-rienced from the adults in her life quickly culminated in her missing classes, avoiding going to school, and then dropping out completely, despite having big dreams of going to university to be a vet. At twenty-five, she was diagnosed with ADHD and found a way to manage the behaviors she was shamed for continuously as a teenager and child. However, the memories of this shame meant she never went back to school and she was constantly worried about speaking up or being too disruptive in the workplace, or even around friends. Her inner dialogue became one of self-hatred. This level of toxic shame can create a wounded inner teen who interrupts our ability to find a stable self-concept and identity as adults.

The Way Forward

Healing your inner teen involves acknowledging these experiences: the times you felt unheard, misunderstood, rejected, angry, or oppressed—and the impact they continue to have. Connecting with your teenage self and providing a space to release these experiences, and the emotional patterns they have created, helps you overcome the wounds carried by this former version of you.

If you want to heal your inner teen, you've got to be able to identify when they have control or are reacting to a situation. I want to return to those indicators from before:

- High rejection sensitivity.

- Uncontrollable anger and outbursts of rage for no apparent reason.

- Self-sabotaging behaviors like procrastination, overspending, emotional eating, and substance abuse.

- Replicating early romantic partners or experiences.

- Regression to adolescent habits and coping mechanisms.

Let's take anger as an example. Often when our wounded teen is speaking up through things like rage, outbursts, or tantrums, it is just a secondary emotional reaction to a deeper sense of injustice, or feeling misunderstood or out of control. It may be that, as a teenager, you weren't given permission to feel emotions intensely, so as an adult you don't have the same level of control. Emotions like rage are stored in the body.

One study found that rage can create muscle tension and automatic arousal in certain areas of the brain. So giving these feelings a physical expression will stop you from doing so inappropriately—and it feels nice to give yourself permission to actually feel, rather than scolding your inner teen as your parents, teachers, and peers used to do in the past. It feels nice to release anger, it's incredibly satisfying, but you need to channel that in a productive way to satisfy both your inner teen's needs and your adult responsibilities as well.

Go to a rage room or a boxing class, provide yourself with a physical catharsis in order to connect with your rage. Or better yet, go to a nice secluded spot out in nature and just scream and yell. Or dance intensely in your room, headphones on, Blink-182 playing, or maybe some *Fearless* by Taylor Swift—classic teenage angst albums.

There's one final method that I want to discuss here, known as the "Adult Chair method." This method, created by the incredible therapist Michelle Chalfant, uses visualization and psychoanalytic techniques to converse with our inner teen. I want you to imagine three chairs in front of you, one symbolizing your childhood self, one symbolizing your inner teen, and finally one for your current self. You sit with these three chairs and you speak to each of these versions of yourself as if you were the therapist. What's making you upset right now? What's bothering you? What are you angry or frustrated about? What do you need from me?

Creating this open dialogue with your past and the memories contained in these versions of you allows you to better understand what teenage experiences have remained with you all these years. And if they have remained with you, it's likely they have had a lasting emotional impact. This method also allows you to get into the mind of your past self and see exactly where the insecurity, rage, and fear have come from. In response, imagine what this version of you needs to hear. Tell them that it does get better. That they find love. They find friendship. They learn to accept the parts of them they disliked so much. That everything works out.

Similar to inner-child healing, when you see yourself as this innocent, scared past version of you, your inner dialogue will naturally become more empathetic and kind. Some people find these techniques quite strange, but it is your responsibility to process how your teenage memories and experiences have shaped you. Part of that is integrating them into the current version of yourself, finding a place where these experiences sit in your current reality. This is just one exercise that allows us to understand what our adult selves crave, by looking back at what we didn't receive as children or teenagers.

> With anything in life, you have a choice. You can choose to be gentle, or you can choose to be hard on yourself. That decision is yours, but you can't hate yourself into loving yourself.

> Make friends with who you are. Your past self helped get you here. Whatever they went through, whatever mistakes

they made, whatever you cringe at now, these were the things that allowed you to be who you are now.

You are the main adult in your life now. You are the parent. Make sure your inner child and your inner teen know they are safe with you.

CHAPTER IV

The Gift of Loneliness

THE FURTHER WE get into our twenties, the more we realize that all of us are struggling with some kind of loneliness. Even the busiest, most social person you know, online or in real life, has moments of isolation and longing for deeper connections. We feel lonely even when we're surrounded by people, lonely even after a full day with those we love, lonely even when we know we need downtime. Surely we must be the only ones feeling this way, or everyone would be talking about it more? It seems that the secret doesn't lie in the quantity of social interaction we are having, but our perception of isolation. Further, the more we fear loneliness, the more powerful it becomes. Perhaps the solution is to run toward it, rather than away.

The Rise of Loneliness

It's no secret that loneliness among twenty- to twenty-nine-year-olds is on the rise. We don't need statistics to tell us something many of us are observing in real time: in a world that has never been more connected, our level of disconnection is reaching new heights. As a generation, we are suffering. It's ironic that as technology has provided us with so many ways to stay in touch, it has actually lessened our ability to meaningfully and authentically connect in real life, perhaps because we are so overexposed to this form of semi-connection that online life brings. Researchers have been searching for an explanation, looking at factors from genetics to global life-changing events, including the pandemic and of course the rise of social media, but I want to offer my own Gen Z theory.

It all starts with our perception of loneliness. Contrary to popular belief, feeling lonely is neither rare nor something to be afraid of. There is such a stigma around admitting that we feel lonely. We think it means something is wrong with us, that if we were to come out and say, "I feel lonely," people will assume we aren't socially desirable enough to make friends, we're unenjoyable to be around, people don't like us. Ninety-nine percent of the time, in my personal opinion, this isn't true. **Loneliness is simply an emotional reaction to our environment and our experiences, but also our subjective threshold for how much connection we need.** It is an evolutionary cue telling us it's time to reconnect, not something that defines your character or says anything about who you are. Loneliness feels so intense because social connection is so vital to our needs and survival that our body wants to ensure we have a natural drive to obtain a sense of connectedness, as much as we have a natural drive to eat and drink and sleep.

Repeated and consistent human interaction is a core psychological ingredient for our mental health and well-being. But on a more evolutionary level, humans dislike feeling alone or isolated because, in the past, our survival rested on feeling connected with others. It rested on belonging to a group. Membership in a group provided us with security, with access to food, shelter, mating partners, and protection. If we were to strike out on our own or were shunned from the group, our chances of long-term survival were slim. Loneliness acts as a neural mechanism to draw us back into the protection of a group. Though loneliness may be painful, the reaction it incites—to return to human connectedness—is a much better alternative to being killed by a hungry beast or dying from exposure, as was likely the case back in the day if we rejected our social group.

The True Meaning of Loneliness

I think we have lost sight of this evolutionary explanation. We no longer see loneliness for what it really is, but as something to be afraid of due to the stigma attached to it. Sometimes this stigma is self-applied and arises because we perceive that we are not meeting the expectations for the quantity and quality of experiences we should be having in our twenties. We are sold this really contrived and romanticized narrative that our twenties are the "best years of our lives." If these are the best years of our lives, we've got to make the most of them because things will surely go downhill from here! So we think we should be surrounded by friends, seeing people every day of the week, dating, constantly socializing, building that large circle of people we trust—this is the time when we meet our forever friends. Loneliness is a problem for the elderly, not for twenty-somethings. When this isn't our experience, we feel like a failure, which only exacerbates our perception and sensitivity to loneliness.

Counter to conventional wisdom, our twenties are not necessarily the best years of our lives for making memories or building relationships. A poll conducted by YouGov in 2021 found that, among 13,557 American adults, most actually believe the best decade is the one they're in. The exception was people in their sixties and seventies, who fondly indicated it was their thirties. It's only while you're in your twenties that this decade has this elevated sense of importance, but rest easy: the best is seemingly yet to come.

It certainly doesn't help that this decade is naturally one of significant transitions and experiences that are inherently lonely at times. It is a period that our previously mentioned and favorite psychoanalyst, Erik Erikson, called the battle between identity and isolation, in which we are pushing for those committed relationships while simultaneously undergoing a number of life changes that force us into isolation. We graduate high school and leave the security of a convenient, built-in community to go out into the world on our own. For most of us, that involves saying goodbye to friendships and connections that we'll naturally outgrow. The first eighteen years of our lives are very much cut-and-paste. And then suddenly you're twenty-three, one of your friends is about to get married, some of your friends are still in college, half of you are working full-time, another one is off in Peru exploring the world—you're scattered across the country and friendship is no longer convenient. There's also the fact that, as our circumstances and environment change, we are changing as well.

The person I was at twenty-one, let alone eighteen, is so, so different from who I am now. So our ability to connect and feel seen also changes, especially as we step into a new identity. If we don't really know ourselves yet, it's hard to feel that others can know us deeply. For most, our twenties are the time when we move out of our family home and leave the orbit of the family unit—specifically our parents. At first it might feel incredibly liberating—perhaps even overdue—to be free of parental supervision and to have independence. But it's also very comforting to have that stable support system to come home to. It provides the belonging we need as a species, and in its absence there can be a bit of an emotional vortex. We might go through our first breakup, experiencing for the first time what it feels like to be so close to someone, spend 80 percent of our time with them, and then have that connection disappear almost overnight. In the aftermath, we find ourselves clawing back into the friendships we've neglected while we've been consumed by love.

There are some other typical events and experiences that contribute to social isolation the further we get into our twenties. As we enter the workplace, the time we have to build and maintain healthy connections is minimized by our paid obligations. Socializing is reserved for the hours before nine a.m. and after five p.m. We simply have less time. Our priorities change, not just with work and our careers, but with the entry of prominent long-term romantic partners. We all know what it's like to watch a friend enter a new relationship and know our friendship is now going to come in second. This series of events and transitions contributes to a monumental sense of isolation and, in part, confusion about what happens next—whether we just have to accept that our social lives are bound to diminish as we age or continue to feel like something is lacking.

While this feeling is unpleasant and even damaging at times, I believe that when we fear loneliness and villainize this emotional experience, we actually deprive ourselves of the many benefits it has to offer. If we don't learn how to be alone and are so fearful of this reaction that we rush into any new friendship or relationship that presents itself, we actually do more harm than good.

We are being controlled by the feeling and allowing it to stifle our growth, rather than accepting it as part of the human experience.

There is something sacred in solitude, in knowing that you will always have yourself, that you can be your own best friend, you can leave behind those relationships and what feels comfortable, even if loneliness is a side effect.

The other hard truth is that, at some point, you are going to feel lonely no matter how hard you try to avoid it. Your circumstances will change, something may interrupt your normal pattern of socializing, or your threshold for avoiding loneliness becomes so high that even you cannot satisfy it. One way of seeing loneliness is as a discrepancy between our actual and desired level of connection. This shows us how our tolerance for loneliness is subjective, based on the level of interaction we actually want, but also how we can perhaps become too reliant on others as a way to avoid negative feelings. Our desired level of connection can increase beyond what is physically possible within any given day, until we find ourselves lonely in a crowded room, even among those we love the most, because we are so focused on avoiding loneliness that we aren't actually getting what we need out of our relationships.

Valuing Solitude

Time spent alone is so important, especially in our twenties. It allows us to actually enjoy the time we spend with others, understand which relationships might be better left in the past, develop a better understanding of ourselves, and become more independent because we are not reliant on the company of others to do the things we want. Solitude allows us to really think deeply about who we are and what we want. I've seen these benefits for myself.

When I was twenty years old, I went through a heartbreak so devastating and isolating I thought the only solution to my grief was complete solitude. I needed my sadness to completely take over before I could move through it. I needed to be alone with the emotion instead of distracting myself with the company of others. To be honest, I had become so reliant on this person—but also so anxious about my friends abandoning me—that I wanted to force myself to be alone just to prove that everything could fall apart, I could be the loneliest I'd ever be, and I would still do okay.

So I spent two months by myself back in the town where I spent my childhood. Every day, I would walk alone along the beach, hike alone, wake up when I wanted, spend my days making silly pottery creations and my nights crying, refusing to pick up the phone and call someone because I thought what I needed was to manage this by myself. It was almost like self-imposed exile. I can admit now: That definitely wasn't the answer. That level of extreme solitude is not something I would endorse.

However, in that period I experienced the kind of magnificent growth you only see in fictionalized coming-of-age movies. I had never been clearer about what I wanted my future to look like. It allowed me to regain my confidence in my own abilities, because each day I learned to rely on myself, to listen to my intuition, to manage my emotions on my own. An increasing number of studies are providing evidence that solitude increases productivity and that loneliness improves empathy and leads to greater feelings of independence and reduced stress. In those moments of loneliness, whether self-enforced or involuntary, we often don't see the many ways we are being allowed to grow, how truly sacred our solitude is. **In a world that is more connected than ever, it is a radical act to accept your loneliness as a normal, if not beneficial, part of the human experience.**

This doesn't mean you have to constantly be excited by your loneliness or just "get over it." It is still, naturally, very uncomfortable, but that doesn't mean it has to be your enemy, if you a) recognize that it's normal and will pass, and b) embrace some of the opportunities it provides. If you want to embrace solitude, you have to start before you begin to feel lonely. **Being able to tolerate loneliness is a skill, and that skill needs to be practiced, so that when the time comes that your loneliness is not voluntary, you know what to do.** Don't panic. Find time during your week to do solitary activities. It could be as simple as going to the movies alone or to a new café by yourself, or taking solo day trips. With each of these experiences, you'll slowly adjust and train your mind to accept loneliness as part of your reality. Therefore, you'll see fewer of the negative emotional side effects.

Another way to embrace loneliness is to acknowledge that it is a natural response to a need of yours not being met, and that need doesn't always have a social origin. Sometimes loneliness emerges from not feeling connected with yourself, and no amount of excessive socializing will restore your most crucial relationship—the relationship you have with yourself. The natural instinct is to minimize this feeling by filling up your social calendar, but at the end of the night or the end of the week, you will find yourself back in the same position. Lonely, lost, wondering why your back-to-back engagements didn't help.

If you can, spend a day each week filling up your own cup so that you can, first, feel connected with yourself and, second, give

your full self when you do see friends, rather than running your social battery flat. As the age-old saying goes, quality over quantity, and that applies to our social interactions as well. Schedule activities with friends you actually enjoy, rather than just filling the empty space in your calendar with whatever you can.

Finally, explore your own secret gardens. Our secret gardens are the private parts of us that only we get to enjoy, the things we are inspired by that other people would be surprised to know. It's the part of ourselves we keep behind lock and key because it is so precious. The things we do when no one is around. It could be that you feel joy toward the strangest things, like people-watching or seeing old people hold hands. It could be your creativity, the small songs you make up in your head, how interesting your dreams are, how deeply you love, how much care you show animals, the poems you write in your notes app, how dedicated you are to your goals, your spirituality, your great music taste, your secret special talent. These are the parts of you that don't require external validation and you can find peace in when you feel disconnected from those around you. In our secret gardens, we are protected from loneliness.

It's important to pause here and acknowledge that loneliness is not "opt in." Some of the above examples approach loneliness as an inevitable future worry, not something we are currently experiencing. But loneliness affects everyone, and many of us are held up in its depths right now. Loneliness is one of the universal truths of human existence, not something to be ashamed of or to run from. You have all the necessary tools and relationships to feel connected once again. In those moments of feeling completely powerless over the feeling, I want to offer you four important mantras for pushing through.

I haven't met all the people who will love me. Life is long, and there are beautiful people and connections in my future that I can't foresee. I am so excited for the moments I will meet these people.

I am never truly alone. My brain has just convinced me I am as a survival mechanism. There are people who love me even if I am incapable of seeing it right now.

Nothing stays the same forever. This feeling will pass, as all good and bad things in life do.

My loneliness is my friend. I will take this opportunity to grow my self-knowledge and get in touch with what I want and what I value.

- - - - - - - - -

CHAPTER V

Mental Health—The Conversations We Aren't Having

WE'VE SPOKEN A lot about the challenges of our twenties so far, but one subject we've only touched the surface of is our mental health. It's ironic that this should come at the end of my book, considering that for many of us our mental health exists at the center of our lives during this decade. It can be the black cloud over our everyday, the surprise visits from our anxious thoughts when we least expect them, the days we want to stay in bed but force ourselves to keep going even as the world loses color and interest. It's the thoughts and impulses we can't control, the milestones and goals that seem just a bit harder, the string that binds so many of our experiences together. It's also incredibly isolating. When an illness originates in our mind, it is difficult to share with others, because it's so uniquely personal and, at times, indescribable.

How can we explain something that we can't see, can't touch, can't articulate? How can we make people understand something that is as unique and complicated as us, and therefore receive the empathy and support we need? Our experiences are so hard to see, and when they can be seen, people feel uncomfortable. It means we face a catch-22: pretend to be okay and never receive the support we need, or be open about our health and be stigmatized instead. It's a battle I understand really well.

When I was fourteen, I had my first panic attack. On the surface level it was about death and how inevitable it felt, but deeper than that it was about a lack of control and anxiety over the future. Once I'd had the first one, they never really went away. They would come in response to more than just my internal worries: friends, exams, my body, my family. I could go a few months feeling completely stable, only to suddenly have a breakdown on the train on a random Monday evening.

By nineteen, my anxiety had been joined by depression. Clinical research tells us this is a classic combination, the unhappy couple of the mental health world. At my lowest points during my twenties so far, I would make constant lists of things to look forward to in order to stop myself from thinking about the alternative. Life felt so heavy that the gravity of it all would keep me in bed for days, only rising to eat from my stockpile of frozen meals. I worried that I shouldn't have kids because of how crippling I assumed postpartum depression would be for me, that I maybe wouldn't survive it, or would never find someone to love me enough during my rough days to want me for my bright ones. The worst moment for me, which I rarely speak about, was the time my boyfriend admitted me to the hospital, calling in my parents from out of state to come and take care of me. Eventually they sent me home with some sedatives and a number to call if things got bad again. It hasn't been that bad again yet, but as anyone with a mental illness will tell you, it always feels like there's a countdown going on somewhere, ticking away until the symptoms start up again and reality takes on that different, disturbing, distressing hue.

To some extent society has come a long way in how we talk about this subject. But in writing about my experiences, I still considered what you, the reader, would think of me. Whether, in your mind, I'm now an unreliable narrator, less trustworthy, weak. Did I embarrass myself? Did I make you uncomfortable? There is an internalized stigma still present in these narratives. We may be better at acknowledging the existence of mental illness, its impact, talking about it with our mates, but there are a number of conversations we aren't having that still create a global deficit in understanding. These are the conversations I wish I'd had earlier, ones that would have offered information, recognition, and above all else: hope.

Conversation One: Mental Health Is Not "One Size Fits All"

About 13 percent of the world's population has a mental health disorder. The number is likely far higher when we consider the lower rates of reporting in countries with high levels of prejudice and stigma or with underdeveloped healthcare systems and mental health services. Regardless, that's a huge number of people and they make up a large portion of society: Shouldn't mental illness be a lot more visible? How come every eighth person we encounter on the street doesn't appear mentally ill? That's because we have been taught that poor mental health is meant to look a certain way, when it actually looks entirely different for everyone, the same way we all have different personalities, values, interests, or preferences.

In movies, the media, the news, and so on, people with mental health problems are typically depicted as one of two stereotypes: **the violent or the sad—but not complex.** The violent depiction of mental illness is the one I think we commonly encounter in the news. It's the person who has a complete mental break, can no longer control their impulses, becomes totally detached from reality, and proceeds to be aggressive to others. We see countless articles and news stories depicting mentally unwell people like this, when in truth, people with serious mental health conditions are much more likely to be victims of violent crimes than perpetrators. People who are receiving support and treatment are no more violent than anybody else in the community, but this narrative serves to villainize mental illness.

In contrast to the violent archetype, we have the sad stereotype. We often see this play out in film and television, depicting people who experience poor mental health as sluggish, isolated, unable to function in society. This portrayal is equally dangerous, because it is just as limiting. It depicts us as helpless individuals who are unable to live fulfilling lives, perpetuating this myth that mental illness resigns you to living a bleak and joyless existence. Again, not true. People with mental illnesses go on to run for government, start businesses, start families, create beautiful art, live beautiful lives, form community, and thrive.

So many of us cannot see ourselves in either stereotype, and even when we can, the narrative is still simplistic and incomplete. Each of us experiences this differently. Each of us has a different combination of symptoms, a different reality, a different personality, a different support network and upbringing, a different journey. When we apply a one-size-fits-all approach, it means so many of our unique experiences are excluded as soon as they don't meet people's expectations for what a mentally unwell person looks like. It keeps people invisible both to the system and to others, because if you don't present in a certain way, you must be "putting it on." In that sense, it also keeps the stigma alive, a stigma that says poor mental health is dangerous, disorderly, dysfunctional, and therefore shameful.

The *Diagnostic and Statistical Manual of Mental Disorders,* or *DSM*—the ultimate guidebook on mental health conditions, from mood disorders such as anxiety and depression to psychotic disorders and neurodevelopmental disorders, among many others—lists over three hundred different mental health conditions. Not all of those fall into the violent or sad category. Even within that, there are thousands of unique criteria people can either meet or not meet, each of which forms a unique profile, and even those criteria aren't exactly specific. One of the *DSM* criteria for major depressive disorder is a "markedly diminished interest or pleasure in all, or almost all, activities most of the day, nearly every day," also known as anhedonia. For one person, that might look like social withdrawal, wanting to stay at home all day; for another it may be no longer finding the motivation to enjoy hobbies but still wanting to see friends, or still pursuing hobbies but being completely indifferent to experiences like holidays, going out to eat, celebrations, or hitting major milestones. Or you could have none of that but a great deal of fatigue and feelings of emptiness.

Your experience does not have to meet the criteria of what others expect a mentally unwell person to look like. Mental illness is not for appearances; it should not have to meet others' expectations. Just because you don't "look" depressed, or anxious, or psychotic, or overwhelmed, doesn't mean that it's not your daily reality.

Conversation Two: You're Not Broken Just Because Your Reality Is Different

Just because your reality is different doesn't mean you're broken or damaged goods. Sometimes the hard things we experience make us believe we are, by default, hard to love. Who would take on a "burden" even we don't want to carry: the burden of seeing the world and ourselves differently, and occasionally harshly? The burden of not being "normal," as if such a thing exists. This is one of the greatest fallacies our mental health convinces us of, and it is influenced by the remnants of a society that has long overly pathologized and criminalized emotional and mental distress or differences.

The thing that I've found, time and time again, is that people who battle with their minds are often more compassionate, more honest, more loving, more forgiving, more emotive than most people—all of which makes them excellent partners, friends, companions, and children. For centuries there has been a known relationship between mental illness and creativity. Some types of neurodivergence give people incredible abilities and sometimes even the label of "savant"—an exceptionally talented person or genius when it comes to a specific domain like mathematics, or memory, or languages. We are exceptionally resilient, self-aware, and introspective; we go on to form communities among ourselves and other people with our lived experience. We change attitudes and promote open conversations.

This isn't to suggest that mental health conditions seemingly have "perks" or "benefits." It's more that if people won't accept you because your reality is different, they are the ones missing out by closing themselves off. **You are not your mental health condition. You are more than that.** You deserve someone who loves you, mental health and all—not IN SPITE of it. The other reason we need to retire this idea that we are "broken" is because it implicitly emphasizes that we need to be "fixed." **You don't need saving; you need support.** There will always be people who glamorize mental health disorders or who project themselves onto our experiences in order to live out some version of themselves through us. They want to be the savior.

In psychology, the "savior complex" refers to the strong tendency some people have to seek out others who rely on them for help or assistance in order to feel like a good person. These are the people who want to "fix" or "save" us. When we examine their motivations more deeply, these people benefit from your needing them; they have ulterior motives to keep you stuck in a dark place. It's not always conscious, but if your relationship has been founded on someone else's savior complex, and those are the roles you've self-assigned, it's hard for you to learn other ways to cope and manage, because it means you might need them less. And they might, therefore, need you less as well.

Mental illness does not make you broken, as if you were once whole before things shifted, or as if you were born missing something essential. When we stop using this language, it stops us from feeling like a burden, like someone who needs fixing. Then we're just individuals with a different reality, one that has a legitimate place in—and is a benefit to—society.

Conversation Three: It Won't Be Like This Forever

When you're struggling with mental health, one of the most annoying things you can hear is "It gets better." You probably know it's true, but it doesn't bring the kind of comfort people think it will. How can we focus on "better" when we're just trying to survive? "Better" is for people who have the mental energy and resources to plan for the future. But I'm going to be that person today and tell you: It might not get better all at once, but the only thing promised in life is change. The bad times are not excluded here. They will change into better times as well.

One of the most existential and terrifying thoughts I had when I was at my lowest points was that I was going to be like this forever. I remember my mum saying to me, "This is never going to go away, it will always be part of your life in some capacity, so you'll have to find a way to cope." She wasn't wrong, and I knew it at the time, but that wasn't the complete story. Struggling with our mental health is like surfing a wave: sometimes you are in a flow state and it becomes completely reflexive, you don't think about it at all; other times you're being flung off the board, into the rushing water, and, for lack of a better word, drowning. As you gain coping skills, as you learn to preempt certain episodes, as you make adjustments to your life, as you become more informed, better understand what you need from your loved ones, find the right therapist or people, you get better at surfing the waves. You gain expertise. Of course, there are times when a rogue wave will still knock you off, but you will have the experience to know you'll make it back on the board eventually.

It may be comforting to know that, even among people with some of the most serious mental illnesses, the older we get the milder our symptoms become. Aging seems to be a powerful antidote and is associated with an improvement in mental health. I guess as our physical and cognitive functions decline, we have one thing to look forward to. But right now, in our twenties, it's the trenches. Everything about the human experience and the adult experience is new to us, including the mental distress and lows that come with it. Be gentle with yourself—this was not a choice. Mental illness is not "opt in" and you didn't get to choose this reality or the way your brain works, so you have no reason to blame yourself for the way things have turned out or the ways it makes your life different.

You have to hold on to what is good in life, what is real, what you can control, and what your future will bring, knowing that there is a way forward for you—as there was for me, as there was for the millions of people who have come before you, fought the same battles, and survived. So many of the most brilliant parts of your life haven't happened yet, and they won't happen until your thirties, your forties, maybe even your eighties. I want you to be there to see it and to be able to look back at what this decade has brought you: the lessons, the hardship, the resilience—and know that it was you all along who had your back and pulled you through.

There is no one way mental health "should" look. Your experience is valid even if it doesn't match what people expect.

Mental illness doesn't make you broken. You don't need fixing, or saving, or to hide away.

The right people will stay by you. The best people will show up for you.

Your story is still being written. Within the triumphs and joy, there will be hard times that you will meet with resilience. Hold out for the future you and the hindsight they will bring to your situation.

Conclusion

This decade is important, but it's not everything. You would be forgiven for thinking it is, given the overall theme of this book. But for all the pressure placed on our twenties to be "the best years of our lives," there are still many more years, and many more decades, yet to come. At thirty, you are still so young and have your whole life ahead of you, and at forty, the same goes. Not all your decisions need to be made right away. You're not required to have all the answers just yet, and you probably never will. Besides, how boring would it be if you did? It would strip all the excitement from our lives if, by our twenties, we already knew how the next fifty years were going to go. If we knew who we'd end up with, the names of all the friends we would ever meet, what our job would end up being, where we would live, and how much money we would inevitably make . . . Where's the fun in that? May as well pack up and go home right now. The chaos and confusion definitely feel uncomfortable, but it's better than a predictable and lifeless alternative, so lean in. Lean in to how lost you feel, lean in to the heartbreak, the isolation, the career anxiety, because although it feels awkward and difficult now, you will eventually look back at this time fondly and find that the chaos was the foundation for some amazing memories and lessons.

Another big idea to keep in mind? Don't take yourself too seriously! It may sound hypocritical of me to say, but there is such a thing as being too self-aware, and it strips a lot of the joy out of life. I've found myself in that mindset before, trying to draw an invisible line between all my experiences, or seeking some explanation for the present in the past, or searching for the final thing I needed to "heal" in myself to finally be happy. Here's what I've learned.

First, hyperawareness made me miserable. Second, not everything has an answer, scientific explanation, or solution. Sometimes things just happen or are felt for no rhyme or reason, and you'll run yourself into the ground trying to apply meaning to them. Give yourself a break from overanalyzing your life for a second, step back from the self-help content, and just sit in your life and feel. Oftentimes in our search for a reason or a solution to our biggest problems, we end up losing touch with what it means to just be human and to feel, hold, touch, and experience this existence. Being present is sometimes the greatest antidote and the greatest gift you can give yourself in your search for clarity.

Finally, it may be unsettling to hear, but nothing about this decade is a unique experience. Not your situationship, or your quarter-life crisis, your loneliness, or your career confusion. Somewhere in the world someone is going through the exact same thing as you. I find a lot of comfort in knowing that there is a twenty-five-year-old in Vietnam or Kenya, Ireland or New Zealand, worrying about job security, watching their parents get older, feeling like they don't have enough friends—and yet we all figure it out. You and all these other people are on the same team, living through the same emotional turbulence.

So, as you close this book, I hope you take with you a sense of reassurance. Whether it's a quarter-life crisis, your identity, your love life, your friendships, your career path, your finances, your past: you're going to figure it out. **You're going to survive. It's all**

going to make sense one day. The struggles you face are not a sign of failure, but of growth. The moments of doubt are just as important as the moments of certainty, and the journey is far from over. Embrace the uncertainty, lean in to the discomfort, and trust that, in time, everything will fall into place, because you are still, at the end of the day, a person in progress.

Acknowledgments

My favorite part of any book has always been the acknowledgments because they feel so intimate. It feels surreal to be writing my own. When I first started writing this book, it was like a dream sequence. Part of me forgot the book was ever going to be published, because just the act of writing a book has been a life-long goal since I was a child, and it felt so strange that it was actually happening, especially a book that felt as important as this. I recently went looking through my childhood journals and found an entry from when I was nine years old that listed my number-one goal in life: Be an author.

I want to thank the listeners of *The Psychology of Your 20s* above all else for making this possible. I feel connected to each one of you through our shared experiences, knowing that somewhere across the world someone is listening to my words and thinking, "I thought I was the only one." It is cliché, but you have all changed my life, and my gratitude for our community of kind, thoughtful, intelligent individuals is overflowing.

My agent, Shelby Schenkman. My wish for any podcaster or creator is to find their Shelby. She takes the smallest dreams and makes them bigger and greater than you can ever imagine. I am so grateful she found me. I also want to thank Joanna Orland at United Talent Agency for her support and joy.

Dan Milaschewski, my literary agent, for always making sure I knew my worth as a new writer, and who came on board with so much enthusiasm and encouragement. I'm always excited for our random NYC catch-ups.

I'd also like to thank my many colleagues at Nous for not only allowing me but helping me to balance a full-time job, my podcast, and this book all at once. Your patience and encouragement was an important part of this journey.

My editors, Marnie Cochran and Katherine Leak at Rodale Books. None of this would be possible without your trust, reinforcement, expertise, and valuable contributions. Thank you for always finding a way to work with our crazy time zones; hopefully this means the end of late night and early morning Zoom calls for a bit.

To my mum. Thank you for introducing us to *This American Life* and every podcast under the sun when we were kids, and thank you for being supportive of all my choices, even when they weren't the most stable. You are my hero. To my dad, I think you understand me better than anyone. I'm so glad we have a relationship where we can speak so openly about our struggles and feelings. Thank you for making me feel seen. My sisters, Ellie and Hannah, thank you for making me a big sister; I can't wait to keep growing old with you both.

My Panda and Missy Chrissy, not only grandparents but also dear friends (but pretty amazing grandparents as well). Thank you for the baked goods, traditions, and warm memories.

My grandma Val, thank you for creating the most magical moments and home for all your grandchildren. And to my late Pa, you raised a scraggly brood of curious souls who love each other more than anything, and I know you would be so proud. We miss you.

My partner, Tom, for being so patient and wise and for making me laugh. You taught me true love. How did I get so lucky?

Finally, I say that our friends are the relationships that define this decade more than any other, and I've learned that from experience. Kate, thank you for sharing my anxieties about the world and being so silly with me, always. Meg, thank you for being my sounding board and a true rock in my life for all these years. Jack, thank you for listening to every small or big idea I have and always telling me to go for it. I also want to thank my dear friends Erin, Steph, Sarah, Gracie, Zoe, EJ, Erika, and many others, for always hyping me up and letting me cancel as many plans, phone calls, and dinners as I needed to get this book done. Thank you to my office buddies, Alex and Sally, for holding me up and being my trusted advisors.

This feels like a historical document for me, one that I'll return to when my own children are going through their twenties and I've long forgotten what it feels like. Thank you for reading.

Notes

Section I: The Quarter-Life Opportunity

Chapter I: Welcome to Your Quarter-Life Crisis

8 **Our brains are not particularly great:** Grupe, D. W., & Nitschke, J. B. (2013). Uncertainty and Anticipation in Anxiety: An Integrated Neurobiological and Psychological Perspective. *Nature Reviews Neuroscience, 14*(7), 488–501.

8 **The American psychologist Abraham Maslow:** Maslow, A. H. (1954). *Motivation and Personality.* Harper & Row.

8 **In 2020, a group of researchers:** Kim, E. S., Shiba, K., Boehm, J. K., & Kubzansky, L. D. (2020). Sense of Purpose in Life and Five Health Behaviors in Older Adults. *Preventive Medicine, 139,* 106172.

Chapter II: The Art of Fucking Up

15 **The Olympic snowboarder Lindsey Jacobellis:** Pinelli, B. (March 21, 2024). Olympic Snowboardcross Champion Lindsey Jacobellis Shows No Sign of Slowing Down. Team USA. teamusa.com/news/2024/march/21/olympic-snowboardcross-champion-lindsey-jacobellis-shows-no-sign-of-slowing-down.

15 **Back in 1997, researchers:** Dunbar, R., Duncan, N., & Marriott, A. (1997). Human Conversational Behavior. *Human Nature, 8*(3), 231–246.

17 **In the 2015 study:** Aczel, B., Palfi, B., & Kekecs, Z. (2015). What Is Stupid? People's Conception of Unintelligent Behavior. *Intelligence, 53,* 51–58.

17 **the "Dunning-Kruger effect":** Gaze, E. C. (October 3, 2023). The Dunning-Kruger Effect Isn't What You Think It Is. *Scientific American.*

23 the term "failure deprived": Bennett, J. (June 24, 2017). On Campus, Failure Is on the Syllabus. *The New York Times*. nytimes.com/2017/06/24/fashion/fear-of-failure.html.

Chapter III: Risky Business

30 Fear is what keeps us safe: Adolphs, R. (2013). The Biology of Fear. *Current Biology, 23*(2).

32 There are three kinds of people: Durlauf, S., & Blume, L. (2008). Risk Aversion. In *The New Palgrave Dictionary of Economics*. Palgrave Macmillan.

33 A paper by researchers: Eisenberg, A. E., Baron, J., & Seligman, M. E. P. (1998). Individual Differences in Risk Aversion and Anxiety. University of Pennsylvania. sas.upenn.edu/~baron/papers.htm/amyold.html.

34 Bounded risks are amazing: School of Life (March 13, 2024). On Bounded and Unbounded Tasks. theschooloflife.com/article/on-bounded-and-unbounded-tasks/.

Chapter IV: The Paradox of Choice

41 the poet Sylvia Plath: Plath, S. (1963). *The Bell Jar*. Heinemann.

42 In 2000, psychologists: Iyengar, S. S., & Lepper, M. R. (2000). When Choice Is Demotivating: Can One Desire Too Much of a Good Thing? *Journal of Personality and Social Psychology, 79*(6), 995–1006.

44 one of my favorite studies: Roese, N. J., & Summerville, A. (2005). What We Regret Most . . . And Why. *Personality and Social Psychology Bulletin, 31*(9), 1273–1285.

44 The average person tends: How Many Career Changes in a Lifetime? University of Queensland (2023). study.uq.edu.au/stories/how-many-career-changes-lifetime.

45 Each of us has a way: Ramachandran, V. S., Vajanaphanich, M., & Chunharas, C. (2016). Calendars in the Brain: Their Perceptual Characteristics and Possible Neural Substrate. *Neurocase, 22*(5), 461–465.

Chapter V: The Battle for Authenticity

50 Researchers normally list: Cartwright, T., Hulbert-Williams, L., Evans, G., & Hulbert-Williams, N. (2023). Measuring Authentic Living from In-

ternal and External Perspectives: A Novel Measure of Self-Authenticity. *Social Sciences & Humanities Open, 8*(1), 100698.

51 **known as the "false self":** Winnicott, D. W. (1960). Ego Distortion in Terms of the True and False Self. In *The Maturational Process and the Facilitating Environment* (pp. 140–152). International Universities Press.

54 **It also creates a "spotlight effect":** Gilovich, T., Medvec, V. H., & Savitsky, K. (2000). The Spotlight Effect in Social Judgment: An Egocentric Bias in Estimates of the Salience of One's Own Actions and Appearance. *Journal of Personality and Social Psychology, 78*(2), 211–222.

55 **Start with a big list:** Carr, B. (April 11, 2013). Live Your Core Values: 10-Minute Exercise to Increase Your Success. TapRooT Root Cause Analysis. taproot.com/live-your-core-values-exercise-to-increase-your-success/.

56 **Your flow state is when you feel:** Gold, J., & Ciorciari, J. (2020). A Review on the Role of the Neuroscience of Flow States in the Modern World. *Behavioral Sciences, 10*(9), 137.

56 **The coiner of this term:** Csikszentmihalyi, M. (2008). Flow, the Secret to Happiness. TED Talk. ted.com/talks/mihaly_csikszentmihalyi_flow_the_secret_to_happiness.

Section II: Love on the Brain

Chapter I: The Psychology of Attraction

64 **Things like scent, facial symmetry:** Nahman, H. (March 30, 2022). Why Are We Obsessed with Symmetrical Faces? An Investigation. *The Guardian.* theguardian.com/lifeandstyle/2022/mar/30/symmetry-filters-tiktok-symmetrical-faces-beauty.

65 **Those personal preferences:** Feinberg, D. R., Jones, B. C., Little, A. C., Burt, D. M., & Perrett, D. I. (2005). Manipulations of Fundamental and Formant Frequencies Influence the Attractiveness of Human Male Voices. *Animal Behavior, 69*(3), 561–568.

65 **We've all heard the myth:** Strachey, J., Freud, A., Strachey, A., & Tyson, A. (1961). The Dissolution of the Oedipus Complex. In *The Standard Edition*

of the Complete Psychological Works of Sigmund Freud (pp. 173–179). Hogarth Press.

65 **For women and girls:** Khan, M., & Haider, K. (2015). Girls' First Love: Their Fathers. Freudian Theory Electra Complex. *Research Journal of Language, Literature and Humanities, 2*(11), 1–4.

65 **we are really attracted:** Gordon, A. (March 27, 2022). The Role of Familiarity in Attraction. *Psychology Today.* psychologytoday.com/au/blog/between-you-and-me/202203/the-role-familiarity-in-attraction.

65 **the formula for attraction:** Goddard, N. (2012). Social Psychology. In *Core Psychiatry* (pp. 63–82). Saunders Elsevier.

66 **One of my favorite studies:** Faur, S., & Laursen, B. (2022). Classroom Seat Proximity Predicts Friendship Formation. *Frontiers in Psychology, 13.*

66 **Other research conducted:** Anton, C. E., & Lawrence, C. (2014). Home Is Where the Heart Is: The Effect of Place of Residence on Place Attachment and Community Participation. *Journal of Environmental Psychology, 40,* 451–461.

67 **people assume that "opposites attract":** Philipp-Muller, A., Wallace, L. E., Sawicki, V., Patton, K. M., & Wegener, D. T. (2020). Understanding When Similarity-Induced Affective Attraction Predicts Willingness to Affiliate: An Attitude Strength Perspective. *Frontiers in Psychology, 11.*

67 **When we share similar attitudes:** Hillman, J. G., Fowlie, D. I., & MacDonald, T. K. (2022). Social Verification Theory: A New Way to Conceptualize Validation, Dissonance, and Belonging. *Personality and Social Psychology Review, 27*(3), 309–331.

67 **In a number of studies:** Stevens, G., Owens, D., & Schaefer, E. C. (1990). Education and Attractiveness in Marriage Choices. *Social Psychology Quarterly, 53*(1), 62–70; Kent. M (2015). Most Americans Marry Within Their Race. Population Reference Bureau. prb.org/resources/most-americans-marry-within-their-race/; Van der Wal, R. C., Litzellachner, L. F., Karremans, J. C., Buiter, N., Breukel, J., & Maio, G. R. (2023). Values in Romantic Relationships. *Personality and Social Psychology Bulletin, 50*(7), 1066–1079.

68 **Psychologists Paul Ingram and Michael Morris:** Ingram, P., & Morris, M. W. (2007). Do People Mix at Mixers? Structure, Homophily, and the "Life of the Party." *Administrative Science Quarterly, 52*(4), 558–585.

68 **If you want a concrete estimate:** Hall, J. A. (2018). How Many Hours

Does It Take to Make a Friend? *Journal of Social and Personal Relationships, 36*(4), 1278–1296.

69 **One estimate by a researcher:** Grover, N. (July 12, 2021). Two-Thirds of Couples Start Out as Friends, Research Finds. *The Guardian.* theguardian .com/lifeandstyle/2021/jul/12/two-thirds-of-couples-start-out-as-friends -research-finds.

70 **principle known as the "scarcity effect":** Vinas, A., Blanco, F., & Matute, H. (2023). Scarcity Affects Cognitive Biases: The Case of the Illusion of Causality. *Acta Psychologica, 239,* 104007.

71 **a sign of an intensity addiction:** Earp, B. D., Wudarczyk, O. A., Foddy, B., & Savulescu, J. (2017). Addicted to Love: What Is Love Addiction and When Should It Be Treated? *Philosophy, Psychiatry, & Psychology, 24*(1), 77–92.

72 **One theory always drives this home:** Sternberg, R. J. (2007). Triangulating Love. In Oord, T. J. (ed.), *The Altruism Reader: Selections from Writings on Love, Religion, and Science* (p. 332). Templeton Foundation.

Chapter II: Myth-Busting Your Attachment Style

74 **Many people incorrectly diagnose:** Mickelson, K. D., Kessler, R. C., & Shaver, P. R. (1997). Adult Attachment in a Nationally Representative Sample. *Journal of Personality and Social Psychology, 73*(5), 1092–1106.

75 **The idea of attachment styles:** Bretherton, I. (1992). The Origins of Attachment Theory: John Bowlby and Mary Ainsworth. *Developmental Psychology, 28*(5), 759–775.

76 **Ainsworth demonstrated this:** Ainsworth, M. D. S., Blehar, M. C., Waters, E., & Wall, S. N. (2015 [1978]). *Patterns of Attachment: A Psychological Study of the Strange Situation.* Routledge.

76 **Our early patterns of relating:** Hazan, C., & Shaver, P. (1987). Romantic Love Conceptualized as an Attachment Process. *Journal of Personality and Social Psychology, 52*(3), 511–524.

77 **They feel anxious:** Simpson, J. A., & Rholes, W. S. (2017). Adult Attachment, Stress, and Romantic Relationships. *Current Opinion in Psychology, 13,* 19–24.

78 **no single experience creates:** Bowlby, J. (2001). Forty-Four Juvenile Thieves: Their Characters and Home-Life. In *The Mark of Cain* (pp. 155–162). Routledge.

80 **Research in psychology and neuroscience:** Andriopoulou, P. (2021). Healing Attachment Trauma in Adult Psychotherapy: The Role of Limited Reparenting. *European Journal of Psychotherapy & Counselling, 23*(4), 468–482.

80 **recent studies into adult romantic relationships:** Kansky, J., & Allen, J. P. (2018). Long-Term Risks and Possible Benefits Associated with Late Adolescent Romantic Relationship Quality. *Journal of Youth and Adolescence, 47*(7), 1531–1544; Moore, S., & Leung, C. (2002). Young People's Romantic Attachment Styles and Their Associations with Well-Being. *Journal of Adolescence, 25*(2), 243–255.

80 **Conscious remembering is especially powerful:** Schacter, D. L., & Thakral, P. P. (2024). Constructive Memory and Conscious Experience. *Journal of Cognitive Neuroscience, 36*(8), 1567–1577.

83 **One of the most fascinating:** Rubin, K. H., Dwyer, K. M., Booth-LaForce, C., Kim, A. H., Burgess, K. B., & Rose-Krasnor, L. (2004). Attachment, Friendship, and Psychosocial Functioning in Early Adolescence. *Journal of Early Adolescence, 24*(4), 326–356.

85 **researchers have begun:** Main, M., & Solomon, J. (1986). Discovery of a New, Insecure-Disorganized/Disoriented Attachment Pattern. *Affective Development in Infancy, 18*(1), 32–46.

Chapter III: Repeating History in Relationships

87 **There are myriad ways:** Darling Montero, M. (December 7, 2017). Is History Repeating Itself in Your Relationships? *HuffPost.* huffpost.com/entry /is-history-repeating-itse_b_672518.

88 **Repetition compulsion occurs:** Bibring, E. (1943). The Conception of the Repetition Compulsion. *Psychoanalytic Quarterly, 12*(4): 486–519.

89 **Repeating history in relationships may also occur:** Bibring, Conception of the Repetition Compulsion.

89 **On a more biological and neurological level:** Cooke, S. F. (2006). Plasticity in the Human Central Nervous System. *Brain, 129*(7), 1659–1673.

90 **Fantasy bonding occurs:** Firestone, R., & Catlett, J. (1985). *The Fantasy Bond: Structure of Psychological Defenses.* Human Sciences Press.

91 **In the pioneering study:** Felmlee, D. H. (1995). Fatal Attractions: Affection and Disaffection in Intimate Relationships. *Journal of Social and Personal Relationships, 12*(2), 295–311.

Chapter IV: The Stigma of Being Single

98 **One 2019 study:** Stavrova, O. (2019). Having a Happy Spouse Is Associated with Lowered Risk of Mortality. *Psychological Science, 30*(5), 798–803.

99 **"single-shaming" is on the rise:** Klein, J. (December 13, 2022). "Single Shaming": Why People Jump to Judge the Un-Partnered. *BBC News.* bbc.com/worklife/article/20220405-single-shaming-why-people-jump-to-judge-the-un-partnered.

100 **Gender schema theory was introduced:** Bem, S. L. (1981). Gender Schema Theory: A Cognitive Account of Sex Typing. *Psychological Review, 88*(4), 354–364.

101 **Some studies even suggest:** Patrick, W. (February 28, 2021). Why So Many Single Women Without Children Are Happy. *Psychology Today.* psychologytoday.com/au/blog/why-bad-looks-good/202102/why-so-many-single-women-without-children-are-happy.

102 **In 2020, a group of researchers:** Apostolou, M.; O, J.; & Esposito, G. (2020). Singles' Reasons for Being Single: Empirical Evidence from an Evolutionary Perspective. *Frontiers in Psychology, 11.*

104 **As conceived by Baptist pastor:** Chapman, G. (2016). *The 5 Love Languages.* Moody Publishers.

105 **definitely gets a few things wrong:** Grady, C. (February 14, 2024). What the 5 Love Languages Get Right, and What They Get Very Wrong. *Vox.* vox.com/culture/24067506/5-love-languages-gary-chapman.

106 **known as "self-soothing touch":** Dreisoerner, A., Junker, N. M., Schlotz, W., Heimrich, J., Bloemeke, S., Ditzen, B., & van Dick, R. (2021). Self-Soothing Touch and Being Hugged Reduce Cortisol Responses to Stress: A Randomized Controlled Trial on Stress, Physical Touch, and Social Identity. *Comprehensive Psychoneuroendocrinology, 8,* 100091.

Chapter V: Unrequited Love and Situationships

110 **People high in sociosexuality:** Blasco-Belled, A., Zyskowska, E., Terebu, M., Włodarska, K. A., & Rogoza, R. (2021). Sociosexual Orientations and Well-Being: Differences Across Gender. *International Journal of Sexual Health, 34*(2), 254–266.

111 **We don't like feeling lonely:** Spielmann, S. S., MacDonald, G., Maxwell, J. A., Joel, S., Peragine, D., Muise, A., & Impett, E. A. (2013). Settling for

Less Out of Fear of Being Single. *Journal of Personality and Social Psychology, 105*(6), 1049–1073.

112 **For example, childhood exclusion:** Salmon, G., James, A., & Smith, D. M. (1998). Bullying in Schools: Self-Reported Anxiety, Depression, and Self-Esteem in Secondary School Children. *BMJ, 317*(7163), 924–925.

112 **In psychology, commitment readiness is:** Hadden, B., Agnew, C., & Tan, K. (2018). Commitment Readiness and Relationship Formation. *Personality and Social Psychology Bulletin, 44*(8), 1242–1257.

113 **The sunk-cost fallacy occurs when:** Arkes, H. R., & Blumer, C. (1985). The Psychology of Sunk Cost. *Organizational Behavior and Human Decision Processes, 35*(1), 124–140.

114 **We may think we want a relationship:** Keppler, N. (November 9, 2018). The Psychology of Commitment Phobia. *Vice.* vice.com/en/article/is-fear-of-commitment-real-what-to-do/.

Chapter VI: Heartbreak—Hurting, Healing, and Thriving

121 **This theory proposes that:** Fisher, H. E., Xu, X., Aron, A., & Brown, L. L. (2016). Intense, Passionate, Romantic Love: A Natural Addiction? How the Fields That Investigate Romance and Substance Abuse Can Inform Each Other. *Frontiers in Psychology, 7,* 687.

121 **These chemicals are the same:** Zou, Z., Song, H., Zhang, Y., & Zhang, X. (2016). Romantic Love vs. Drug Addiction May Inspire a New Treatment for Addiction. *Frontiers in Psychology, 7,* 1436.

121 **When researchers conducted studies:** Fisher, H. E., Brown, L. L., Aron, A., Strong, G., & Mashek, D. (2010). Reward, Addiction, and Emotion Regulation Systems Associated with Rejection in Love. *Journal of Neurophysiology, 104*(1), 51–60.

123 **This experience is quite literally painful:** Kross, E., Berman, M. G., Mischel, W., Smith, E. E., & Wager, T. D. (2011). Social Rejection Shares Somatosensory Representations with Physical Pain. *Proceedings of the National Academy of Sciences, 108*(15), 6270–6275.

123 **the loss of friends that often accompanies:** DePaulo, B. (August 3, 2022). The Pain and Shock of Losing Custody of Friends After a Breakup. *Psychology Today.* psychologytoday.com/au/blog/living-single/202208/the-pain-and-shock-losing-custody-friends-after-breakup.

124 **Certain studies have tried:** Lewandowski, G. W., & Bizzoco, N. M. (2007).

Addition Through Subtraction: Growth Following the Dissolution of a Low Quality Relationship. *Journal of Positive Psychology, 2*(1), 40–54; Divorce Takes 18 Months to Get Over. *The Telegraph* (October 30, 2009). telegraph.co.uk/news/uknews/6464020/Divorce-takes-18-months-to-get-over.html.

126 **In psychology, therapists like to talk:** Kübler-Ross, E. (1969). *On Death and Dying: What the Dying Have to Teach Doctors, Nurses, Clergy and Their Own Families.* Scribner.

130 **These involuntary memory flare-ups:** Jabr, F. (February 20, 2024). Mind-Pops: Psychologists Begin to Study an Unusual Form of Proustian Memory. *Scientific American.* scientificamerican.com/article/mind-pops/.

131 **The final explanation has to do:** Rosen, A. (May 30, 2024). How to Offer Support and Find Strength on a Trauma Anniversary. Johns Hopkins Bloomberg School of Public Health. publichealth.jhu.edu/2024/the-anniversary-effect-of-traumatic-experiences.

132 **known as the "Pollyanna principle":** Dember, W. N., & Penwell, L. (1980). Happiness, Depression, and the Pollyanna Principle. *Bulletin of the Psychonomic Society, 15*(5), 321–323.

133 **Closure occurs when:** McDonald, M. (2023). *Unbroken: The Trauma Response Is Never Wrong.* Sounds True.

133 **When we lack that closure:** Christensen, J. P. (2018). Human Cognition and Narrative Closure. In *The Routledge Handbook of Classics and Cognitive Theory* (pp. 139–155). Routledge.

135 **a study on rebound relationships:** Brumbaugh, C. C., & Fraley, R. C. (2014). Too Fast, Too Soon? An Empirical Investigation into Rebound Relationships. *Journal of Social and Personal Relationships, 32*(1), 99–118.

Chapter VII: Friendship—A Reason, a Season, a Lifetime

138 **There have been numerous studies:** Choi, K. W., Stein, M. B., Nishimi, K. M., Ge, T., Coleman, J. R. I., Chen, C.-Y., Ratanatharathorn, A., et al. (2020). An Exposure-Wide and Mendelian Randomization Approach to Identifying Modifiable Factors for the Prevention of Depression. *American Journal of Psychiatry, 177*(10), 944–954; Abrams, Z. (June 1, 2023). The Science of Why Friendship Keeps Us Healthy. *Monitor on Psychology, 54*(4), 42. apa.org/monitor/2023/06/cover-story-science-friendship.

138 **one of the most noteworthy:** Holt-Lunstad, J., Smith, T. B., & Layton,

J. B. (2010). Social Relationships and Mortality Risk: A Meta-Analytic Review. *PLoS Medicine, 7*(7), e1000316.

139 **There's also been recent research:** Bond, R. M., Fariss, C. J., Jones, J. J., Kramer, A. D., Marlow, C., Settle, J. E., & Fowler, J. H. (2012). A 61-Million-Person Experiment in Social Influence and Political Mobilization. *Nature, 489*(7415), 295–298.

139 **Scientists studying friendship in 2018:** Parkinson, C., Kleinbaum, A. M., & Wheatley, T. (2018). Similar Neural Responses Predict Friendship. *Nature Communications, 9*, 332.

140 **In one 2020 study:** Apostolou, M., & Keramari, D. (2020). What Prevents People from Making Friends: A Taxonomy of Reasons. *Personality and Individual Differences, 163*, 110043.

146 **Friendship breakups are especially hard:** Cesur-Soysal, G., & Arı, E. (2022). How We Disenfranchise Grief for Self and Other: An Empirical Study. *OMEGA—Journal of Death and Dying, 89*(2), 530–549.

147 **In the 1990s, the psychologist:** Dunbar, R. I. M. (1992). Neocortex Size as a Constraint on Group Size in Primates. *Journal of Human Evolution, 22*(6), 469–493.

Section III: Work in Progress

Chapter I: Imposter Syndrome and Self-Sabotage

156 **In some of the worst cases:** Maslow, A. H. (1971). *The Farther Reaches of Human Nature*. Penguin.

158 **A study conducted by KPMG:** Paulise, L. (August 3, 2023). 75% of Women Executives Experience Imposter Syndrome in the Workplace. *Forbes*. forbes.com/sites/lucianapaulise/2023/03/08/75-of-women-executives -experience-imposter-syndrome-in-the-workplace/.

158 **In fact, the initial research:** Clance, P. R., & Imes, S. A. (1978). The Imposter Phenomenon in High Achieving Women: Dynamics and Therapeutic Intervention. *Psychotherapy: Theory, Research & Practice, 15*(3), 241–247.

159 **In Australia, we have a term:** Feather, N. T. (1989). Attitudes Towards the High Achiever: The Fall of the Tall Poppy. *Australian Journal of Psychology, 41*(3), 239–267.

161 **In 1991, a group of researchers:** Herman, J. L., Kolk, B. A., & Perry, J. C. (1991). Childhood Origins of Self-Destructive Behavior. *American Journal of Psychiatry, 148*(12), 1665–1671.

162 **Freud was one of the first clinicians:** Kernberg, O. (2009). The Concept of the Death Drive: A Clinical Perspective. *International Journal of Psychoanalysis, 90*(5), 1009–1023.

Chapter II: Career Anxiety and the Myth of the Dream Job

171 **In 2019, a team of researchers:** James, S., Mallman, M., & Midford, S. (2019). University Students, Career Uncertainty, and the Culture of Authenticity. *Journal of Youth Studies, 24*(4), 466–480.

176 **For their book *Ikigai*:** García, H., & Miralles, F. (2017). *Ikigai: The Japanese Secret to a Long and Happy Life*. Penguin.

176 **exclusive club of five "blue zones":** Buettner, D., & Skemp, S. (2016). Blue Zones. *American Journal of Lifestyle Medicine, 10*(5), 318–321.

177 **This concept was introduced by:** Simon, H. A. (1956). Rational Choice and the Structure of the Environment. *Psychological Review, 63*(2), 129–138.

179 **It's no surprise that satisficers:** Lufkin, B. (March 30, 2021). Do "Maximisers" or "Satisficers" Make Better Decisions? *BBC News.* bbc.com/worklife/article/20210329-do-maximisers-or-satisficers-make-better-decisions.

180 **A recent longitudinal study:** Zhenjing, G., Chupradit, S., Ku, K. Y., Nassani, A. A., & Haffar, M. (2022). Impact of Employees' Workplace Environment on Employees' Performance: A Multi-Mediation Model. *Frontiers in Public Health, 10,* 890400.

Chapter III: Burnt-Out or Still Burning?

184 **In 2020, the American Psychological Association:** Abramson, A. (2020). Burnout and Stress Are Everywhere. *Monitor on Psychology, 53*(1), 72. apa.org/monitor/2022/01/special-burnout-stress.

184 **It also seems that the people:** Smith, M. (March 14, 2023). Burnout Is on

the Rise Worldwide—and Gen Z, Young Millennials and Women Are the Most Stressed. *CNBC*. cnbc.com/2023/03/14/burnout-is-on-the-rise-gen-z -millennials-and-women-are-the-most-stressed.html.

186 **professional and personal hazard:** Burn-Out an "Occupational Phenomenon": International Classification of Diseases. World Health Organization (May 28, 2019). who.int/news/item/28-05-2019-burn-out-an-occupational -phenomenon-international-classification-of-diseases.

187 **The term was coined:** Malesic, J. (2023). *The End of Burnout: Why Work Drains Us and How to Build Better Lives.* University of California Press.

187 **Freudenberger saw burnout occurring:** Freudenberger, H. J. (1974). Staff Burn-Out. *Journal of Social Issues, 30*(1), 159–165.

190 **Chronic high achievers:** Smits, J. C. (November 1, 2011). Field Guide to the Overachiever. *Psychology Today.* psychologytoday.com/au/articles/201111 /field-guide-the-overachiever.

Chapter IV: Money, Money, Money

196 **This takes its toll:** Ryu, S., & Fan, L. (2022). The Relationship Between Financial Worries and Psychological Distress Among U.S. Adults. *Journal of Family and Economic Issues, 44*(1), 16–33.

197 **"financial phobia":** Shapiro, G. K., & Burchell, B. J. (2012). Measuring Financial Anxiety. *Journal of Neuroscience, Psychology, and Economics, 5*(2), 92–103.

197 **In a pioneering study:** Bachelor, L. (February 2, 2003). Feel the Fear and Face the Finance. *The Guardian.* theguardian.com/money/2003/feb/02 /observercashsection.theobserver.

197 **The groups impacted the most:** Elsesser, K. (October 4, 2022). Women's Financial Health Hits Five-Year Low, According to New Survey. *Forbes.* forbes.com/sites/kimelsesser/2022/10/04/heres-why-women-are-worrying -about-money-more-than-men-according-to-new-survey/.

198 **In 2011, researchers:** Klontz, B., Britt, S. L., Mentzer, J., & Klontz, T. (2011). Money Beliefs and Financial Behaviors: Development of the Klontz Money Script Inventory. *Journal of Financial Therapy, 2*(1), 1–18.

199 **In 2013, a group of researchers:** Griskevicius, V., Ackerman, J. M., Cantú, S. M., Delton, A. W., Robertson, T. E., Simpson, J. A., Thompson, M. E., et al. (2013). When the Economy Falters, Do People Spend or Save? Re-

sponses to Resource Scarcity Depend on Childhood Environments. *Psychological Science, 24*(2), 197–205.

201 **If we avoid it long enough:** Duhigg, C. (2021). *The Power of Habit: Why We Do What We Do in Life and Business.* Random House.

205 **The act of purchasing something:** Rodrigues, R. I., Lopes, P., & Varela, M. (2021). Factors Affecting Impulse Buying Behavior of Consumers. *Frontiers in Psychology, 12,* 697080.

206 **creates a sense of loss aversion:** Sediyama, C. Y. N., de Castro Martins, C., Teodoro, M. L. M. (2020). Association of Loss Aversion, Personality Traits, Depressive, Anxious, and Suicidal Symptoms: Systematic Review. *Clinical Neuropsychiatry, 17*(5), 286–294.

Section IV: Everybody Is Healing from Something

Chapter I: Family Ties

213 **There's a famous quote:** Larkin, P. (2001). *Collected Poems.* Faber and Faber.

215 **Then there are things they:** Likhar, A., Baghel, P., & Patil, M. (2022). Early Childhood Development and Social Determinants. *Cureus, 14*(9), e29500.

215 **Recent estimates tell us:** Zwir, I., Arnedo, J., Del-Val, C., Pulkki-Råback, L., Konte, B., Yang, S. S., Romero-Zaliz, R., et al. (2018). Uncovering the Complex Genetics of Human Character. *Molecular Psychiatry, 25*(10), 2295–2312.

216 **The Big Five are as ominous:** Soldz, S., & Vaillant, G. E. (1999). The Big Five Personality Traits and the Life Course: A 45-Year Longitudinal Study. *Journal of Research in Personality, 33*(2), 208–232.

216 **In one of psychology's most groundbreaking:** Bandura, A., Ross, D., & Ross, S. A. (1961). Transmission of Aggression Through Imitation of Aggressive Models. *Journal of Abnormal and Social Psychology, 63*(3), 575–582.

219 **A 2005 survey showed:** Lyons, L. (April 3, 2005). Teens Stay True to Parents' Political Perspectives. Gallup. news.gallup.com/poll/14515/teens-stay-true-parents-political-perspectives.aspx.

221 **area where that becomes really apparent:** Jones, C. C., & Young, S. L. (2021). The Mother-Daughter Body Image Connection: The Perceived Role of Mothers' Thoughts, Words, and Actions. *Journal of Family Communication, 21*(2), 118–126.

223 **Abuse of any sort has the capacity:** Ibrahim, P., Almeida, D., Nagy, C., & Turecki, G. (2021). Molecular Impacts of Childhood Abuse on the Human Brain. *Neurobiology of Stress, 15,* 100343.

223 **studies conducted by McGill University researchers:** Lutz, P. E., Tanti, A., Gasecka, A., Barnett-Burns, S., Kim, J. J., Zhou, Y., Chen, G. G., et al. (2017). Association of a History of Child Abuse with Impaired Myelination in the Anterior Cingulate Cortex: Convergent Epigenetic, Transcriptional, and Morphological Evidence. *American Journal of Psychiatry, 174*(12), 1185–1194.

223 **I interviewed people:** Scott, J., & Matthews, B. (2023). The Australian Child Maltreatment Study. *Medical Journal of Australia, 218*(6), 3–56.

228 **We revert back:** Hunt, E. (December 6, 2023). I'm an Adult. Why Do I Regress Under My Parents' Roof? *The Guardian.* theguardian.com /wellness/2023/dec/06/adult-millennials-gen-z-regression-to-childhood.

Chapter II: Healing Your Inner Child

233 **This form of healing:** Davis, S. (July 13, 2020). The Wounded Inner Child. CPTSD Foundation. cptsdfoundation.org/2020/07/13/the-wounded-inner -child/.

233 **Who you were as an infant:** Sjöblom, M., Öhrling, K., Prellwitz, M., & Kostenius, C. (2016). Health Throughout the Lifespan: The Phenomenon of the Inner Child Reflected in Events During Childhood Experienced by Older Persons. *International Journal of Qualitative Studies on Health and Well-Being, 11*(1), 31486.

238 **Recent literature has acknowledged:** Marici, M., Clipa, O., Runcan, R., & Pîrghie, L. (2023). Is Rejection, Parental Abandonment or Neglect a Trigger for Higher Perceived Shame and Guilt in Adolescents? *Healthcare, 11*(12), 1724.

239 **This concept, introduced by:** Freyd, J. J. (1996). *Betrayal Trauma: The Logic of Forgetting Childhood Abuse.* Harvard University Press.

241 **From infancy, children strive to:** Over, H. (2016). The Origins of Belong-

ing: Social Motivation in Infants and Young Children. *Philosophical Transactions of the Royal Society B: Biological Sciences, 371*(1686), 20150072.

243 **The basis for inner-child healing:** Jackman, R. (2020). *Healing Your Lost Inner Child: How to Stop Impulsive Reactions, Set Healthy Boundaries and Embrace an Authentic Life.* Practical Wisdom Press.

243 **The longer you suppress them:** Bukar, A., Abdullah, A., Opara, J. A., Abdulkadir, M., & Hassan, A. (May 2019). Catharsis as a Therapy: An Overview on Health and Human Development. *Journal of Physical Health and Sports Medicine,* 31–35.

246 **A study published in 2019:** Mastandrea, S., Fagioli, S., & Biasi, V. (2019). Art and Psychological Well-Being: Linking the Brain to the Aesthetic Emotion. *Frontiers in Psychology, 10,* 739.

246 **Engaging in play:** Ho, W. W. (2022). Influence of Play on Positive Psychological Development in Emerging Adulthood: A Serial Mediation Model. *Frontiers in Psychology, 13,* 1057557.

Chapter III: Healing Your Inner Teen

251 **The psychoanalyst Erik Erikson:** Weiland, S. (1993). Erik Erikson: Ages, Stages, and Stories. *American Society on Aging, 17*(2), 17–22.

252 **The brain starts to remove connections:** Spear, L. P. (2013). Adolescent Neurodevelopment. *Journal of Adolescent Health, 52*(2), S7–S13.

252 **Some recent studies have suggested:** Kundakovic, M., & Rocks, D. (2022). Sex Hormone Fluctuation and Increased Female Risk for Depression and Anxiety Disorders: From Clinical Evidence to Molecular Mechanisms. *Frontiers in Neuroendocrinology, 66,* 101010.

256 **One 2013 study:** Smith, C. V., & Shaffer, M. J. (2013). Gone but Not Forgotten: Virginity Loss and Current Sexual Satisfaction. *Journal of Sex & Marital Therapy, 39*(2), 96–111.

257 **This role reversal disrupts:** Dariotis, J. K., Chen, F. R., Park, Y. R., Nowak, M. K., French, K. M., & Codamon, A. M. (2023). Parentification Vulnerability, Reactivity, Resilience, and Thriving: A Mixed Methods Systematic Literature Review. *International Journal of Environmental Research and Public Health, 20*(13), 6197.

258 **Shame is a powerful psychological tool:** Stuewig, J., Tangney, J. P., Heigel, C.,

Harty, L., & McCloskey, L. (2010). Shaming, Blaming, and Maiming: Functional Links Among the Moral Emotions, Externalization of Blame, and Aggression. *Journal of Research in Personality, 44*(1), 91–102.

260 **rage can create muscle tension:** Barusch, A. S. (2023). Angry Bodies. In *Aging Angry: Making Peace with Rage* (pp. 35–43). Oxford University Press.

260 **created by the incredible therapist:** Chalfant, M. (2024). The Adult Chair Model. theadultchair.com/adult-chair-model/.

Chapter IV: The Gift of Loneliness

264 **It is an evolutionary cue:** Cacioppo, J. T., Cacioppo, S., & Boomsma, D. I. (2013). Evolutionary Mechanisms for Loneliness. *Cognition and Emotion, 28*(1), 3–21.

265 **Loneliness is a problem for the elderly:** Lawton, G. (August 19, 2017). Loneliness Is Not Just for Older People. I've Found It Crushing in My 20s. *The Guardian.* theguardian.com/lifeandstyle/2017/aug/19/loneliness-is-not-just-for-older-people-ive-found-it-crushing-in-my-20s.

265 **Counter to conventional wisdom:** Ballard, J. (June 25, 2021). Are Your Twenties Really the Best Years of Your Life? What Americans Think. YouGov.today.yougov.com/society/articles/36637-best-years-of-your-life-decades-age-poll; Stauffer, R. (June 12, 2021). The One-Size-Fits-All Narrative of Your 20s Needs to Change. *The Atlantic.* theatlantic.com/ideas/archive/2021/06/your-20s-dont-have-to-be-the-best-time-of-your-life/619187/.

268 **There is something sacred:** Weinstein, N., Vuorre, M., Adams, M., & Nguyen, T. (2023). Balance Between Solitude and Socializing: Everyday Solitude Time Both Benefits and Harms Well-Being. *Scientific Reports, 13,* 21160.

268 **One way of seeing loneliness:** Danvers, A. F., Efinger, L. D., Mehl, M. R., Helm, P. J., Raison, C. L., Polsinelli, A. J., Moseley, S. A., et al. (2023). Loneliness and Time Alone in Everyday Life: A Descriptive-Exploratory Study of Subjective and Objective Social Isolation. *Journal of Research in Personality, 107,* 104426.

Chapter V: Mental Health—The Conversations We Aren't Having

274 **Clinical research tells us this:** Levine, J., Cole, D. P., Chengappa, K. N., & Gershon, S. (2001). Anxiety Disorders and Major Depression, Together or Apart. *Depression and Anxiety, 14*(2), 94–104.

275 **About 13 percent of the world's population:** World Health Organization (June 8, 2022). Mental Disorders. who.int/news-room/fact-sheets/detail /mental-disorders.

276 **We see countless articles:** Rossa-Roccor, V., Schmid, P., & Steinert, T. (2020). Victimization of People with Severe Mental Illness Outside and Within the Mental Health Care System: Results on Prevalence and Risk Factors from a Multicenter Study. *Frontiers in Psychiatry, 11, 563860.*

278 **For centuries there has been a known relationship:** Andreasen, N. C. (2008). The Relationship Between Creativity and Mood Disorders. *Dialogues in Clinical Neuroscience, 10*(2), 251–255.

280 **Aging seems to be a powerful antidote:** Thomas, M. L., Kaufmann, C. N., Palmer, B. W., Depp, C. A., Martin, A. S., Glorioso, D. K., Thompson, W. K., et al. (2016). Paradoxical Trend for Improvement in Mental Health with Aging. *Journal of Clinical Psychiatry, 77*(8), e1019–e1025.

Index

About the Author

JEMMA SBEG is a prominent mental health advocate and top podcast host based in Sydney, Australia. She's best known for her groundbreaking, globally recognized podcast, *The Psychology of Your 20s,* which she launched independently to make psychological research more relatable to the universal experiences of our twenties. She has a degree and double specialization in psychology from the Australian National University.

Instagram: @thatpsychologypodcast
                  @jemmasbeg

About the Type

This book was set in Sabon, a typeface designed by the well-known German typographer Jan Tschichold (1902–74). Sabon's design is based upon the original letter forms of sixteenth-century French type designer Claude Garamond and was created specifically to be used for three sources: foundry type for hand composition, Linotype, and Monotype. Tschichold named his typeface for the famous Frankfurt typefounder Jacques Sabon (c. 1520–80).